SENA'S
Black Rose

A Different Kind of Love Story

L.K. JONES

PAGE PUBLISHING, INC.
Conneaut Lake, PA

First originally published by Page Publishing 2020

ISBN 978-1-6624-1602-6 (pbk)
ISBN 978-1-6624-1603-3 (digital)

Printed in the United States of America

My sister Beverly Brown, took her own life in 1981. She was just a young girl when mental illness stole her mind and everything she knew. She was beautiful, smart, and very talented. I was inspired to write this book, not knowing it would become my greatest source of healing. Thank you. RIP.

My sister Pat, was called home in 2018. She was a great inspiration to all that knew her. Her kind heart, generosity, and God-fearing spirit will live in our hearts always. RIP.

My sisters Doris, Connie, Carol, and Pam. You are the greatest sisters anyone could have. You are kind, loyal, and my best friends. And also my brother, Paul. Thank you all for your support. I love you.

My mother, Fannie Terry, the greatest mother any child could ask for. Her strength and belief that we should never fight but love each other has stood strong in our lives to this day. It was her love for all of us that taught us there is no love like sisterly love. RIP.

To live moments means death.
To change worlds means a new life.
To move forward takes effort.
While being pushed backward.

—Beverly Brown

FOREWORD

The pain of being seen and not known, of being seen and not loved, the pain of being invisible to the hearts you love, and the joy of living in the heart of another has shaped many a good story. The added layers of being the second-best loved child, the darker-skinned child, made to feel ugly against a mother's need to fight self-hatred, and to see herself in her lighter-skinned child adds to the particulars of this tale's weight.

There are two sisters. To the eye, one seems fortunate and loved; the other wonders what she could do to be as wanted. But the eye's vision distorts what we can see with our brain and our heart. The darker sister, even knowing her lighter-skinned sister's pains, wants the attention so easily given to the beautiful one. Though she hears her sister vomit up her binged food to keep the form people admire, she wants the easy approval her sister receives.

But pain can be a teacher. She learns that happiness is something she must make from her own life on her own terms. It won't be enough to earn the kind of attention her sister receives based as it is on what she can conceal from others. To be seen, she will need to show herself fully and be received by another. And it will need to be by someone she sees and receives.

So we have a love story. And though romance is part of the picture, the hatred and resentment of family is too. The implicit color bias among African Americans living in a country of white women with glowing skin and flowing hair and African American women imitating that glow and flow, wanting to be seen as beautiful, is part of the mosaic. There are confusions among family, sorting out the betrayals and lies and insecurities as each person works out their answer to the question "Can someone love me?" It is a constant presence. And at the heart of the novel, a woman becomes self-confident and aware as she sorts through life's ugliness and its beauty.

I read an early version of this book about twenty-five years ago. Since then, it has matured in its author's mind and has come out with the richness, complexity, and unity of a good wine stored in a well-made barrel. You will meet a strong mind facing the demands of life as her heart and body go forth to battle. The battle is the one we all share and fight—to find the people who will become our real family and to find ourselves.

Give the first page of this book a try. You will want to read on. You will want to finish it. You will want to become part of this story as you work out your own battle to live.

Patrick Keyes

ACKNOWLEDGMENTS

Thanks to my English professor, Patrick Keyes, who, after reading an essay I had written in his class, told me, "I would like to see you take this story further." That prompted me to write my very first novel.

Thanks to Dewane and Doris Hughes, who gave me my very first computer to write this novel. You believed in me from day one.

Thanks to my children, Dennis, Ricolyn, Ryan, and Jamie for their undying love and support.

I love you all.

Thanks to my wonderful husband who loves and supports me in all my endeavors. I love you.

Finally, thanks to Page Publishing for reading and accepting my manuscript and turning it into a complete work of art. Thank you, Page Publishing.

Sister ran down the stairs and picked her baby up from the living room couch. T went rushing after her while Mama continued to look out the window. T saw Sister as she went through the door and ran down the stairs after her, calling her, but Sister kept running, her eyes blurred from the tears. Mama noticed a car coming and hollered out the window, calling Sister's name as loud as she could. Henry struggled to get out of his seat belt, calling Sister's name. Sister kept running just as T got to the front door. She and Mama screamed.

* * * * *

"Mama?"

"Yes, Roselyn."

"Why are you crying?"

"Your mommy just told me to tell you she loves you."

"Is she still in heaven?"

"Yes, she will always be in heaven."

"What does Mama do in heaven?" little Roselyn asked.

"Well, honey…she just walks around…walks around heaven all day," I said with tears in my eyes. "Come here and give me a hug. Oh! You're getting to be such a big girl." Roselyn held up her little hand, showing four fingers.

"I'm almost four. Oh…Mama, I just felt the baby move," she said, patting my stomach.

"I know. I felt it too. She can feel you next to her."

"She will be my very own sister?"

"Yes, baby, your very own sister," I said.

"I can't wait."

"I know, sweetie, I know." I rocked her in my arms. The older she got, the more she looked like Sister, except Roselyn is darker, with brown hair.

CHAPTER 1

"Rose!" my sister called to me from downstairs. "Let's go to the corner store."

"Okay, let me brush my hair first," I said. I hated going anywhere with my sister. All the boys would whistle as she went by. Cars would stop, and the boys would yell out, "Hey, baby! What's your name?" It was sickening. My sister had very light skin, and her hair was so wavy and shiny, you could almost see your reflection. I was just the opposite. My hair was short, and my skin was considerably darker, a lot darker than our mother's. She had skin the color of caramel. I loved my father very much. When he died, part of me died too. He did not care that I was darker. He loved me just the same. He used to call me his beautiful black rose. He would get angry with Mama because she would spend more time with my sister. I would hear them arguing late at night. He would say, "Rose is your daughter too."

"I know," Mama would say indifferently. Daddy would get angry and storm out of the room and sleep on the sofa. I would sneak down, crawl under the sheets, and hold on tight to my daddy because I knew that soon the light would come and he would have to leave for work. Before he left, he would pick me up, kiss me on my cheek, and say, "Daddy will be back soon." But one evening, he did not come back. I wilted.

On our way to the store, a friend of my sister approached us and totally ignored my presence. When Sister introduced us, her friend announced, "You don't look alike. You must have different fathers." Enraged, I wanted to grab her throat and wring her neck off her shoulders. But I constrained myself and smiled. I wanted to crawl in a hole. Looking at her, I thought she was no great beauty herself. Sister made excuses so her friend would continue on her way. I never wanted Sister to see my pain.

"Let's go to the Copper Box Club. It's ladies' night," she said on the way home.

"I don't know. Let me think about it," I said, knowing I didn't want to go.

"Okay," Sister said as she abruptly turned.

"Where are you going?" I asked.

"I forgot to get something. You go on ahead."

She went back into the store and bought a large bag of chocolate chip cookies, potato chips, and a box of ice glazed donuts. Mama didn't allow Sister to eat junk food. She said it was bad for her teeth. But I knew it was because she didn't want Sister to be fat. She had an image to uphold—a straight-haired light skinned daughter that was perfect in every way. I could eat Donutland and Mama wouldn't complain once. Sister would put junk food on the ground below her window and pull it up from the inside. I would often find empty wrappers stashed away in her dresser drawers.

We spent a lot of time in our bedrooms. Daddy would always come in and read to me. I had a full-size bed with a canopy dressed in white lace. The floor was covered with white shag carpeting and black throw rugs. I cherished a picture of a single black rose that hung over my bed. I would take it down sometimes and clutch it against my breast to feel my heart beating against it. Sister's room was directly across the hall from mine. Mama's room was at the far end of the hall. I could hear Sister being sick late at night, but I would never go to her. I wanted to, but I didn't. I wouldn't. I couldn't. I heard a knock on my door.

"Who is it?" I asked.

"It's me, Sister."

"Come in."

"Well, are you going?" she asked me.

"Going where?"

"To the Copper Box. Ronnie's going to be there," she said with a smirk.

"How do you know?"

"Keith told me."

"Well…I don't know. My hair is a mess. I have to do more than brush mine."

"Whose fault is that?" Sister answered.

"I guess it's my fault my hair is not soft and wavy like yours."

Sister turned and walked out, leaving my door open and slamming hers. I jumped up, walked to my door, and slammed it. Then I walked to my bed, feeling guilty. It wasn't her fault my hair was nappy and hers was not. I just lay there and drifted into the darkness.

It was 9:00 p.m. I didn't realize I'd slept so long. Groggily, I opened my bedroom door and noticed Sister's light on. I gently knocked on the door.

"Come in, Rose," she said sweetly. I was twiddling my fingers with my head down.

"I just wanted to say I'm sorry. It's not your fault. It's just that I'm tired of being the ugly one or the dark one." Sister raised her shoulders off the bed and gave a motion for me to sit down. She took my hands.

"Rose, look at me." I continued to hold my head down. She let go of my hands and gently put her hand under my chin, lifted my head, and said, "Rose?" When I looked into her eyes, my tears were about to fall. "You are my sister, and I love you. You are not ugly." I could feel the tears heavy on my lids. I held my sister like never before.

"Thank you." Still holding hands, I asked, "But why do we look so different?"

"I don't know, Rose. It just happens that way sometimes." We then heard Mama at the door.

"Come in, Mama," Sister quickly said.

"What's going on in here?"

In unison, we said, "Nothing."

"Why do I see tears in you and your sister's eyes?"

Having my sister sitting next to me gave me an overwhelming sense of security. I stood up, looked Mama in her eyes, and just asked, "Why do I look so different? Look at me. I don't look like either of you." My eyes started to fill up again, and so did Sister's.

I looked into Mama's eyes. She became very nervous, opened her bag, and took out a cigarette, a sure sign something was wrong. She stood up and walked around the room for a minute, shaking her head. I couldn't take it anymore, so I yelled, "Mama, please!"

She walked over to me and said, "I've been dreading this day."

"Should I leave?" Sister asked, starting to get up.

"No!" I grabbed her hand and held it tightly. We both sat down, and Mama began to speak.

"It was a hot evening. A group of friends and I decided we'd cool off at Myers Park. There was a huge pool some of us would use when the weather was nice. That particular evening, the gate surrounding the pool was locked. But one of the boys said he could open it, and he did." The whole time Mama was talking, she never looked up. I noticed a slight tremble in her hands. "We drank a couple of beers and smoked a few joints. One of the girls had taken off all of her clothes and jumped in, so we all did," she said with embarrassment.

"After we finished, David was taking everyone home. He'd decided to take me last because he was kind of sweet on me. We were having so much fun. I thought it would be okay. After he dropped everyone off, he suggested we go back to the pool for a private party. I said no. I was tired and ready to go home. He drove back to the park anyway." I could tell Mama was in pain telling this story. Her shaking became more prominent. She lit cigarette after cigarette. "I asked him, 'Where are you going?' But he didn't answer. I was afraid. I didn't know what to do. I tried to ease my hand on the door and jump out. But he grabbed me! He pulled me back into the seat. I tried to fight him, but he was stronger than I was."

My heart started to beat very fast. I held tight onto Sister's hand for fear of what she was going to say next. This couldn't be what I was thinking. I was becoming hysterical.

"Mama," I said. I was crying and walking over to her. I could feel my body starting to go limp. "Did he?" I couldn't get the words out. Mama raised her head slowly, tears streaming down her face. Without saying a word, she nodded. My legs felt like Jell-O as I felt myself falling. Mama and sister caught me before I hit the floor. They sat me in a chair and covered me with their arms. We cried with every ounce of strength we had. We cried and cried as we continued to hold each other. Mama held me tight.

"I'm sorry. I'm sorry. I love you, Rose. Please know that I love you." We embraced again and rocked each other gently.

That morning, about 3:00 a.m., I could hear my sister being sick in her bathroom. I jumped up and knocked on her door. No one answered. I knocked again, calling her name. I became terrified. On her bed I saw the donut box, potato chips, and cookie bags all empty. My pace quickened. Oh my god! My sister was lying on the bathroom floor with blood coming out of her mouth. I was in shock and put my hands to my mouth and screamed. Mama came running in, out of breath.

"What's the matter?" Mama bucked her eyes in disbelief. "Rose, what happened? Call 911."

Mama and I sat hand in hand in the hospital waiting room. All the harsh things I ever said to my sister flooded back. *God, please give us another chance.* Then I prayed silently.

The doctor approached us. "She's going to be fine. She's suffering from an eating disorder known as bulimia. Have you heard of it?" he asked.

"Yes, I have," Mama said.

"Well, the constant purging and regurgitation has caused her esophagus to rupture slightly. Did either of you notice anything strange about her eating habits?"

It hit me all of a sudden. I'd hear her being sick in her room, but I never thought. *I never went to check,* I thought. I was hoping no one would see the fear on my face. How could I not have checked? She was my sister, for Christ's sake! I could not believe my stupidity.

"Sometimes these things can be hard to spot if the person is being secretive, which most of them are. We'll keep her for a while just to make sure she's okay. She's in bed C. Try not to stay too long. She's exhausted," the doctor explained.

"Thank you," Mama said. We walked over to Sister. She looked terribly frail. She opened her eyes and started to cry.

"I'm sorry," Sister said.

"That's okay, baby," she said with a sensitivity I never heard before.

"Everything's going to be all right." But it wasn't.

CHAPTER 2

The ride home was unusually quiet. Mama was in her own world, smoking one cigarette after another. After all, she'd just told me my father was a rapist and found out that her favorite daughter had an eating disorder. I didn't want to think about it anymore. I just wanted to think about the only man I knew and loved as my father. My brain was on overload with questions. Did he know about Mama being raped? Could Mama have told him I was his? Was this why he loved me so much? Did she tell him I did not belong to him? Was that why he left? *Oh God! Oh God!* I screamed in silence. *Daddy! Daddy!* I could not keep the tears from falling. I saw Mama out of the corner of my eye watching me. She didn't say a word. Why? I was totally exhausted by the time we got home from the hospital, but I didn't want to do or think about anything. I climbed into my bed, took down the picture of my single black rose, and cried into my pillow. "Daddy, Daddy! Why did you leave me?" I cried.

Mama left earlier than usual for work the next morning. I knew she was going to avoid me. But that was okay. There was something I needed to do. Mama kept a box with mementos and old pictures. I wondered if there was a picture of him in there. Mama's room smelled heavy of cigarette smoke. She'd been up smoking all night. Her room was a beautiful royal blue with silver accents everywhere, from her picture frames to her hope chest at the foot of her bed. She even had a silver telephone a friend sent her from Germany. The most beautiful was the wall facing her king-size bed. It was all mirror tiled. She also had a huge walk-in closet. *I'll never find that little box in such a huge closet*, I thought. But there it was on the top shelf among all her shoe-boxes. I slowly reached for it and immediately slowed down when I noticed a picture of my father and me on my tenth birthday. He was so big and strong. "Oh, Daddy, I miss you so much," I said aloud.

I remember Daddy being just as excited as I was that day. He came into my room that morning and sat down next to me and watched me sleep. I knew he was there because he always smelled so good.

"Hi."

"Hi, baby," he said, sitting on the bed next to me.

"What are you doing in here so early?" I asked.

"Well, I just wanted to give you a very special birthday in private."

"What do you mean?"

"I want to give you something special before your mom gets up," he said.

"What?" I asked impatiently.

"When you were first born, I thought you were the most beautiful baby I had ever seen. You had perfect shaped lips and perfect little feet and hands. But mostly, you had the most beautiful dark brown skin. I fell in love with you on sight. So I found this."

"What is it?" I said excitedly.

"I wanted to get you something really special. Something that you could keep forever to remember me always."

I sat straight up in my bed, my eyes widening. "Are you going somewhere?"

"No, honey. Of course not," he answered.

But I knew he wasn't telling me the truth. I'd heard him and Mama arguing the night before about me. I couldn't really hear what they were saying, but I heard my name called several times. I remember hearing them talking about my skin. I couldn't hear them very well. That was the night I went downstairs and crawled under the sheets with my daddy, because Mama had been yelling at him about me. I never knew why. Was she jealous because my daddy loved me? Daddy pulled out of his pajama shirt pocket the most beautiful little black velvet bag with a little red shiny ribbon tied to it. He opened up the bag and gently pulled out some tissue paper with something in it. He slowly pulled out a thin gold chain with a gold locket attached to it. My mouth opened.

"Oh, Daddy, it's lovely," I said, grinning like a Cheshire cat.

"There's a little catch on it. Open it up." He was excited too.

"I can't."

"Here. I'll help you," he said.

"Oh, daddy, it's so pretty," I said.

I grabbed my daddy around his neck and hugged him as tight as I could.

"It's a flower," I said.

"No, baby. It's not just a flower. It's the most beautiful and rare flower there is. It's a black rose."

"I've never seen one before," I said.

"That's because people are used to red roses, yellow roses, even white roses. There aren't too many who like black roses because they're different. That's why I like them so much, because they are different. Its beauty is different from all the others. You know how people tease your little friend down the street because he walks with a limp? Well, they do it because they think he's different. You know how your friends treat you differently because you play with him sometimes?" he said.

"Yeah. But, Daddy, he is always nice to me."

"That's the beauty he has inside. I'm proud of you, baby, for being nice to him. So you see, sweetie, people can't always see the beauty we have inside because they are looking on the outside. This rose has beauty inside as well. You've smelled the fragrance of flowers?" he asked.

"Yes," I said.

"And you can see the beauty it has outside too, right?" he asked.

"Yes," I said, smiling.

"That's how I feel about you. You are just as beautiful outside as you are inside." Daddy must have held on to me for five minutes. When he finally let go, he had tears in his eyes. I knew I would never see him again. I knew now that he was trying to tell me something.

I started to smile when I came across a picture of my sister and me. She was always so very pretty. People would come over and always talk about how pretty she was.

One very warm day in July, Mama was combing my hair. I was seven years old. Mama really didn't like combing my hair because of the kinks, so she would always tug my hair really hard and put it up in one ponytail. I would have this big giant Afro puff sitting on top of my head. I hated it. It felt like someone was going to pick me up any minute and dust the furniture or mop the floor with the top of my head. My sister's hair always got special attention. Her hair was not kinky at all. It was long, black, and wavy. Mama would practically play with it and tell her how pretty it was. She'd make numerous ponytails and put pretty barrettes all over her head. As young as I was, I remember feeling different. Mama's friend Marilyn came over that day. She was tall, light, and kind of flirtatious and very loud. I didn't like her because she would always give my sister candy or gum when she thought I wasn't looking. My sister would come out and tease me about it. Mama would just let it happen. I would go upstairs and cry in my closet, sometimes for hours. Mama never even missed me.

I heard the phone ringing in my room. *Shit!* I thought. *Who is that this time of morning?* I quickly put the box down and ran to answer the phone.

"Hello?" I said, quick and out of breath.

"Hi, Rose. It's me."

"Oh, how are you feeling?" I asked her.

"I'm feeling much better now," Sister replied. "Where's Mama? I just tried calling her at the office, but she wasn't there."

"Huh! I don't know," I said, wondering myself where she might be.

"She left really early this morning. I thought she went straight to work, but I guess not."

"I left something cooking on the stove, so I'll have to call you back," I said.

She probably knew I was lying. I never cooked, especially early in the morning.

"Oh! If Mama calls, have her give me a call," Sister said.

"All right. Bye."

I ran back into Mama's room and put the box away in a hurry. Since she wasn't at work, I didn't want her to come home and find me in her room. As I was lifting the box, I felt a small hard piece of something. It was a small key taped to the bottom of the box. I became very curious.

"Now, why does Mama have this key taped to this box?" My eyes started to quickly scan the room for anything I thought that key might belong to. But then I heard Mama's key opening the front door. I quickly ran back into my room, closed the door, and jumped into my bed. I thought she heard me, but she didn't.

"Rose?" she said softly.

Trying to sound half asleep, I answered, "Yeah, Mama, is that you? I thought you were gone."

"Oh, not yet. I'll be leaving soon though. Did your sister call?"

"I don't remember. I talked to someone. It might have been her. I don't know. I was still sleeping," I said.

Why did Mama just lie like that? I thought. What was she up to this morning? I got out of bed. The robe I had on had become wrinkled. I went to see where Mama was. Her door was opened just a little bit. She was on the phone talking to someone, but I couldn't hear who she was talking to. So I slowly opened her door. She must have heard me because she got off the phone quickly.

"Oh, Rose!" she said. "You startled me."

"I'm sorry, Mama. I thought you heard me coming."

"Now, Rose, you know I can't hear you walking on the carpet."

"Oh yeah, that's right," I said.

"Why is your robe so wrinkled?" she asked.

I wanted to ask Mama about **him**, but I didn't know how. So I just blurted something out.

"Mama," I said. "Where is my father now?"

"What?" she said nervously.

"You know...**him**."

"I don't know, Rose. I never saw him again after that."

"Well, does he know about me?"

"No."

"Why?"

I could tell she was getting angry and nervous at me for asking so many questions. I just wanted to know. I couldn't stop thinking about it. I wondered why she didn't abort me.

"Why should he, Rose?" she screamed. "Do you think he honestly deserved to know? He raped me, for God's sake! All I ever wanted to do is forget about that horrible night. But you won't let me!"

The pain I was feeling was new to me, even though I always knew something was different about me.

"Don't you think I have a right to know, Mama?" I fired back. "How long were you planning on keeping this secret from me? How could you not have told me my father was a low-life skank! Is that why you always treated me differently from Sister?!" Mama really got on the defensive when I said that.

"I never treated you differently from your sister. How can you say that?"

"Because it's true. One year we had all planned to go to Disney World. I don't remember how old we were, except that we were little. Remember?"

"Yes, I remember," she said.

"Remember how your rich white friends from work decided they wanted to come along and bring their kids?"

"Yes."

"Mama, you knew how much I wanted to go to Disney World that summer, and because I hit a girl back for hitting me, you made me stay with neighbors. You didn't want me to come with."

"No, Rose. That's not true and you know it." She scowled.

"And Sister had just failed one of her summer school courses. Was that fair?" I asked.

"No, Rose. I don't remember any of that! I think you're lying."

"Okay, Mama, you never believe anything I say anyway, so what made me think this would be any different? Daddy was the only person who ever listened to me!" I shouted. I stormed out of Mama's room and slammed her door. I hated her just then. I paced back and forth in my bedroom. I had to find out something; I kept pacing and pacing. *Think! Rose, think!* Someone must have said something about it.

Grandma Lucy had to know something. I could go down for a visit.

My grandma Lucy was from the old school. She never had very much education, so she talked with that old back home drawl. She was raised in Mississippi and had lived there all her life. My grandma was damn near ninety years old with the mentality of someone in their fifties. She was a sweet old lady, hair pure white from age. She always wore one long braid wrapped around her head and walked with one hand on her hip that she broke in a fall. My grandma looked just like Mama, except my grandma was darker. I could tell Grandma had been beautiful…once. I called her Grammy. She called me Ro, and I loved her very much.

Sister stayed in the hospital for a week. I waited until she came home from the hospital, and then I left. I took the Greyhound to Mississippi because I wanted to think for a while. Grammy didn't know I was coming. I wanted this to be a surprise. In Mississippi, you could get off the bus anywhere you wanted to.

CHAPTER 3

I had the bus driver let me off as close as he could to Grammy's house, but it wasn't close enough. I hitched a ride with an old friend of Grammy's who was on her way to the corner market. She remembered only that I was her granddaughter. She asked how Mama was and if she'd be coming as well. I said no, I was the only one, and I wanted it to be a surprise and could she let me out so I could walk up to the house. I spotted Grammy's house in the distance. It looked a lot smaller and shabbier than I remembered, and it needed a paint job. The faded blue reminded me of her. The house looked so alone. I saw her sitting on the porch. Grammy didn't look very well to me. It had been five years since I had last seen her. I asked the driver to stop and let me out and thanked her. Grammy noticed us stopping at the edge of the dirt road, but she still didn't know it was me. I saw her stand up to get a better view. Both my hands were full with luggage, so I slowly walked up the road with a big smile on my face. As I got closer, Grammy had a strange look on her face as in disbelief. I knew she recognized me when I saw her put down the bowl she had and put her hands to her face. She tried to hurry down the steps. "Be careful, Grammy," I said in a low whisper. I put my luggage down and ran to my Grammy.

"She's dead. Yo mama's dead," Grammy said jokingly.

"No, Grammy. Hell won't have her," I said, smiling.

We stared at each other for a few seconds and started laughing. Feeling my Grammy's arms around me gave me the feeling of security and belonging I never received from Mama.

Grammy lived in a small three-bedroom house. It wasn't dirty, but you could tell that it wasn't as nice as it once was. Her age kept her from cleaning as well as she used to. Mama tried to get her to move in with her years ago, but Grammy said she was born there and would die there. So Mama never mentioned it again. I never believed Mama wanted her to live with us anyway. Grammy acted too much like a nigger. Grammy knew Mama always tried to be something she wasn't. Grammy hated that about her.

Her house had that old people smell of liniments and mothballs, with an added attraction of salt pork cooking on the stove for the beans she was shelling.

"Put yo grips in that room at the top of the stairs," Grammy said. I climbed the familiar stairs, listening to the squeaks from my steps. "Ya hungry, chile?" I heard Grammy call from downstairs. "I got some pole beans with salt poke in 'em, some fried conebread, and rice wit red eye gravy. It'll be ready soon," Grammy said. I hadn't had food like that in a long time. Since Mama had gotten so white, all we seemed to have any more was tuna noodle casserole. Old people had a way with food. Grammy's food always did taste good. I could hardly wait.

After dinner, Grammy turned on the TV and sat in her favorite rocking chair. She reached down right beside her chair and picked up the quilt she had been working on. She slowly started to rock and hum an old church hymn. "Ro, suga, would you put the set on channel nine? It's time fa the rifaman."

"Sure, you still watch that show?" I asked.

"Honey, chile, yes indeed. It puts me in the mind of my husband when he use to go huntin'. Those was some fine times. Yes indeed, yes indeed." She chuckled as she rocked back and forth. I hated to move. I hadn't eaten that much in a long time. It was just delicious. "So tell me, chile, how's yo mama and sistah doin'?"

"Mama didn't call you?"

"No, chile. I ain't talk to yo mamas since I broke my hip a ways back."

"How come?"

"Oh nah, don't you go worryin' yosef 'bout me and yo mama. I ain't hurtin' none, and neder is she. All right?" Grammy said with a disturbed smile.

Something was strange about Mama and Grammy not speaking to each other. I wondered if this had anything to do with me.

"Grammy," I said, "would you like for me to scratch your head for you?"

"Oh…baby, sho would! Would you plat it to fa me too, sweetie?" she asked.

"Oh, Grammy, nobody says plat anymore. It's braid," I said, laughing. "Where do you keep your comb, brush, and hair oil?"

"Well, there's some Royal Crown next to my bed, and the comb and brush is in the bathroom cupboard."

Grammy had beautiful white hair. When I unpinned her braid, it fell clear down to the middle of her back. It was soft, with just a little frizz to it.

"Grammy? Do you have any pictures of all of us? I want to do a scrapbook. It'll keep me from getting bored."

"Well, sho I do. There's a box up in the attic just loaded wit pitchas."

I quickly finished scratching and braiding her hair so I could take a look in the attic, which was dusty and full of cobwebs. I turned on the light, looked around, and saw the trunk Grammy was talking about. I went over to it and opened it up. It was full of stuff—old pictures, costume jewelry, screws, tacks, mothballs. You name it, it was there. There was also a diary with no name on it, locked. After seeing the diary, I forgot about everything else. I closed the trunk and ran downstairs to ask Grammy about it. But just as I stepped on to the last step, a light bulb went on in my head. What if she said I couldn't read it? I made a U-turn and ran upstairs to my bedroom. I wanted to see if I could pry it open without damage. I went downstairs to say good night so that I wouldn't be disturbed.

"Ro? Did you find what you was lookin' fa?"

"I didn't finish looking yet. I'm tired, so I thought I would look again tomorrow." I gave Grammy a tight hug and scurried up the steps to my room and closed the door. I looked around the room to see if there was anything I could find to pry open the lock. I tried a safety pin. That didn't work. I then took a bobby pin out of my hair and sat back down on the bed and tried and tried. I was trying so hard I broke out in a sweat. When I finally realized I wasn't going to get it open, I threw it across the room in anger and lay on my bed and started to think about what kind of man this David was. I hardly ever dreamed unless I was in a state of unrest or excited about something. That night, I dreamed about a man I had never seen. My father. The rapist.

I was a little girl, about seven or eight, and I was sleeping on the most beautiful pink billowy cloud. Suddenly, a man gently sat beside me. "Rose, wake up, sweetheart. I have something for you." He smelled so good, I knew it couldn't be anyone but my daddy. I turned over, but I didn't see anyone.

"Daddy?" I asked. "Where are you?"

He said, "I'm here, angel. I'm right here." But this time, when he spoke, the good smell went away. All I could smell was alcohol and reefer.

I quickly sat up and yelled, "You're not my daddy! My daddy smells good."

He said, "Yes, baby, I am your daddy. I'll prove it. Remember this?" I still couldn't see him. A locket appeared in front of me, hanging in thin air. But the locket didn't have that shiny new look like it once did. I opened it and saw a picture of a wilted black rose. The voice then said. "Give Daddy a kiss."

"No! Go away! You're not my daddy. Where is my daddy?" I shouted. I felt a sensation, hands touching me in places I shouldn't be touched.

I started kicking and screaming. I was screaming so loud, my Grammy heard me.

"Ro! Ro! Ro! Wake up! Wake up!"

I could feel my Grammy shaking me. I opened my eyes and held on to Grammy.

"My father," I said, trying to catch my breath.

"Steven," Grammy said.

"No. David," I said.

Grammy's eyes widened, and she sat back on the bed in wonderment. I started to cry hysterically. Grammy quickly held me and said, "Don't cry, baby. Grammy's here. Yo grammy's riiight here. You hush up nah. Thangs gon be all right afta while," she said.

"But, Grammy."

"Hush up nah. You get some rest."

Grammy kissed me on the forehead, pulled the sheets over me, and walked slowly out of the room with one hand on her hip. I knew that the rest of her night would be as restless as mine. I felt bad about that.

Grammy went downstairs and called Mama. Mama was busy doing laundry, so Sister answered the phone:

"Hello, is that you, Sistah?" Grammy asked.

"Yes, hi, Grandma. How are you doing? I haven't talked to you in such a long time."

"Oh, chile, the Lawd takes care of us old folks. I heard you had a bout wit the stomach flu. hope you feelin' betta," she said.

"I feel much better, Grandma."

"Well, that's good, chile. Can I speak to yo mama?"

"Mama!" Sister yelled from her bed. "Grandma's on the phone."

I purposely told Grammy Sister had the stomach flu. Sister was okay, and I didn't want to worry Grammy about something she had no control over. Mama always called Grammy by her first name. I never understood why. Perhaps it was because her and Mama were never really close.

"Hi, Lucilla," Mama said with a happy pretense.

"What you been telling that po chile?" Grammy asked.

"What are you talking about?" Mama said.

"That po chile woke up in a cold sweat, talkin' bout that no good nigga," said Grammy

"What no good nigger are you talking about? And believe me, I've known plenty," Mama said.

"David," Grammy said rather loudly. "What you been tellin' them churen? You ought to be ashamed of yosef, lyin' to them churen like that. The Lawd is gon whoop you good, and I hope I'm right there watchin'," Grammy said angrily.

"I know what I'm doing, Lucilla," Mama said with resentment. "What has Rose been saying anyway? Sister?" Mama whispered. "Hand me my cigarettes."

"Nothin'. That chile woke up screamin' and hollerin'. I thought somebody was in my house. She had one of those scary ni...night dreams," Grammy struggled out. "Besides, I know ya. I birthed you. I know you done tole some kinda lie."

Mama became very frustrated. "Nightmares. Nightmares. Gee! I got to go. Bye!"

* * * * *

Sister talked with Mama that night. She told me about it one night when I wanted to put the pieces of my life together. Her version of the conversation went like this:

"Mama? What did grandma want?" Sister asked.

"Oh, she said something about Rose having a nightmare."

"Is Rose okay?"

"Sure, she's fine. You know your grandmother. She makes a big deal out of nothing with her no talking ass. Oh! That woman knows she upsets me so," Mama said, slamming her cigarette butt out in the ashtray.

"Mama, did you and Rose get a chance to talk about what happened?"

"If you could call it that. I really don't want to talk about that just now. How are you feeling, sweetie?" Mama asked.

"I'm fine, Mama."

"Sister, I've been wanting to talk to you. The doctor suggested that it's possible you might need some kind of counseling for your eating disorder. But I told him I thought you would be fine and that counseling wasn't necessary. Don't you agree?"

"Yes, Mama, sure," Sister said.

Sister wasn't sure herself what the problem was. I hadn't thought how all of this might have affected my sister through the years. After all, Mama treating her better was no fault of hers. There were times

I know now that Sister was hurt by the way Mama was treating me. When Sister and I were teenagers, when I was sixteen, we had just been invited to our first party. It was so exciting because boys were going to be there. We spent that whole day primping, doing our hair, polishing our nails, and I must say my sister and I looked very cute that night. Just as we were getting ready to leave, Mama asked me, "Rose, did you get the laundry done like you were supposed to?"

I could tell by the sound of her voice that she was not going to let me go to the party. My heart started to race.

"We always do the laundry on Saturdays," I told her. Tears formed on my eyes, and I could feel my voice starting to tremble.

"As long as you are black and ugly and live in my house, you will do as I say. Do you understand me, Rose?"

I didn't answer. I gave her the coldest stare I could.

"Now march up to your room and don't come out until I say so."

The tears were pouring by this time. I looked at Sister and ran upstairs to my bedroom and quietly closed the door. I knew if I slammed it, Mama would come rushing up, and I really didn't want to see or talk to her. I saw the hurt in Sister's eyes. I heard Mama say to her, "Go on, baby. You can go to the party. Have a good time."

Sister left, but soon after I heard footsteps coming up the stairs. I thought Mama was coming back to give me a hard time. It was Sister. She sat down beside me.

"Rose, don't cry." She sounded like she was going to cry herself.

"Why does Mama hate me so much?" I asked as I turned to face Sister.

"I don't think Mama hates you. I think she's just crazy," Sister said. We laughed.

"Aren't you going to the party?" I asked.

"No, I don't want to leave you alone. Besides, I don't want to go if you're not going to be there." That's when I realized that she really loved me. But I wasn't going to let her miss the party because of me.

"No! Sister, you go on, and tell me everything when you get back. I especially want to know who's with who and if Keisha is still hanging out with that skuzz bucket Tyrone." We both laughed a little. Then she left. But I could tell the hurt was still there.

When Sister arrived at the party, it was in full swing. Everyone was talking, dancing, or eating. The food was set up buffet style with party wings, salads, trays, and assortments of drinks. Sister kept staring at the food table and sauntered over to it, taking a little bit of everything, just tasting it and tasting it and tasting it. Realizing what she had just done, she walked swiftly to the restroom and made herself throw up.

When Sister came in, Mama asked about the party. She said it was fine and continued upstairs without stopping, climbed into bed, curled up next to me, and drifted off to sleep.

Sister and I weren't always on good terms. There were times when we tore into each other with a real vengeance. Sister was so beautiful that I was always jealous of her beautiful hair, her thin lips, and her complexion. There was only one thing she had that I didn't want—her flat ass.

For some reason, I always blamed Sister for the things that were happening in our lives. She was so pretty. I actually thought I hated her. I realized I only hated her because of Mama. I had no way of fighting Mama, so I took all my frustrations out on Sister.

One time, it went like this:

"Sister? Can I borrow your white blouse, the one with the lace on the collar?"

"I don't know… Rose, you know that's my favorite blouse."

"Oh, please. It'll go perfect with the pants I want to wear tonight. I promise I'll take very good care of it. I'll let you borrow something of mine," I offered.

"Okay, Rose. You can borrow it."

"Thanks. I promise I'll take good care of it."

A week later, Sister came to me, asking about the whereabouts of her blouse. And of course, I just felt like being mean.

"Rose, where is my white blouse you borrowed last week?"

"What white blouse?" I asked. I just wanted to give her a hard time.

"My white blouse with the lace on the collar," she said angrily.

"I don't know. I hung it back in your closet," I said.

"No, you did not, Rose. Why are you lying?"

Sister came into my room and started looking through my closet. She did not see her blouse hanging up on the pole. So she started searching my dirty laundry sitting on the closet floor. She spotted it balled up and wrinkled in the corner of my closet. She snatched it up off the floor.

"Rose! Why is my white blouse on the floor? Don't ever ask to borrow anything else of mine again!"

"I don't want to borrow anything else of yours!" I shouted back.

"I let you borrow my things, then you act like you don't give a shit about it!"

"I don't!"

I know my sister could have slapped me just then. I didn't care. I just liked making her angry sometimes. I later apologized and told her I had planned to put the blouse in the cleaners, and of course she forgave me.

* * * * *

I've been here at Grammy's house for three weeks, and she hadn't said a word about my father. Maybe she didn't know anything. I had decided not to think about him anymore. College was getting ready to start in a few weeks, and I needed to spend time thinking about classes and what I wanted to do with my life.

CHAPTER 4

When I returned home, I had received a scholarship to attend CSU in Long Beach, California, after submitting essays I had written. I was ecstatic to be in college. No Mama to tell me what to do. Sometimes I think us young people go to college just to get away from our parents. My college major was writing. I loved to write. Funny how I loved writing but hated doing research. Even so, I wanted to be a famous author.

I was assigned to share a room with Nina Schumaker. She was black, tall, very attractive, and had been class valedictorian. I knew we would get along well.

I assumed college would make me forget about my father, but it didn't. I still wanted to know about him, what he did for a living. Why did I have this desperate need to know him? He was a rapist. I shouldn't care anything at all about what he did. And I wanted to know if I looked like him.

After three weeks, I was missing Sister horribly. She called me to see how I was enjoying college life. I told her I liked it a lot. I told her about my friend Nina. She wanted to meet her and asked about the party Nina and I were going to. It was the first party we'd been invited to. Of course, they had several scattered about the campus. But this was the first one we were actually invited to.

I was in a frenzy trying to get my hair just right for the party tonight. Nina and I went to the mall and spent a fortune on just the right outfits.

"Nina, how do you think I look?"

"Girl, that's a bad outfit you have on. You're going to stop traffic in that bad mama jama!"

If I were white, my face would have been beet red from all the blushing I was doing. I did look good.

"Well, hey, girl, you look good too," I said with a huge grin on my face.

"Let's go."

When we arrived, the DJ was playing a song called "Short Dick Man." The crowd was poppin'. I could feel my adrenaline kicked in. I was ready. My body started to sway. We stood to the side because we didn't know many people. Then we spotted Kiki and Samara. We all lived in the same dorm. We decided to go over to where they were sitting. I liked Kiki and Samara a lot. Kiki was short for Keisha. She was short with short hair she tried to dye blond. It turned out to be redder. We told her it still looked nice, and it did. Kiki liked partying. She didn't give a shit about who thought what. She did just what she wanted. I think that's why Samara hung around her so much. Samara maintained a 4.0 grade point average. She was also very attractive and light with shoulder-length hair that she kept together at all times. One side of her head was cut just to the top of her ear. It was nice. Samara was very confident, loud, spoke her mind, and didn't give a damn who didn't like it. When they saw us, they waved their hands for us to come over and join them.

"Samara and I have been here for an hour already, and it's been nonstop dancing," Kiki said, moving to the beat of the music.

"Rose, you want a drink? Tonight they're on the house," Nina asked.

"Sure, I'll have a Sex on the Beach." I never knew what was in that drink, but it was pink and tasted delicious. After a couple of sips, I started to feel strange. I grabbed onto the back of a chair and sat down.

Nina saw me and asked, "Girl, are you okay?"

Lying, I said, "These shoes are kind of tight on my feet."

My heart started to race. "Calm down, Rose. You're okay," I said to myself and took long slow breaths. After a while, the feeling left because I started dancing in my chair. I was feeling good. A couple of hours had passed, and things were really heating up. I'd had two more drinks, was feeling no pain, and was laughing and talking. I even danced a couple of times. It was great.

There was a fine man standing over in the corner. He was tall and dark, a mixture of Denzel Washington and Steven Seagal rolled into one. He wore a long ponytail in the back of his head. His perm job was excellent, but he looked too old to be in with this crowd. He wore all black. I saw him watching me from the time I arrived. At first, I was too nervous to look at him, but after the drinks kicked in, I couldn't keep my eyes off him. He gave me a light smile to let me know he saw me looking at him. Of course, I smiled back. I saw him rise off the wall. My heart jumped. Oh my god! *He's coming over here*, I thought. As he approached the table where we were all sitting, everyone sitting there thought he was coming for them. Then suddenly, he reached out his hand to me. He had long slender fingers, manicured to perfection. You could almost see the red showing through my skin. You could almost see the green showing through theirs. I had a buzz going, so I got up very slowly to keep from stumbling. As we glided onto the dance floor, I was captivated.

"You look very lovely tonight. Mind if I ask your name?" I thought I would melt when I heard the tone of his voice. It was heavy but not too deep. He towered over me. The DJ was in a dusty mode by this time and was playing "Love Won't Let Me Wait," a slow jam. He took my hand and gently placed it around his taut waist. The other he placed around his neck. We slowly started to move.

Trying my best to sound sexy, I responded, "Rose."

"Rose, that's a beautiful name. It's also one of my favorite flowers," he added.

"Mine too."

"My name is David Jamal. Everyone calls me Jamal."

"Hi, Jamal."

Then came the silence. He smelled so good. My nipples started to harden just from his scent alone. He reminded me a lot of my daddy, not the way he looked but the way he smelled and carried himself. When the song was over, I hated letting him go. He looked at me and gave me a light bow and whispered, "Thank you, Rose. I hope to see you again." My mind was saying, *Ask for my number. Please, ask for my number.* But he didn't. This guy was a real gentleman. I was ready to believe nothing would top that. I attended a lot of parties after that, hoping to see Jamal again, but no such luck. Even though I didn't know him, I found myself thinking about him a lot.

I decided to sit down and write my sister a letter as I did every week. I had just finished telling her about Jamal when someone knocked on my door.

"Who is it?"

"I have a package for Rose Sinclair." I quickly opened the door.

"I'm Rose Sinclair," I said anxiously.

"Please, sign here." I reached in my pocket, pulled out a dollar, and handed it to him.

We both said thank you as I closed the door. I could tell it was flowers by the shape of the box. A dozen long-stemmed red roses delighted my eyes. I searched for the card. "I'd like to see you again. If you are free for dinner, please call my office at 555-7327. I'm here until six. Jamal."

"Oh my god! Oh my god!" I opened the door and ran down the hall to Kiki's room. I knocked loud and hard until someone came to the door.

"Who is it? Man! I can't get any studying done around her." Kiki scowled.

"It's me, Rose. Hurry up! Open the door!" I couldn't keep still. It felt like my feet had a mind of their own. Showing all my teeth, I said, "Kiki, look!"

"Roses! Who gave you those?"

"Jamal." We looked at each other for a second, screamed, and raised our hands and gave each other a high five. "He wants to take me to dinner. And guess what else." I was losing my breath. "He has an office number." We screamed again and started jumping up and down.

"When?" Kiki was almost as excited as I was.

"Well, he left his number for me to call him." Kiki grabbed me by my arm and pulled me into her room.

"What are you waiting for? Let's call him. Come in here and use my phone."

I nervously dialed the numbers I saw on the card. "It's ringing. Shhh. Hello, may I speak with Jamal David please? This is Rose Sinclair calling."

The operator sounded as if she was expecting me to call when she said, "One moment, please." Of course, I could have been imagining things.

"Good afternoon, this is Jamal. Can I help you?" My heart skipped a beat when I heard his voice.

"Jamal, hi, this is Rose. I just received your flowers. Thank you. They're lovely."

"My pleasure." I could hear his smile.

I didn't know what to say next. There was that silence again. Luckily, he asked me, "Rose, are you free for dinner tonight?"

Ecstatically, I said, "Yes."

"How about seven thirty? I'll pick you up at Linn Hall."

"Seven thirty is fine. I'll be there." I was glad the conversation came to an end. I thought I was going to drop dead from lack of oxygen any minute. When I got off the phone, I put my hand up to my chest to feel just how fast my heart was beating.

"What did he say, Rose? What did he say?"

Hardly believing it myself, I said, "He wants to take me to dinner…tonight! You have to help me, Kiki. Let me borrow something of yours."

"Sure. What?"

We looked through Kiki's closet. She had beautiful clothes. She had this black dress I'd been dying to wear. It was a little short, but that was how I wanted it.

"Yes, that one would be perfect for you." I completely forgot about the letter I was writing to Sister. I decided to wait until after my date to finish it so that I could tell her about it. I had two hours to get ready. That wasn't nearly enough time.

I felt like Cinderella preparing for the ball. My roommate wasn't in yet, so I decided to treat myself like a princess. I laid the dress out on the bed, went to the closet, and pulled out my black heels. I sat them on the floor right under the dress, then laid out my black hose and my underwear, the black lace ones. We didn't have bathtubs in our dorms, so I went down the hall where there was a small bathroom with a tub. I ran hot water for a lavender-scented bubble bath, lit a candle, and turned off the light. I slowly undressed and slid my naked body into a luxuriously phenomenal bath.

While I waited for Jamal in the lobby of Linn Hall, my girlfriends were off in the corner, watching. Jamal pulled up in a white Camry. My eyes widened. I gave a quick glance to my friends, and of course they were giving each other high fives. I heard Samara say, "You go, girl!" I felt…I couldn't even describe how I was feeling. Yes, I could, like Cinderella going to the ball. I thought about my daddy just then. He used to tell me that someday, I would grow up and go on my first date. I couldn't believe how fast that time went. I thought, *Daddy, I wish you could see me now.* I gave a quick wave to the girls and went down the steps to meet my prince. I could tell he had just gotten his hair done again. There was not a kink to be found. He looked good! He was still wearing his ponytail, and what a beautiful ponytail. It was about six inches long, close to the nape of his neck. He wore tailored black slacks, a black silk shirt by Pierre Cardin, black Stacy Adams, and to top it all off, he wore Grey Flannel cologne. It was the same cologne he wore when we danced. After dinner, we went dancing at the Fantasy Disco. As I would have suspected, Jamal brought me home at a decent hour, walked me to my dorm room, kissed my hand, and told me he had a wonderful time. Of course, I returned the compliment. After watching his cute buns walk down the hall, I quietly closed my door. I sat on the side of my bed, mesmerized by the wonderful time I had just had. I was startled by a sudden knock on the door. Kiki, Samara, and Nina came charging in. They were all saying at the same time, "What happened? Tell us about it." Then they noticed my rose lying on the bed.

Kiki asked, "Did he give you another rose?"

I picked it up, put it up to my nose to smell it, and said, "Yes, he did." We all started jumping up and screaming. Later, we sat on the bed. I started to undress while I was talking. "It was wonderful. He took me to dinner at Red Lobster and told me to order anything I wanted, so of course I had crab legs. He ordered wine for us. Some kind of French Chablis. It tasted fabulous. Then he took me to the Fantasy Disco." When I said that, all the girls gasped. Samara was amazed.

"You went to the Fantasy?"

"Girl, yes. And it was all that!" We all started laughing.

Nina stood up and boldly asked, "What I wanna know is did you bust a slob?" They all started giggling and laughing.

"No, but his lips sure were tempting. I got wet every time I looked at his lips." They all fell out when I said that. We were rolling on the floor, laughing.

"When are you going to see him again?" Nina asked.

"You know what, I don't know. We never talked about that." There was an eerie silence.

Nina then asked, "Well, at least he has your number, right?"

"Yes," I said quietly. Kiki and Samara got up to leave because they had early classes the next day. "Thanks again for letting me borrow your dress."

"Oh sure. Any time. Good night."

"Good night," I said. "See you in class tomorrow."

CHAPTER 5

It was time for spring break. I really wanted to go home. I needed a break from college. Sister was excited about me coming home. She told me she made a special effort to make sure my room was clean and smelling fresh. Even though the ride was only a few hours, by the time I got to Oakland, I was exhausted. Mama and Sister were waiting for me when I arrived. Sister was the first one I saw before I got off the bus. She was standing on her toes, trying to see me. As soon as she did, she started smiling, jumping, and waving. I was just as happy to see her. We both started hugging and kissing.

"Oh, Rose, look at you. You look so nice," Sister said. "I like those jeans. You look older too."

I took that as a compliment. "Thanks, Sister. Hi, Mama."

"How was your ride, baby?"

"It was fine." I could tell the tension was still there, maybe because we never got anything settled. I was going to find that bastard if it killed me. Then I thought, he was not the bastard. I was. Sister never could stand the tension between us.

"Let's go home," she said. "I made a special dinner for you." Sister picked up one of my bags and walked to the car. When I went inside the house, the smell of different foods intermixing was heavenly. It felt really good to be back home. I could hardly wait to get to my bedroom. Sister was right behind me, bringing up my bag. Proudly, Sister asked, "Well, what do you think?"

"It looks great, Sister. Thank you." I appreciated it, but I really didn't like anyone messing around in my room.

Sister had prepared fried chicken, sweet potatoes, cabbage, and mashed potatoes with brown gravy. She also made gingerbread for dessert.

"Sister, I can't believe you cooked this all by yourself. You never liked cooking. How did you learn to cook so well and so fast?" I could tell she was happy about what I had just said. Unlike me, I could tell when she was blushing.

"I have a cooking class at school," Sister said proudly.

Mama had to add her two cents. But wouldn't you know it, it was negative. "I told Sister she's not going to be cooking all this fattening food. She won't be able to get a date for the prom if she keeps on cooking like she's been doing."

I thought she wouldn't have to worry. Sister kind of lacked on seasoning.

"I already have a date for the prom," she gloated. Mama had a funny look on her face when Sister said she had a date for the prom.

"With who?" Mama asked.

"Tweety," Sister said.

"What the hell is a Tweety?" Mama snapped.

"A friend from school, Mama. The one that calls here for me all the time."

"How come you didn't tell me you had a date for the prom?"

"I don't know. I just never got around to it, I guess."

"I want this Tweety to come to the house before he takes you to the prom."

I could tell things weren't going well between Mama and Sister. Mama wasn't as sweet to her as she used to be. Sister just said, "Okay, fine," left the dinner table, and went upstairs, which made things really awkward for me. I hadn't been alone with Mama since that argument we had just before I went to visit Grammy.

"So, Rose, how are things at the college? Have you made a lot of new friends?"

"Yes, Mama, I have." I didn't want to sit and carry on a meaningless conversation with her, so I made my excuses and went upstairs.

I had an overwhelming feeling that Sister needed to talk to me. I softly knocked on Sister's door and went in. She was lying facedown on her bed. "Sister, hi," I said as if I was seeing her for the first time. I sat down on the foot of her bed. "How are you doing, sweetie?" I could see tears starting to form in her eyes. Something wasn't right. I never used to feel my sister's pain. I guess I was so wrapped up in my own that I actually thought she was a part of the problem. It hurt me to see her so unhappy. She only had this year to finish, and then she could come to college with me. It would be great to have her there. Just seeing the tears forming on her eyes brought a lump to my throat. "What's the matter, Sister? Are you and Mama having problems?" My sister turned over and sat up. She wanted to say something, but I could tell she was having trouble getting the words out. I looked at her strangely because I saw something that I had never seen before when I looked into her eyes. I became frightened. This fear brought tears to my eyes. Sister put both her arms around me and sobbed, sobbing with every ounce of her strength. My heart was beating fast. I grabbed her by the shoulders, looked deep into her eyes, and demanded she tell me what was wrong.

"I can't," she said. "I can't, I can't, I can't." She dropped back down on the bed and continued sobbing. I got down on my knees so that I could be face-to-face with her.

"Sister, tell me, sweetie. What's the matter? Why are you crying?" I was getting angry. I thought if I threatened her, she'd give in. "Okay, I'll go and ask Mama then."

"No, don't!"

"Why not? Sister? Why not?"

"Because I hate her! I hate her!" I had a feeling things were bad between them, but I never imagined Sister would say something like that. I thought I was the only one that hated Mama. I held on tight to my sister and shared her tears. Exhausted, we rocked each other gently until we fell into a semi peaceful slumber.

I woke up early, about 3:00 a.m. As I was trying to get up, Sister woke up. Still half asleep, she asked me, "Where are you going?"

"I do have my own room, you know," I said, trying to keep my voice down.

"I know, but don't leave now. Let's talk for a little while."

"Sister, it's three a.m."

"I know, but at least we do talk now. For once in my life, I feel like I have an older sister."

"I know, Sister, and I'm sorry for that. I'm sorry for a lot of things. I'm sorry for the way I treated you. I'm sorry for ignoring you when you were sick a lot of nights. But most of all, I'm sorry for blaming you for what Mama did to me."

"After you left for college, I thought Mama would be especially nice to me, but she was a real bitch. I don't know how to explain it. It's weird. She has this thing about color. She didn't really like any of my dark-skinned friends. It's just the way she would act when they came over. Like I was too good to be playing with them. And when any of my white friends or my real light skinned friends came over, she'd offer them cookies, pop, whatever we had. But when my dark-skinned friends would eat something, she would complain about how she can't keep food in here to feed my friends. The funny thing is, I don't think she was aware of it," Sister said.

"Well, I think she knows just what she was doing," I said. "If she didn't think she could love me, why didn't she just abort me? Have you ever heard her mention anything about David?"

"No, I never have. Did Mama tell you anything about him?"

"Nope, I just don't understand why she won't tell me anything about him. I think I deserve to know. It's my right to know." The more I started talking about him, the angrier I was becoming. Besides, I wanted to know what was bothering Sister last night. "Sister, why were you crying last night?" I asked suddenly.

"No reason. I'm just depressed a lot, that's all."

"Then why are you depressed?"

"I don't know. Sometimes I feel strange."

"Strange how? Sister?"

"Sometimes I feel like someone's following me."

"Have you told Mama about this?"

"No."

"Sister! You have to tell Mama about this."

"What do you think she'll do?"

"I don't know, but you have to tell someone. What are you afraid of?"

"Everyone's going to think I'm crazy."

"Oh, Sister, come on! Because someone's following you, we're going to think you're crazy? That doesn't make sense. It happens to people all the time."

"Rose," Sister said. "I haven't told you everything."

I was starting to worry. "What do you mean? What everything?" Sister then got up, went into her closet, reached up on her top shelf, and retrieved a large bag of sour cream and cheddar potato chips. She opened the bag and started eating them while she was talking.

"Rose," she said. "He raped me!"

"Oh my god! Sister! Oh my god! Did you call the police? Where was Mama? Did he hurt you?" I was frantic.

Sister quietly said, "I didn't tell anyone."

"What! What! You didn't tell anyone! Why not!" I started pacing back and forth. "I can't believe this! You didn't tell anyone!" I started pacing faster, moving my hands wildly. Sister started chewing faster. "And stop eating those chips. Sister! I thought you were smarter than that! I can't be—"

"Rose," Sister interrupted. "There was no one there." I looked at Sister, confused.

"What? What do you mean there was no one there?" I was looking at Sister strangely because I just didn't understand what she was saying. I then sat down on the bed.

Sister continued, "I mean, I could feel him in me, but no one was there." Sister picked up the bag of chips again. I snatched them away from her.

"Stop it and look at me!"

"Eating calms me down!" she said.

"Do you want to end up in the hospital again?" I said. "Sister, that doesn't make sense. What do you mean there was no one there?" I could tell I was upsetting her, but I didn't care.

"See! I told you. It sounds crazy. That's why I haven't told anyone."

"Are you sure, Sister? How could there not have been anyone there?" I had a very hard time grasping what Sister was saying to me. All this time I thought it was Mama. I really didn't know what to say to Sister after that. I told her if it happened again to call me right away at school. I didn't say anything to Mama, but I was tempted. This could be serious. Could things like that really happen? I just didn't know what to think. Last night, she seemed more upset. This morning, she acted as if it was no big deal. Strange. I had decided not to say anything to Mama until I noticed some food wrappers sneaking out of her bottom dresser drawer. I was concerned. The next day was Saturday. I heard Sister make a date for the mall. I decided to talk to Mama then.

CHAPTER 6

Mama and Sister had dates. Only Mama didn't know about Sister's date because Sister waited for Mama to leave first. Sister knew to get back before Mama. I had the whole evening to myself, and what a glorious feeling it was. I decided to take one of my fabulous candlelight baths. Only this time, I decided to leave the door open. The last candlelight bath I took, I was getting ready for my date with Jamal. The thought gave me goose bumps. Mama had some body gel on the shelf. I took it down to see what kind it was. "Azure Body Gel, hmmm." I took the cap off. "This smells delicious," I said. I poured gel all over my body. The aroma of Azure permeated the house. Mama also had some Red Door cologne. It smelled heavenly, so of course I sprayed a little on my neck, a little on my chest, a little inside my knees, you know, a little. All of a sudden, I caught a glimpse of my entire nude body in Mama's full-length mirror. I stopped in my tracks. As I looked at myself, I thought, *Not a bad looking body, breast high, good. Stomach is tight. Good!* As I turned around, I thought about what Wesley Snipes said in the movie *New Jack City*: "Gotta look for the pimples on the booty." Uh! Just as I thought, I had a very nice ass. *Hey, I'm ready.* Since Mama wasn't home, I thought I would put on one of her gowns. They were elegant; the satin felt good sliding across my skin. The radio was playing the latest version of "Giving Him Something He Can Feel." So you know I had to pretend like I was one of En Vogue. I was really getting into it when the phone rang.

"Hello?" When I heard the voice on the other end of the phone, I thought I would die.

"Hello, Rose," he said.

"Jamal?" I was ecstatic.

"Yes, I was in town, so I thought I would give you a call. I hope it's not too late."

"No," I said, trying hard to keep my composure.

"Well," he said hesitantly. "I thought I might come over for a little while. I'm only about a block away. If that's okay."

Happily, I said, "Sure, if you don't mind seeing me in my nightclothes."

"It's not a problem for me," he said.

I could tell he was smiling when he said that, then added, "I'll be there in a minute."

I quickly ran into the bathroom and removed my pink sponge rollers. I did a quick comb job on my hair and threw on some lipstick and a pair of Mama's gold hoop earrings. I quickly looked in Mama's mirror. The gown I was wearing was quite lovely. It was a beautiful fuchsia with spaghetti straps. It flowed flawlessly to the floor, simple yet elegant. I had just put on the robe to complete the ensemble when the doorbell rang. My heart stopped. Just as I opened the door, I realized I'd forgotten to put on underwear.

"Hi."

"Hi, Rose," Jamal said. He stood there and stared at me for a while and then said, "You look simply gorgeous."

Smiling, I said, "Thank you, Jamal. You look quite handsome yourself." I led him to the sofa. "Have a seat," I added. Jamal handed me a chilled bottle of champagne. I took it and went to the kitchen to get two of Mama's best champagne glasses. When I returned, he of course took the bottle, popped the cork, and filled our glasses. "Would you like to hear some music?" I asked.

"That sounds great," he responded.

"What brings you to town?"

"I had some business to take care of. I'll be leaving first thing in the morning going back," he said.

"I'm really surprised to see you. I didn't think you would remember where I lived."

"Well, I didn't actually remember. I put your address in my Rolodex so that I wouldn't forget it."

Mama had some old tapes, and since Jamal was older, I decided to play one of them. I liked a lot of the tapes Mama had, like the one I decided to play by Anglo Saxon Brown called "The Man I Love." I was hoping Jamal would ask me to dance. But he didn't. Instead we sat and sipped champagne. We had become so comfortable talking and being with each other. He kept looking at me in a way that I'd never seen before. It wasn't threatening, but direct. After two glasses of champagne, I was feeling pretty good. I decided to pump up the volume with Luther Vandross, hoping this would prompt Jamal to ask me to dance. But it didn't. So I had to take matters into my own hands, by reaching mine out and asking him to dance.

"May I have this dance, sir?" I said very eloquently.

Jamal stood up, took a bow, and said, "Yes, you may."

I could tell the champagne was in effect. Because this man felt good! I had my hands around his neck, and he had his around my waist. The satin I was wearing caused his hands to glide over my body in a way that would make the devil crawl in a hole and die. We slowed down the movement of dancing and just stood there and rocked. I could feel his heart beating against mine. I could also feel his love rising. He slowly pulled his body away from mine, still holding me around my waist. He was looking at my lips with great intensity and I his, and then we kissed. Somewhere far in the back of my mind, I wondered if Sister was having as great a time as I was.

When she filled me in on her evening, it went something like this:

"Tweety, I really appreciate your doing this for me. I don't know what I would do if it wasn't for you," she said.

Tweety and Sister had been friends now for a couple of years. They had the kind of friendship that was hard to find today. They would do anything for each other.

"So what about prom night? Your mama is expecting you to go, right?" Tweety asked.

"Yes, I told her I was going with you."

"So you want me to come and pick you up at eight? Take you to meet your friend, then pick you up at your friends at two a.m. Right?"

"Yep."

"I don't know why you just won't tell her what's up."

"Tweety, you don't know my mother. And besides, this is my business. She doesn't have to know every fuss and fart I do."

"But she might be okay with it."

"Okay with it?"

"Did you tell Rose?"

"No. If I tell Rose, she'll hate me. I know it."

"You're going to have to tell them sooner or later, and it's not going to get any easier," Tweety replied.

"I know it. I don't care so much about Mama finding out. It's Rose I worry about," Sister said.

"Why are you so worried about Rose finding out?"

"Well, because Rose and I have been getting along really good. And I don't want to mess that up. Rose and I have been through a lot, and I know she'll stand by me no matter what. But to tell her I'm a lesbian, Tweety, I don't know."

"Why don't you go home and tell her now? Your mom's not home. This would be the perfect time."

"No! Not yet."

"Why not?"

"She was really looking forward to having the house to herself with no disturbances."

"Come on, chicken. Let's go get some ice cream." Tweety snickered.

Sister smiled and said, "You got some nerve, Tweety."

Jamal was all that and more. I loved kissing him. His lips were soft just like I imagined they'd be. Even after the song was over, we just stood there, kissing and kissing. And just by standing very close to him, I could tell he was very well endowed.

"Would you like another glass of champagne?" I asked him. I felt like I needed to get away from him for a minute. Things were getting pretty heated up. I liked it. Jamal must have gotten a little embarrassed about his manhood taking a stand. He pulled his shirt out of his jeans. I could feel him watching every move I made. It was getting late. I knew that Sister would be home soon. She might not understand if she came home and found me in Mama's gown and a man sitting on the couch. I went back into the living room to tell Jamal it was getting late and I thought he should leave. When I went into the living room and sat down on the couch, I started to tell him, but he put his finger up to my lips and said "Shhh" and kissed me passionately. If I were a block of ice, I would have become a puddle of warm water. Then I felt his hand gently cup one of my breasts. When he noticed my nipple was hard, I heard him moan sweetly. I knew he had to leave. I politely moved his hand.

He looked into my eyes and said, "Call me as soon as you get back to school."

I returned the look and said, "I will." We smiled at each other, kissed once more, and he left.

CHAPTER 7

It was a beautiful Saturday morning. I awakened to the delightful sounds of birds chirping in the sunlight. I felt great. I wondered what time Mama and Sister got in. The sweet smell of bacon cooking tickled my nose, so I got up, showered, and went downstairs to see who the chef was.

"Good morning, Rose," Sister said. She was very cheery as well.

"Good morning, Sister," I said and went over and gave her a big hug.

In shock, Sister asked me, "What was that for?"

"Oh, nothing. I just wanted to let you know how much I love you," I answered.

Sister looked at me strangely and said, "I love you too, Rose." Then she paused, and asked, "Do you want some breakfast?"

"Sounds good to me. What's gotten into you this morning?"

"Oh, nothing. It's just a great morning," Sister answered.

"Isn't it though?" I replied. We gave a quick glance at each other and started to laugh. It felt good to laugh along with Sister. She looked at me as if she could tell I was blushing.

"How was your night last night? Did you get bored in this house alone?"

"No." Sister could read the look on my face.

"Oh! Rose, you had a man over here, didn't you? Who was he? That man you met at school, wasn't it?" Sister smiled. "Well, what's his name?" Sister anxiously waited.

"Jamal."

"Oh, Jamal, I like that. How old is he? Is he in one of your classes?"

"Whoa, Nelly, slow down. I can only answer one question at a time," I said. "I met him at a party I went to with some friends. I'm not really sure how old he is. He looks like he could be at least thirty-five. Didn't I tell you about him when I wrote?"

"Maybe. But are you crazy! Mama's going to kill you!"

"Shhh! Be quiet. Mama's going to hear you."

"No, she won't," Sister said.

"How do you know she won't?"

"Mama's not here. She didn't come in last night."

"You said that like she does it all the time."

"She does."

"Does she have a boyfriend or something?" I asked.

"I don't know, but something is keeping her out. And you know what, Rose? I really don't care. It gives me time to myself, and I like that. But, Rose, tell me about this new man in your life. Does he feel the same way about you?"

"You know, at first I didn't think so, because so much time would lapse before he'd call me, but last night I saw something in his eyes when he looked at me. It gave me a warm feeling all over."

"What does he look like?"

"He's tall, dark skinned, oh! And, Sister, he has the most beautiful hair. He keeps it well-groomed and wears it in a ponytail. Umph! He's gorgeous."

"He sounds like it. When will I meet him?"

"As soon as I meet Tweety." We paused. Sister smiled.

"I'm just curious, Sister. What's up with that name, *Tweety?*" Sister chuckled as she told the story of how Tweety got his name.

"Tweety liked this yellow girl. I mean, this person had a lot of yellow in their skin. Tweety was in love. Remember the cartoon Tweety and Sylvester? That was my Tweety and his friend. Tweety was always chasing after someone who hated his guts too. So everyone started calling him Tweety. Besides that, he looks like a bird, a beautiful bird. Tall, slender, dark skinned with the most beautiful slanted eyes, girl!" She paused before saying, "Very light brown eyes. He is fine."

"Sister, what time did you get in last night?"

"About…twelve thirty. I peeped in your room. You were sound asleep, so I turned off your TV."

"Do you want some orange juice?"

"Yes, please. Sister, this is really good. The eggs came out perfect. What are your plans for today? Didn't I hear you say something about going to the mall?"

"Yeah, I am going with my girlfriend," Sister explained.

"Do I know her? What's her name?" Sister got up to get the marmalade out of the refrigerator.

"I don't think you know her. Her name is Brenda." Sister took a breath and looked at me. "Rose, the last year or two, we've become pretty close, wouldn't you say?"

"Yes, I'd say so. It's great too," I said, smiling.

"Sooooo, I can tell you anything, right?" Sister said, sounding dubious.

"You know you can, Sister. What's the matter? Is there something wrong?"

"Oh no, no, nothing's wrong. I'm just not sure I want to tell you."

"Oh, come on now. Didn't we agree to trust each other?"

"Yes, but this is different. Your feelings about me might change. I think that's what I'm mostly afraid of."

"My feelings for you would never change. It's taken us too long to get to this point. Stop procrastinating. What do you want to tell me? Come on now. Stop washing the dishes. Come over here. Sit next to me and tell me," I said rather sternly.

"Well, let me think for a minute how I want to say this. Okay, I'm just going to blurt it out. Daddy always loved you more. I used to go through changes because of it. I never told anyone. But a lot of times, when we were in the same room together, Daddy ignored me a lot. I remember one time when we were little, Daddy was playing horsey back ride, and you came into the room and sat down on the couch with your sad face. Daddy immediately stopped playing with me and took you out for a walk. I bet you don't remember that, do you, Rose?"

I put my head down and started playing with my fingers, because I knew what Sister was saying to be true. Even now, I treasure that thought.

"Yes, I do remember that, and the only reason Daddy took me out that day was because Mama had just finished yelling at me for no reason."

"But I was his daughter too, and sometimes he acted as if I wasn't. Sometimes I felt more like a neighbor's kid than his. Some mornings, I would come downstairs and find you and him asleep on the sofa bed. You would be curled up around him. I was jealous, Rose. I was." Sister's voice was shaking a little. I didn't realize it then, but Daddy did spend a lot more time with me. Funny, again I didn't realize the impact this must have had on Sister. After all, she was his daughter too. "I think that's why I was mean to you a lot. I didn't know how to express the jealousy I was feeling. I thought it was your fault Daddy didn't like me as much." What Sister was saying was beginning to make me angry.

"Hold up! Hold up! Daddy did love you. The only reason Daddy showed me so much attention was because you were getting all of Mama's love."

"What!"

"It's true, Sister. Mama never pampered me the way she pampered you. Mama would go shopping and bring you all sorts of pretty dresses and hair stuff. She would always bring me these cheap little short sets. And then when it was time to go somewhere, she'd say I couldn't go because I didn't have anything to wear. She knew it! Because she would never buy me any dresses. And you know what? I don't think she wanted to take me anywhere. I really believe she felt like if she took us anywhere together, she would have to explain how I turned out to be so dark when she was married to a white man. And you know what else? I believe that's why Mama and Daddy argued so much. I would hear them. Daddy was always telling Mama that I was her daughter too. I heard him say that quite a few times. Mama would always straighten up for a while, but then she would start treating me the same way. Like I didn't belong. But you know what, Sister? I am going to find out who and where David is if it's the last thing I do. It's not that I want to have a relationship with him. I just want to know who and where he is. I want to look him in his face and call him by name the dog that he is."

As much as I tried not to, I started to cry.

"I just can't understand why Mama didn't tell me. I could understand her not telling me when I was little, Sister, but I'm an adult now. Do you think Grammy knows?" By this time, Sister was standing over me, rubbing my back. "I don't want you to feel sorry for me, Sister, because you also suffered because of Mama's secret, and we still are. I wake up in a cold sweat because of nightmares. I think if I just knew something about him, you know what I mean? Do you think I'm wrong for wanting to know? Sister?"

"No, Rose. Of course not. If it were me, I'd want to know. Grammy might know. I mean, she should know. She's Mama's mama."

"I don't know, Sister. Mama was a slick ass. I'm sure she got away with a lot of shit," I said.

"Yeah, I'm sure she did," Sister agreed.

"I wonder where her ass is at anyway."

"I don't know." Just then, the phone rang. I got up quickly to answer it. I thought it might have been Mama calling. I didn't know why, but I was a little worried about her. It wasn't Mama. It was a long-distance call from the hospital in Vicksburg, Mississippi.

CHAPTER 8

"May I speak with Rose Sinclair, please?" the voice said. I could tell she was not a native Mississippian because she lacked that Southern drawl.

"Yes, this is Rose Sinclair."

"I'm Nurse Johnson calling from Mercy Hospital in Vicksburg. Your grandmother gave me this number."

When the nurse said *your grandmother*, I cut in very quickly, saying, "Is my grandmother okay?" I was almost in hysterics.

"Yes. For now your grandmother is fine. She is resting comfortably," the nurse said.

"What do you mean she's fine for now? What's the matter with her?" I reached for a chair because I felt like I was going to pass out. I could vaguely hear Sister in the background. She was trying to ask me what was wrong. But I just quickly waved my hands at her to be quiet until I got off the phone.

"Your grandmother has had a heart attack. We have her stable now, but it was touch and go there for a while. She's asking for her family to come up."

"Can I talk to her?" I asked.

"We thought it best not to have a phone in her room so she could get as much rest as possible," the nurse said.

"Sure, sure, I understand. Tell Grammy we will be there as soon as we can. Thank you, Nurse Johnson. Goodbye. Oh my god! Oh my god!"

"Rose! What's the matter with Grandma?" Sister took my hands from my face and whispered, "What's the matter with Grandma?"

Preoccupied with what I just heard, I looked at Sister and said, "Grammy's dying." Sister embraced me, and we rocked and rocked. I suddenly raised my shoulders from Sister. "We have to find Mama. I want to leave on the next bus."

"Okay, Rose. I'll comb through her telephone book to see if I can find out where she is."

"Sister?" I called from the other room. "You're coming with, aren't you?"

"Of course. I wasn't as close to grandma as you were, but I loved her too. Besides, I know you need me to be there." Sister gave me a quick wink and scurried up the steps to Mama's room to look for her telephone book. I loved my sister. We never did find out where Mama was, so we borrowed one of her many credit cards, left her a note, and took off to Mississippi to see Grammy.

Sister and I hardly said a word to each other on the bus. I really didn't care though.

Everything I saw reminded me of my Grammy. There were two young kids stealing apples; you could tell they were stealing by the way they were looking over their shoulders. It reminded me of the time Grandma caught us. I closed my eyes.

Cora Lee was a little girl who came up the road to play with us every day. She was a skinny little thing. Her hair was short and nappy. Her mama was too lazy to comb it. It was always flat in the back and sticking straight up on top. She was bad. Sister and I loved it. We were all sitting on a huge tree limb of this old oak tree. Grammy said she sat under that same tree when she was a little girl. Cora looked across the road and spotted Mr. B's apple tree. "Hey, y'all, Mr. B ain't home. Let's go swipe some apples."

"Last one there has to carry all the apples!" I said, and off we went. And wouldn't you know it, I had to carry all the apples. "I hope Grammy isn't in the kitchen 'cause if she is, that's our butt," I whispered to Sister. Grammy's kitchen window had a good view of Mr. B's apple tree.

"You watch the house, and I'll pick fast." But then we spotted old man Kramer pissin' behind some bushes. Cora Lee said, "Who got they

slingshot? Come on, Rose, nah! I know you got yours." Against my better judgment, I handed it to her.

I asked, "What you gonna do with it?" She looked at me kind of sneaky.

"Watch this," she said. Cora was serious with what she was about to do. She made an ugly face. One eye was closed. Her lips were twisted. She was aiming carefully with a small pebble she had been tossing earlier. All of a sudden, she let the pebble fly. We all ducked behind Mr. B's apple tree. Mr. Kramer jumped ten feet high. Cora Lee then looked back at us, nodding, proud of what she'd done. "Who say a white man can't jump?" We were laughing so hard, we didn't hear Grammy coming. She had a long black belt in her hand. I could see and hear her now.

"Wait till I get my hands on y'all." There she was, rushing toward us. Her apron looked like a flag waving. She had a pair of her old draws on her head, with just a little bit of hair sticking out. She had on a blue and white striped dress, falling just past her knees. You could even see the knots tied in her stockings. Her fat legs were moving. When we spotted her, we took off, running back toward the house. We could hear Grammy yelling, "Cora Lee, you get yo fast tail home, you hear me!" Grammy was serious mad. She never liked us stealing.

When I opened my eyes, I noticed my face was wet. I didn't realize I had been crying.

"Are you okay, Rose?" Sister asked me.

"Yes, I'm fine. I just want to see Grammy."

We dropped our bags at Grammy's house and went directly to the hospital.

"Can we have a pass to Lucilla Barnes's room please? Thank you," I said. Grammy's room was on the third floor. I was very anxious to see her. When we walked into her room, she was asleep. Her braid was unwrapped and hanging down on one side. She looked frail and darker than usual. Sister had not seen Grammy in many years.

"Oh my god!" Sister said. "She looks so old, and she looks just like Mama." We walked over to her bed, and I picked up her hand and gently rubbed the backside of it. She stirred a little and opened her eyes. Her eyes widened when she noticed Sister and me standing there. She smiled.

"Hi, Grammy. How are you feeling?" I said. Grammy didn't say anything. She kept staring at Sister.

With a weakened voice, Grammy asked, "Sista, is that you, chile?"

"Yes, Grandma. How are you feeling?"

"Oh, you know, chile, yo granny's gettin' old. The good Lawd is preparing fo you granny to come home." Sister frowned.

"Don't talk like that," I said. "You're going to be with us a long time yet." It was hard getting that lie out. I'm sure Grammy knew that was just what it was. She chuckled.

"Me and Sister are going to the house and freshen up some, and we'll be back. Okay, Grammy?"

"Okay, chile, I'll be here. Yo ole granny ain't goin' nowhere till the good Lawd say so, go on."

I just wanted to make sure Grammy was okay. I was exhausted from the bus ride. All I wanted to do was take a hot bath and go to bed.

We were starving and couldn't wait to see what Grammy had to eat. All she had in the refrigerator were buttermilk, a half-eaten pan of cornbread, and a small bowl of pinto beans that was starting to go bad. "Pew!" Luckily, she had frozen some collard greens and fried corn with cut up pieces of okra. Sister made a fresh pan of corn-bread, and we ate like pigs. I thought, *Tomorrow I'll go to the Hi and Low grocery store up the street.* We still had Mama's credit card. I was more exhausted when I finished eating, so I decided to stretch out on Grammy's couch because Sister had already claimed the rocking chair.

"Turn on the TV, Sister, please," I asked.

"I'm tired too. You turn on the TV. You're the closest," Sister responded.

"Shit!" I said. One of my favorite movies was on—*The Five Pennies.* I loved the music score. Louis Armstrong was fabulous, and so was Danny Kaye. Sister and I both fell asleep during the movie. We were suddenly awakened by the telephone.

"Hello?"

"Rose, is that you?" It was Mama.

"Yes, Mama, it's me. Where were you? Did you just get home?"

"No, I've been home, but you and Sister must not have gotten there yet when I first tried to call. How's Lucilla doing?"

"Well, we were only at the hospital for a little while, but she seems fine. I could tell she was a little weak though. So are you coming or what?"

"Yes, Ms. Smarty-pants, I'm coming. I just wanted to talk to you girls first to see how Lucilla was. Tell her I'm on my way. Okay, Rose? Where is Sister?"

"In the chair sleeping."

"All right. I'll see you in a bit. Bye."

"Who was that?" Sister asked.

"It was Mama. She said she's on her way. Well, I suppose we should be getting back to the hospital. I know Grammy is probably wondering where we are."

"Yes, I'm sure," Sister replied.

I didn't rest very well. I remembered my nightmare. Being here made me think about David. I felt really depressed. Sister could see it, too, because she asked me what was the matter. I couldn't answer her because I didn't know myself. When we got to the hospital, the receptionist told me the nurse wanted to talk to me. My heart started to beat rapidly. Something more was wrong with Grammy. The nurse told me she tried to get a hold of me, but the line was busy. Grammy's test didn't look good. The nurse sat Sister and me down and said Grammy's heart wasn't strong enough to take another heart attack.

"What do you mean another heart attack?" I was confused.

"This is not the first heart attack your grandmother has had. Before, she would never allow me to call you. We had explained to her that another heart attack might prove fatal. It's when she had this last one that she allowed me to call you," the nurse said.

"You mean my grandmother knows she's going to die?" I said with tears in my eyes.

"Yes, I'm afraid she does," the nurse said.

"How long does she have?" I asked.

"It's really hard to say. That depends on her heart." Sister was quiet through this whole conversation. She came over to me and held my hand, and we both started to weep. The nurse said she would give us some time alone.

"Let's go, Sister. Grammy is waiting to see us."

I saw Grammy differently when I saw her this time. I tried hard to keep my tears under control, but it was like they had a mind of their own. She looked so frail, but she was beautiful. Knowing she was going to die didn't seem to bother her. Maybe she was tired. Sister stood on the other side of the bed and held her hand and gently kissed her on her beautiful white hair. "I bet Grammy was hot when she was a teenager," I told Sister. I often wondered how life was for her, raising two daughters without a husband. She had a husband, but he died in a tractor accident many, many years ago. Grammy refused to remarry. She loved that man with all her heart and said no one would ever replace him. No one ever did.

"Sister, we have to call T." T was short for Aunt Fannie. I hadn't seen her in a very long time, but I liked her a lot. She was tall, thin, and very attractive. She kept an immaculate house and took shit off no one. She moved to Chicago when she was nineteen to work in one of the largest county hospitals there was. She still worked there today. My aunt never had any children. She said being a mother was not her cup of tea.

I could tell Grammy was enjoying me brushing her hair. I heard her purr just a little bit before opening her eyes.

"Hi, Grammy." I was trying hard to sound cheerful.

"I knowed that was you, Ro," Grammy said. "I could always tell when you had them fingers of yourn in my head. Yo mama here yet?"

"Not yet," Sister said. "But she called to say she was on her way."

Shifting from her right to her left side, Grammy softly said, "She betta hurrup."

My heart skipped a beat when she said that.

"Grammy," I said, "You have such beautiful hair."

"Oh, chile, my mama had long pretty hair, and so did huh mama."

"Sistuh? How you been doin'? I don't hear much from you."

"I've just been keeping myself busy, Grandma. You know." Sister looked at me and hunched her shoulders.

"When you mama get here, I want you girls to leave us alone. I got somethin' I wanna talk to yo mama bout."

"Mama won't get here until later tonight, so she'll probably see you first thing in the morning. Can I get you something to drink? Some water or juice?" I asked her.

"Some juice is fine, baby. Thank you." The nurse came in and said Grammy had to go down for some more tests. We could come back tomorrow morning.

Mama got in about 4:00 a.m. Sister and I had fallen asleep downstairs because we knew she was coming, and we wanted to be sure we heard her knock. Mama's knock startled me.

"Hi, Rose. How's Lucilla?"

"Mama! Where were you? We called all over, looking for you. When you know you're not coming home, you could at least let somebody know something," I said angrily.

"Well, Rose…was you worried?" she asked with a silly smirk on her face.

"No, I was not worried, just concerned a little." Mama held her head up and started to sniff.

"What's that smell? Oh! Hi, Sister. I didn't see you sitting there. How come you girls are down here? What is that smell?" she asked again.

"We left some greens sitting on the stove all night," Sister said. "We wanted to make sure we heard you knock. But now that you're here, I'm going up. Good night."

"How's Lucilla?" Mama asked. "Oh, good night, Sister."

"Good night, Sister. Are you going to the hospital in the morning?" I asked her.

"No, I think I'll sleep in. How's Mama?" she asked me again.

"Maybe you better sit down."

Mama put her hands to her face and asked, "Rose, Mama's not dead, is she?"

"No, Mama. Grammy's not dead." I actually saw relief in her face. "But she has degenerative heart failure. She's dying." Mama just sat there. I didn't know what to say next, so I just sat there until Mama collected herself. Then I saw something I had never seen before. Mama was crying.

Mama was already gone to see Grammy when we got up the next morning. I wondered what Grammy had to talk to Mama about that she didn't want us to hear. I still thought Grammy knew a whole lot more than she was telling.

I didn't find out till it was almost too late.

Mama stood in the doorway of Grammy's room for a minute before going over and giving her a kiss and a hug. "Hi, Lucilla. How are you feeling this morning?"

"Oh, chile, the Lawd don't give us no mo than we can bear. He's done good by me."

"I saw the nurse as I came in. She said she thinks the doctor is going to be letting you out of here soon. This heart attack was very mild. But he doesn't want you doing anything strenuous. So I think I'll stay down here for a while and make sure you're doing everything you are supposed to." Mama noticed Grammy was very quiet. "What's the matter, Lucilla? What's on your mind?"

"It's time you tell them churen the truth." Grammy looked Mama straight in the eye. "This shit has gone on too long. Nah, them beautiful girls a yourn deserve to know the truth."

"Oh, what do you know, Mama? My girls are just fine."

"No, chile, they not. I can see all the pain and hurt in that oldest chile's eyes. She needs to know the truth. I don't want to go meet my maker knowin' you haven't told them po churen about their daddy." Grammy was struggling, trying to sit up.

"Lay down, lay down. I'll let you up." Mama went to the foot of the bed to let her up electronically. Mama turned her back and went to look out of the huge window. "I don't think they need to know. My girls are doing just fine, I told you." Mama and Grammy were starting to get angry. "Mama, okay, that's enough. You're starting to get upset. I didn't come up for this, Mama, please! Calm down." The nurse came in, looked at the heart monitor, and told Mama she had to leave. She tried to give

Grammy a quick peck on the cheek and tell her she would see her later. Grammy turned her cheek away from Mama and closed her eyes. Mama stared at Grammy for a few seconds and left.

I heard Mama come in the door. "How's Grammy today, Mama?"

"She's just fine, Rose. She told me to tell you and Sister hi."

"Mama, I'm going to get ready and leave."

"Leave! You just got here. Where are you going?"

"Mama, I'm due back in school Wednesday. I need to go home and pack. I really hate to, with Grammy being sick. But if anything happens, call me, and I'll be back in a flash. Okay? Besides, I called the hospital, and they said Grammy was doing fine. She can come home in a week."

"So when are you leaving?"

"I'm catching the nine forty-five tomorrow morning. Mama, I wanted to talk to you about something before I leave though. I'm concerned about Sister. Where is Sister?"

I didn't want her to overhear. That would be all I need for Sister not to trust me. I was going back to school. Someone had to know. Unfortunately, it was Mama.

"She went for a walk. What is it, Rose? Shit!"

"How do I say this?" I paused. "Don't get excited until you hear me out, okay, Mama?" Mama just nodded yes. "Sister told me she was raped." I could see Mama's whole expression change. She rose. But when I saw her start to open her mouth, I quickly spoke. "Wait, wait, wait! Before you get excited, she told me that she could not see the person. No one was really there. She said she could feel the person inside her, but there was no one there."

"Wait! What? What does she mean there was no one there?"

"That's what she said. I didn't know what to make of it. It scared me. She doesn't know I'm talking to you about it. Mama, please don't tell her. I just wanted you to keep an eye on her." Mama was spacing out. I didn't blame her. "Mama!"

"All right! I heard you!"

"Well, I'm going to get dressed and go see Grammy and say goodbye."

It was such a beautiful spring afternoon. I wanted to feel the breezes and smell the flowers along the way, so I walked, taking a shortcut through a field of wildflowers. There were reds, purples, white, and yellows, every color imaginable. The flowers looked happy dancing to the music of the wind. I picked a bunch for Grammy. When I was a little girl, after school I'd bring Grammy flowers from this field every day. How long ago that seemed. But the most beautiful was a field of red, white, and purple lilies swaying in the wind. I could see it in the distance like a fine choir. I picked up a long twig and started to run, faster and faster. As I approached them, I could smell their sweet nectar. I stopped, mesmerized by their glory. I closed my eyes and listened to the wind. It went past one ear and then the next. I followed it with my twig raised slightly in the air, and then I whispered, *Sing for me.* I listened closely to their leaves and heard the music of lilies.

Grammy was up sitting in a chair while the nurses changed her linen. She seemed preoccupied with something. Mama seemed a little out of sorts too. I wondered what they talked about. I didn't dare to ask.

"Hi, Grammy. Wow, look at you sitting up in this chair. Are you feeling better?" Grammy didn't say anything. She just sat there and stared out the window. "Grammy?"

"Oh, Ro, honey, I didn't hear you come in."

"You scared me. I thought something was wrong."

"Oh, baby, yo ole Grammy's fine. I just stay so tied." Grammy did look tired. Very tired.

"Grammy, I picked you some fresh wildflowers. Aren't they pretty?"

"Yes, baby, very pretty."

"What's the matter, Grammy?" Grammy didn't like it when she thought I was worried about something. "Come here, Ro. Sit next to Grammy. Ro, never let anythang or anyone destroy yo life. Remember that you are just as important as anyone else. You hear what I say? Always rememba, no matta where I am, yo Grammy loves you very much. Grammy don't have long fa this world, but no matta what, I'll be watchin'." As I listened to Grammy speak, I knew it was possible I might not see her alive again. I knelt down next to Grammy like I did when I was a little girl and sobbed heavily into her lap. I could feel her rubbing my hair like she used to do. I held on tight to her legs and wished as hard as I could that I was that little girl again, sitting down next to Grammy and holding her leg like a pillow, sucking my thumb until I fell asleep against her.

It was hard telling Grammy I was leaving the next day. After telling her, she looked at me as if she knew she would never see me again. It was hard saying bye to Sister too. She didn't say much except that she loved me.

CHAPTER 9

It was nice going back to school. I missed my friends. I called to let them know when I was coming in. Nina met me at the bus station.

"Hey, girl! How was your spring break? I had a ball. My mother bought me all kinds of new clothes. You're welcome to borrow them sometimes," Nina said, smiling.

"All right."

"What's the matter, Rose?"

"Oh, nothing. I'm just tired, I guess. Hey, do you have a joint? Girl, would you believe I haven't had one since I left?"

"You've got to be kidding."

"Um hm." Nina immediately reached down in her purse and said happily, "Here you go, girl. Light it up. Have you talked to Jamal?"

"Yeah, girl. He called me at my mom's and came over. He looked good! I really like him a lot. He seems to like me a lot too. He told me to call him as soon as I got back. Are Kiki and Samara back yet?"

"Yep, they got in yesterday."

"But you know something, Nina, I think Jamal is ready."

Nina held her head down, cocked her eyes up at me, and said, "Ready for what?"

Then I gave her a look to see if she would get what I was talking about. "You think so? How do you know? Did he say so?"

"No, he didn't actually say so. His body language told me."

"His body language?" Nina's eyes widened. "Oh, girl, he didn't have a…"

"Yes, he did, girl!" We both started laughing.

"What do you think? Are you ready? This music on the radio is dead. Reach back and hand me my CD case. Just look in it and hand me Mary J. Blige."

"I didn't know you had her CD."

"I just bought it a few days ago. I had to have it."

"I'm not sure. I mean, I get excited just being around him. I get excited when he kisses me. And when he touches me…yes! I think I am." We both screamed again. "No, I don't know." As we pulled up to the dorm, Kiki and Samara were standing there, waiting. When they saw the car, they both came running over. We were really glad to see each other. Kiki and Samara had just come from the store. They bought a forty-ounce bottle of beer. It was chilling in the refrigerator. When we went up to the room, Nina pulled from under her bed a shoebox top with bud on it.

"Let's get this party started!" Samara yelled.

Kiki went over to the stereo and popped Kut Klose into the CD player. We all waved one hand in the air and said, "Heyyy" when the song came on. Yes, it really was good to be back with my friends.

I missed my writing class. Especially when I thought about how fine the instructor was. He wasn't very tall, kept his light brown beard trimmed lightly, and always wore those funky looking jeans. There was something sexy about him. He wanted to know while we were away if there was anything interesting to write about. Man! Have I got a lot to write about. I think I was in love with Jamal. My sister was losing her mind. My mother acted as if she had some sort of secret life. My Grammy was dying. And to top it all off, I didn't find out shit about my father. Hell yeah! I had a lot to write about. So now we've been assigned to write a poem about the bullshit. I didn't care though; I still thought he was cute.

I didn't feel like company tonight. I just wanted to climb in my bed and watch television or read. But then David kept popping into my brain. I didn't want to think about him anymore. So he raped your mother and you were born. GET OVER IT! I couldn't. I just wanted to know who he was. I wondered if he was still a rapist. I wondered if I saw him and didn't know it was him. *Oh God! Please help me. Please help me get over this.* Why did I ever have to find this out? Sometimes I felt it would have been better if I didn't know. Did he ever think about me? Did he know I existed? Why did I care? I felt so confused. *God! Help me please.* I decided to do my homework. If I had to think about him, I might as well write my poem about him. How could I write a poem about a man I didn't even know? Who was this man, my father? Mama knew.

Mama Knows
Who is this man, my father
Who stole from my mama in the dead of night
Who is this man, my father
Let me see, come into the light
Who is this man, my father
Who left me without a name
Who is this man, my father
Who filled my family with secrets and shame
Who is this man, my father
Who never gave us a crust of bread
Who is this man, my father
Mama knows

I fell asleep shortly after that and dreamed about Jamal.

* * * * *

Mama said Grammy was doing better, but it would only be a matter of time. Sister left shortly after I did. She, too, had to get back to school. Mama only stayed a couple of weeks after that. She said Grammy was getting on her nerves royally. With the help of Grammy's insurance, Mama hired a nurse to come in every day to take care of Grammy. Then she left.

I was going to miss the stories Grammy would tell about Mama and her. Mama was a little hotsy-totsy, trying to play Ms. Innocent.

Grammy told me a story about when Mama was fourteen years old. Grammy had a strict rule about her daughters and their boyfriends. Grammy would let their boyfriends come over and sit on the porch, but only if she was home. Auntie and Mama were sitting on the front porch when an ice cream van parked in front of the house. Auntie and Mama went up to the truck and flirted with the two boys that worked in it. One of the boys asked Auntie if she wanted to go for a ride. She knew they would get in trouble, but their mama wasn't due home from work for another hour. So they thought they would be slick and get in the van. Grammy's friend was watching the house as she always did when Grammy was gone. Grammy had friends that secretly watched her girls whenever Grammy wasn't around. Anyway, one of Grammy's friends reported to her that she saw her two girls riding around in an ice cream truck. Grammy didn't say anything. But later that night, when Auntie and Mama were asleep, Grammy came up the stairs with her ironing cord and commenced to whooping on their asses. Auntie and Mama jumped up in shock, rubbing their butts, asking, "Ouch! What did we do?"

All Grammy said was, well, she didn't actually say it. She sang it as she whooped them. "I won't some iiiiice cream! I want some iiiiice cream!" Mama and T bucked their eyes at her. They knew they were in trouble. I thought about it whenever I saw an ice cream truck.

CHAPTER 10

Jamal and I were going pretty strong. We would go out every weekend to a movie or out to dinner. But this weekend, the girls and me were having a slumber party. Nina was in charge of getting some bud. I was in charge of getting the beer. Kiki was in charge of dips and chips. And Samara was in charge of the music. We invited Connie Wilkens. We all liked Connie. She was black, short, and very cute. We've hung out with her a couple of times. We also invited Doris McAlister. Doris was so much fun and very attractive. She had hazel eyes, and it was obvious she was mixed. A lot of students didn't like her because she had a lot of men friends. But we didn't care. Doris had a date with a new man but promised to come after that.

Since our bedrooms were too small to accommodate all of us, the housemother said we could use the sitting room at the end of the hall, which was great because it had a fire escape we could go out on and get high.

Everyone was there. We expected Doris at about 11:00 p.m., depending on how her date went. We all brought our favorite blankets and pillows. We had to sneak the beer in, so we put it in a cooler and sat it on the fire escape earlier that day. We were all sitting around and having a good time when Samara blurted out, "I wonder where did Doris go tonight. She said this new man is really cute."

Then Connie asked, "Rose, how's your love life? I heard you and Jamal have been real tight lately."

"Well…" Everyone quickly sat down in a circle. "Before I say anything, I want everybody to promise that what I said, no matter how big or how small, will stay in this room, or I ain't telling y'all asses shit."

"Wait! Wait! Wait! Should I turn off the light for this woooo," Kiki howled. I picked up my pillow, threw it at her, and told her to kiss my ass. We all laughed.

"Anyway," I said, "it's real serious, ladies. I think Jamal is ready for a little bump and grind."

"How do you know?" Kiki asked. "Did he say something about it?"

"Nooo, he didn't say anything. A couple times when we were together, his manhood saluted me."

"What did he say?" Nina asked.

"He didn't know I noticed, so I didn't say anything."

"Girl, you better gone get some of that dick." Samara snickered.

"I'm just not so sure I'm ready."

"Ooooooooh, Rose! You're a virgin." We turned around to Connie cracking up. "A virgin!"

"Hold up! Hold up!" Kiki said. "Look, girl, it ain't nothing wrong with being a virgin. Don't let nobody talk you into doing nothing. Because these bastards today, they ain't about shit. It just seems like we still haven't learned anything. We live in the nineties, and women are still letting men misuse and abuse them. Especially with that AIDS shit running rampant out there. Girl, huh, be proud you're a virgin, because it's people out there now wishing they were virgins again. I'm tired of seeing the sistuhs or any woman beat down because a man says I loooove you. Not me! That's why I don't have anyone today. Because if you can't be faithful, I don't want your ass."

"Rose," Connie asked, "what do you want to do?"

"I really like Jamal a lot. I mean, if I sleep with anyone, it would be him. I'm afraid that once we sleep together, things won't be the same."

"What do you mean things won't be the same? If he loves you…" Kiki started waving her hands high up in the air. "Now see, that's just what I mean, if he looooves you. Love don't mean shit anymore."

"Uh uh! Now see, I'm never giving up on love. But I'm not taking love all by itself," Connie said, and then Kiki interrupted.

"What do you mean you're not taking love by itself?"

"I mean, I'm not going to let a man tell me he loves me but then don't come home for two days. That's what I mean. I'm not going to let a man tell me he loves me but he doesn't help me pay the bills if we're living together. That's what I mean. And I'm not going to let a man tell me he loooves me and tell me, 'Aah, baby, I didn't get a chance to stop and get the rubbers. Can't weee?' Hell naw, mothefucka! You either get dressed and go to the drugstore or dream about this pussy tonight!" Everybody fell to the floor, laughing.

Nina stood up and said, "I don't know about you all, but I'm ready for a joint. This beer ain't g'tting' it." Everybody stood and proceeded to the fire escape, beer in hand.

When we went back inside, Samara put on some music. We pretended to be a singing group. We all got the munchies and started in on the chips and dip.

"That's why I got to stop smoking this shit. It makes me eat too much," I said, licking my fingers. "I wonder where Doris is. I thought she'd be here by now."

There were footsteps running down the hall toward us. It was Carolyn from the second floor. "Hey!" she said, barely catching her breath. "Doris is in the hospital. She's been beat and raped."

I froze. I couldn't move. Everyone decided to get dressed and go to the hospital. I saw Nina looking at me. I didn't know what she saw, but she saw something.

"Rose, are you coming with us?" Samara asked. When I didn't respond, she looked at me strangely. All of a sudden, I heard Nina say, "No, Rose and I are staying here. Call us and let us know how Doris is, okay?"

"We will. Bye."

I don't know what came over me, but when Carolyn said rape, it was like my mind froze. It was really hard to explain. I went numb. You'd have thought that I'd been raped. Even though it was my mama that was actually raped. Somehow I felt like I was, because Mama took something from me—my right to know the truth.

"Rose, what's the matter? You're shaking!"

"Nothing, Nina!" Of course, she didn't believe me.

"Rose, you have tears in your eyes and you're trembling. Rose, please, tell me what's wrong. You can trust me. We've been roommates for months now. Have you ever known me to tell anything that you've told me? I take my friendships very seriously. Please, Rose, what's the matter?" Only one thing kept going over and over in my mind.

"What if she's pregnant? What if she's pregnant?" I could feel myself panicking, but I had no control. "Oh my god! Oh my god! Ohhh…"

"Rose, stop it! Now breathe slowly…slowly." When I looked into Nina's eyes, I saw my fear through hers. I slowly started to calm down. "That's it. You're okay," Nina said as she led me to a more comfortable chair. "Come sit down. Now tell me, what's going on with you?"

"Nina, what if she's pregnant?"

"She's not pregnant, Rose."

"How do you know?"

"She takes birth control pills."

"I'm sorry, Nina. I'm sorry."

"That's okay, Rose. Man! I've never seen you act like that before. What brought that on?"

"Nothing. I'm fine now."

"Rose, I'm not going to try and force you to tell me. But I want you to know I'm your friend, and whatever the problem is, I'm here for you. Maybe it would do you some good to talk about it."

I started to weep. I didn't want to, but the tears had a mind of their own. Nina embraced me.

"Oh, Rose! What's wrong?"

"I was so scared."

"Why?"

"Because my mama was raped."

"Was she hurt?"

"Yes. No." I felt dizzy and just wanted to put my head down. "She got pregnant."

"Oh, Rose! What did she do about the baby?"

"You're looking at her."

Nina sat there looking at me, then said, "Rose, I'm sorry. I… no! I'm sorry."

I held my head up and looked at her. Then I heard her finish her thought.

"If your mom had decided to abort you, I wouldn't have you for a best friend."

We didn't say anything for a while, then talked until I fell asleep. I felt cleansed.

We found out later that Doris had a couple of bruises, but she wasn't raped. He tried to rape her but gave up when she started screaming at the top of her lungs. Of course, he denied any of it happened. Once again, shit was shoveled under the carpet, stepped on, and no one seemed to smell it.

I missed Sister. I thought I'd sit down and write her a letter.

CHAPTER 11

Meanwhile, at Mama's house...

Dear Sister

I meant to write this letter a long time ago. I'm still waiting on my pictures. I'm dying to see what this Tweety looks like. What's Mama been doing? Is she still staying out all night? Sister, how have you been doing? Have you had any more experiences or strange feelings? Okay, enough with the questions, right? Guess what, girl. Do you remember Nina, my roommate? We had a long talk. I told her everything. And, Sister, it felt so good that one other person knew besides us. I'll tell you how it came about when I call you next week. Next time I come up, maybe, just maybe, you'll get to meet Jamal, and I'll get to meet the love of your life. Tell Mama I said hello and to keep her behind out of the streets.

PS: I love you.

Rose

"Mama," Sister called to her while reading the letter. "Rose says to tell you hi."

"Oh, was that a letter from Rose?"

"Yes, I'm going out for a while. See you later."

"Take your keys because I'm going out later too!"

Sister grabbed her keys and hurried out the door to see Brenda.

Sister and Brenda had a date for the movies. They went to the movies a lot. They would sit in the back where no one could see their affection for each other.

After the movies, Sister and Brenda went back to Mama's house. Sister knew Mama wouldn't be back for hours. She had a picture of me sitting on top of her bureau. Brenda had never seen me, so she asked Sister who that girl was in the picture.

"That's my sister. Rose."

"Hm," Brenda said.

"Ah! Don't even say it!"

"Say what?"

"We don't look alike. I'm tired of people always telling me we don't look alike!"

"Okay, baby, no need to get upset," Brenda said. "As a matter of fact, I think she does look like you. I think your eyes are similar."

"Thank you, sweetie," Sister said.

"By the way, Sister, when am I going to meet Rose? I've heard so much about her. I'll bet you haven't told her about us, have you?"

"No, I…"

"You said you were going to tell her the last time she was here!"

"I know, okay! I'm scared. I'm chicken, whatever you want to call it. I'll tell her, but only when I feel the time is right! So leave me alone about it, please!"

"All right. Look, we are not going to argue about this. I just wanted to know why you haven't told her. You said you and she was close."

"We are close, and I'm sure Rose would understand, but that doesn't make me any less scared, okay?"

"Whatever!" Brenda said sarcastically. "For all you know, Rose could already suspect. Sister, when did you first know?"

"Know what?"

"When did you first know you wanted to be in the life?"

"I'm not really sure I do know. I mean, there were always boys whistling or screaming out of car windows. That never fazed me. I really hated it. It seemed, I don't know, boys thought I was pretty, but they didn't care anything about what I was feeling. Or where my head was. They don't care about what I want to do with my life. All they saw was a pretty face. I just don't have time for any man that don't have time for me. It seems like it's been that way all my life. Now that I'm older, I know what I want. I want you."

"So what time will your mom get home?"

"It's Saturday. She won't be home tonight."

Sister and Brenda looked at each other, and both ran for the shower.

For whatever reason, Mama decided not to stay out all night that night. Sister heard her keys coming into the lock at 3:00 a.m.

"Oh shit!" Sister said.

"What's the matter, baby?"

"Get up! Mama's home." They were both starting to panic.

Then Brenda whispered, "Wait a minute. It's not like I'm a man. Can't you just tell her you had a friend stay over?"

"Yes, that's it! We need some room deodorizer. Look on the dresser and hand me that bottle of spray I have sitting there. Hurry up!"

Because of the carpeting, Sister couldn't tell when Mama was actually coming up the stairs. Then she heard her lay her keys down on the stand in the hall.

Sister thought Mama was going to peep in her bedroom, but she didn't. Sister and Brenda lay quietly, whispering the rest of that morning.

"We'll get up early and start breakfast. Then I'll introduce you to Mama as a friend from school. She shouldn't have a problem with that. I mean, girls invited other girls to spend the night all the time."

"Sure, Sister. Whatever you say." Brenda fell back to sleep. Sister gently kissed Brenda on the cheek, turned over, and went to sleep too. Sister and Brenda went rushing down the stairs about 8:00 a.m. When they walked into the kitchen, Mama was already sitting there, reading the Sunday paper and drinking coffee.

"Oh! Mama?"

"Good morning, Sister and…"

"Oh, Mama, this is Brenda. She's in one of my classes at school."

"Hello," Brenda said, looking her in the eyes.

"Hello, Brenda. Nice to meet you."

It's been a month since Nina and I talked about Mom being raped. We made a date to go to lunch. I was really looking forward to it. We met at a quaint little place not far from campus. Its decor reminded me of some old movies I'd seen. What stuck in my mind mostly was this huge wagon wheel resting on the wall and that fabulous root beer float I had.

"Nina, this is a really nice place."

"I know. I come here sometimes when I want to be alone to think. Hardly anyone from the campus comes here. I think it might be a little too old-fashioned. I'm glad because I never run into anyone."

"Nina, I never thanked you for coming to my rescue the night of the slumber party."

"Rose, you don't have to thank me."

"You did a lot. I never really talked to anyone about it, and it was eating me up inside."

"I wish you had said something to me sooner, girl! Don't you know you can tell me anything?"

"I know that now, yes. It's not easy telling someone you're the product of a rape."

"I know, Rose. I hate you needed someone to talk to and had no one. I'm glad you can talk to me. You don't ever have to worry about me telling anyone anything that you've told me. I'm your friend, and I don't have a lot of them. I have associates. Besides you, I have only one other friend, and she lives in Chicago, so we don't get a chance to talk or visit much because neither of us can afford it. Rose, I pick my friends carefully. Everyone needs at least one person they can talk to and not worry that this friend might stab them in the back. I want to tell you something that I've never told anyone except my girlfriend in Chicago, and this was when I knew how important friendships are supposed to be. If I didn't consider you my friend, I wouldn't tell you this, okay?"

"Okay..."

"I had this friend. Well, at the time, I thought she was my friend. I had known her since freshman year, and we were juniors. I would tell her everything. I told her when I had sex the first time. I told her about when I'd sneak out at night to be with my boyfriend. At the time, I didn't know she had become friends with this other girl she knew I hated with a passion. My girlfriend told her that I was pregnant and had an abortion. I found out through my girlfriend in Chicago. I didn't know her then, but she came up to me and said, 'I'm Carolyn. Isn't your name Nina?' I said yes. She said, 'I see you all the time. You never mess with anyone. I noticed that you hang with Jenny. Is she a close friend of yours?' I said yes. 'I thought so. You seem so nice I thought you should know.' Know what? I said. 'I heard her tell several people you were pregnant and going to have an abortion.'

"I could have fallen through the floor when I heard those words come out of her mouth. I knew she wasn't lying because Jenny was the only person I told. I was so humiliated and embarrassed, I dropped out of school. Carolyn noticed I had dropped out. She came by my house one evening. Believe it or not, I was really glad to see her. I let her in, and we ended up talking about the pregnancy. She went to the clinic with me. I was so glad I didn't have to do it alone. We've been best friends ever since. Now we take turns calling each other once a month so that we get a chance to talk to each other twice a month. I don't know what I would do without her friendship."

"I'm sure she feels the same way. Before you, I had no one to talk to except my sister."

Then Nina asked, "So have you found out anything new?"

"No. Mama refuses to tell me anything about him. I don't know if it hurts too bad to remember or what it is."

"Well...I don't care. I think you have a right to know, if you want."

"I just can't understand why she won't, especially since I know about him."

"I don't know, Rose. There is something strange about everything you've told me. What do you think that key goes too?"

"I don't know. I've checked everything in the house that a key would belong to."

"That key belongs to something."

"I know." I paused for a minute. "Nina, what are you thinking?"

"You know, Rose, I regret having that abortion."

"Why?"

"Look at you. You are a beautiful black female. If your mama had decided to abort you, you wouldn't exist today. Right now, I would have a beautiful little girl or boy. I've never told anyone this, not even my friend in Chicago. My mother made me have that abortion. I didn't want to, but she made me," Nina said, her voice trembling. "She didn't want to be embarrassed. She didn't give a shit about what I wanted or the toll this might have had on me." Nina cried.

"Nina, I hope you don't mind my asking, but how old were you?"

"I was fifteen. I really wanted the baby. I knew I was young. I also knew having this baby would have changed my life. It could have changed my life for the better. She didn't know. How dare she make a decision that I have to live with the rest of my life. That's why I can understand your situation, Rose. I mean, your mom made a decision that affects you the rest of your life, only hers can be rectified by telling you the truth now. Why she doesn't, I just can't understand. I have nightmares sometimes. Sometimes I wake up so scared and feeling guilty."

"Why do you feel guilty?"

"Because! If I hadn't gotten pregnant in the first place, I wouldn't be going through what I'm going through. I still feel like it's my fault my baby's dead." Nina really started to cry. I got up and went and sat in the booth next to her. She laid her head on my shoulder.

I brushed her hair back with my hand and said, "Nina, we will survive this. I will not be destroyed by this, and neither will you." Nina sat up and agreed with me. She wiped her eyes with a napkin off the table. I wanted to change the subject. "Oh, guess what! *Waiting to Exhale* starts in three weeks."

"Oh…girl! I've been waiting for that movie forever. Did you read the book?" Nina asked.

"Yes, I did. I couldn't put it down. You know Whitney Houston's in the movie. Have you heard the CD? It's bad."

"I know. I heard it. Samara has it."

"You know what? Me, you, Kiki, and Samara should go. Do you have any plans, Rose?"

"No, Jamal is going out of town again. Oh, this is going to be so much fun."

"I know. I can't wait... Rose?"

"Yeah?"

"Never mind. Let's go."

CHAPTER 12

Jamal told me he had something special planned for our date this evening. He wouldn't tell me what it was, but he told me not to have dinner. It was taken care of. I was really excited because he never surprised me with anything before. I asked him to give me a hint so that I would know how to dress. He said however I decided to dress would be fine. I wondered where he could be taking me. Since I didn't know, I decided to wear something cute and simple. Jamal picked me up at 7:00 p.m. sharp. I loved his punctuality.

"Hi, baby," he said. "How was your day?"

"Hi, it's been a long day. I had to do some research for an essay I'm writing. So where are we going?"

"Anxious, are we?"

"Well, of course. You've never surprised me before."

"Okay, hold on. We will be there soon," he said, smiling. I didn't know where we were going, but the area we were riding in was beautiful, and so were the homes. Jamal pulled into the driveway of a duplex apartment building. I didn't let him see me, but I had a strange look on my face. Were we going to visit some friends of his?

"This is a beautiful building. Do you have friends that live here?"

"No, Rose, I live here." My heart stopped.

When we walked into the foyer, I was amazed at what I saw. The first thing I noticed was a vase full of fresh cut red and yellow roses. How beautiful they were. We then walked into a beautiful spacious room with hardwood floors shined to perfection. There was a huge black entertainment system complete with CD ROM, a beautiful oriental rug dressing the middle of his floor, and a beautiful white shag carpeting lying in front of the fireplace, keeping company with a chilling bottle of fine Chardonnay sitting on a silver tray, complete with two long-stem crystal wineglasses. Exquisite!

"Can I take your jacket?"

"Yes."

"Let me show you the rest of my apartment," he said.

A huge lump was building in my throat as I managed the word "Sure."

"This is my favorite room. I love sitting by the fireplace with a glass of wine and a good book or magazine," he said.

"What a nice television. I'm going to have a large screen television someday."

"Well, you can have one now. It's yours whenever you want to watch it," he said, smiling.

"I'm sure," I said, not sure how he meant it.

"I mean it, Rose. You're welcome here anytime." Then I wondered how many women he told that to. "I know what you're thinking, but seriously, Rose, I don't have a lot of women. I just wasn't interested…until now."

I smiled.

"What's that fabulous smell?" I asked.

"Dinner," he said.

"You cooked?"

"Sure, I cooked."

Yes! I thought. *He cooks too.*

"Are you hungry?"

"Starving." I wondered what he cooked. It was probably something exotic. Jamal took my arm and led me into the dining room. I gasped.

"Oh, Jamal! It's lovely." Jamal had the table set beautifully. There were candles and a centerpiece made of roses of all colors, even one black rose in the center.

"Jamal, where did you get the black rose? It's so full and beautiful."

"There's a little shop in Czech Village called International Creations. They carry flowers and exotic plants that are not found in your regular flower shops." He asked if I wanted some wine.

"Yes, thank you." I was anxious to see what Jamal had prepared.

"Okay, here we are." When Jamal uncovered the pan, I was surprised.

"Hamburgers…" I said. "French fries." Jamal seated himself and reached for my plate. To my surprise, the hamburgers were delicious. I kept looking at the centerpiece. Seeing the black rose reminded me of my father.

"Rose, what's the matter?" Jamal asked. "Is there something wrong with the food?"

"No, I think the hamburgers are really good. It's just that I have a thing about black roses."

"Should I take it away?" he said as he started to remove them.

I grabbed his hand and said, "No, I think they're gorgeous. It's just that, well, my father used to call me his beautiful black rose. He gave me a pendant with the picture of a black rose in it. I still wear it. He died when I was just a little girl." Jamal looked at me and reached for my hands.

"I'm sorry, Rose. Come with me and sit by the fire. I'll put on some music." Jamal led me to the carpet, sitting in front of the fireplace. He made sure I was sitting comfortably before he went over to the stereo. "So what happened to your father? If you don't mind my asking."

"I was so young. I really don't remember."

"Well, what about your mom? I'm sure she knows."

I'm sure she does, I thought. "We really didn't talk about it very much."

"Rose, are you an only child?"

"No, I have a sister a little younger than I am. What about you? Do you have any brothers or sisters?"

"Yes, I have a brother three years younger than me and two older sisters."

"I didn't know you had *Waiting to Exhale* CD."

"Oh, yeah, girl, what's the matter? You think I'm too old for this kind of music?" he said, laughing. I laughed too.

"By the way, how old are you?" I asked him.

"I'm thirty-two years young." We both laughed again, and then he said, "Come here, girl." He gently pulled me close to him and kissed me and kissed me and kissed me. "Rose," he said, "I love you." And he kissed me again. The touch of his hands and warmth of the fire built a passion in me beyond belief. When I inhaled the sweet smell of his body, I thought I would lose all control.

"Jamal, stop!" I said, pushing him gently away from me.

"I'm sorry, baby! I guess I just got carried away. Do you want me to take you home? I…" he said as he stood up quickly.

"No, I don't want to go home." I reached for his hand and pulled him back down to where I was. "I just, I don't know. I want you, Jamal. I mean, there's been so many times I imagined us being together. I have so much happening in my life right now. I don't want to make another mistake. I know it sounds corny, and people say what I've said a lot. I didn't understand it until now. You have never given me any reason to believe that this relationship wouldn't work once we made love. I want to be sure. It's one thing I haven't told you that I think you should know."

"What's that?" he said, tilting back a little.

I held my head down and said in a very low voice, "I'm a virgin." He chuckled and put his hand gently under my chin, raising my head.

"Rose, hold your head up. Always hold your head up. When you hold your head up, you see clearer. Never let anyone put you in the position of holding your head down."

I simply nodded with what he was telling me. He made me feel so good about myself just then. I looked directly into his eyes, and he was right. I could see clearer. I could genuinely see that this man cared for me.

"Rose, your being a virgin only makes me love you more. I know you're scared because I'm older and more experienced. You can grow and learn. I'm not asking anything of you except that you be yourself.

It's true. I want to make love to you, but not until it's a mutual decision. I've had many women in my life. I don't want that anymore. I want something more stable. I want to build on something. I'm thirty-two. I want children. Hopefully, the woman I marry does too."

"What kind of woman do you want to spend your life with?" I asked him. I was anxious to know.

"Some men get a bad rap, and truly deserved. I know some of us can be dogs sometimes. I probably was by some woman's definition. But I'm past that now. It's been months since I've slept with a woman."

"Why? I mean, I'm glad, but why?"

"Because I don't want to just fuck! I want something meaningful, something to build on."

"Why me?"

"I don't know. To be perfectly honest, Rose, I don't know. When I saw you that night, my heart skipped a beat, and I'm a man that listens to his heart. I knew I had to at least dance with you."

"What took you so long after that?"

"I wanted to see how I would feel never seeing you again. And obviously, not too good. I thought about you constantly after that night, so I decided to call."

"All this sounds too good to be true. And you know what they say. If it sounds too good to be true, it probably is," I said.

"Yes, I've heard that saying, but time will tell, and I'm giving you as much as you need. You don't have to worry that because you want to take your time, I will go sniffing behind some other skirt, because I won't. I promise you, baby, and I mean what I am saying. Take all the time you need. I want you to be sure—no doubts, no second thoughts, no inhibitions. When we make love for the first time, I want the earth to move." He kissed me passionately, then looked at me and asked, "Did you feel the fire?"

I wrapped myself around him, and I whispered, "Yes! I feel it. I feel it." And we kissed again.

After Jamal dropped me off, I still couldn't get Daddy off my mind. I wondered what he would think about Jamal. He'd have to love him as much as I do. I opened my locket and thought about when he gave it to me. It still brought tears to my eyes. Jamal and Daddy were the only two men who have ever loved me. I looked at the locket and thought out loud, "Daddy, I wish you were here. I need you to tell me what to do. I love Jamal. There's no doubt in my mind about that. He says he'd wait as long as necessary for me. What should I do? Wait?"

"Hi, Rose. When did you get in?" Nina asked.

"About five minutes ago. Where were you? I didn't think anyone was here," I said.

"Down the hall in Kiki and Samara's room. Oh! Rose, you had a phone call."

"Who was it?"

"I don't know. He wouldn't leave a name."

"He? Did he say what he wanted?"

"No, as a matter of fact, he called last week too. But he said he would call you later that evening. I guess he didn't."

"Well, if it's important, he'll call back. What are you doing for the summer?" I asked her.

"I don't know. Probably nothing. What about you? Are you taking Jamal down to meet your family?"

"I haven't said anything to him yet, but I'm going to. Maybe he'll drive. Then I won't have to catch the bus. That would be good."

"How do you think he'll get along with your mom?"

"I don't know, and you know what? I really don't care. Because knowing Mama, she will find something she doesn't like about him."

"Does she know how old he is?"

"Nope!"

"Why not?" she said.

"I just haven't. Mama makes me sick. I guess I feel like she doesn't deserve to know. I mean, she won't tell me anything. Why should I? I know that's childish, but that's how I feel. I will tell her because I do want Jamal to visit me at home over summer break, unless we rent a hotel room or something."

"Have things between you and Jamal gotten that serious?"

"Kind of. We had a real serious talk about sex and our relationship. Girl, he told me that he would wait as long as it takes."

"They all say that, girl. And the next thing you know, some other girl is pregnant."

"That's true. But you know, Nina, there was something, I don't know, something. I could see it in his eyes. Nina, I believe him. Anyway, I've decided to wait. Just in case I read his eyes wrong." Then I asked her, "Do you miss having a man?"

"No...because I date a lot of different men. I don't want a steady relationship. I have too much I want to do. Having a man sometimes slows you down. When I've done all I want to do as a single female, I will find a man. But, sistuh girl! I'm in no rush."

"You know, that makes a lot of sense. I want to be just like you when I grow up," I said, smiling.

"Kiss my ass, Rose," Nina said, returning the smile. She then said., "I'm going to Mickey D's for a burger. Want one?"

"No, I've already had a burger, but thanks anyway," I said. "I think I'll read a couple of chapters and go to bed."

"Oh, Rose, I forgot to tell you! There's a letter for you on the shelf," Nina said, pointing to the envelope sitting on the shelf.

"Okay, thanks. Bye."

Finally, Sister wrote back. She didn't have very much to say, except that Mama had been staying out more and more.

Dear Rose,

I was glad when I received your letter. I had a nice time at the school dance. Remember how Mama said she wanted to meet Tweety? Well, she never stayed home long enough to meet him. She wasn't even there when I got dressed for the dance. She promised me she would. When I asked her about it, she apologized and said something came up that she had to take care of. I was like, whatever! Anyway, the dance was nice. I had a really nice time. I want you to meet my friend. I have something really important to tell you about my friend. Maybe I can come up and visit. Am

I allowed? I don't know what the visiting policy is. Let me know. When are you coming home for summer vacation? I know Mama won't be home hardly at all. I asked Mama if she had a man she's not telling anybody about. All she would say is "Maybe." She makes me so sick sometimes. If I can come down for Christmas instead of you coming here, please, please, let me know. I need a vacation away from this place. If I can't come there, I will still be glad to see you. PS, Mama did tell me to tell you hello.

Luv, Sister

Sister was in her room, lying down. It was late. She heard Mama yelling at someone on the phone. Sister got up to hear more. Sister went to her door and cracked it open so she could hear better.

"Look! You said you would never call here again! I don't know. No! If you do, I'll call the police. Why! I know! You just want to get a whole lot of shit started! Yes, you do! Because! I know you! Yeah, right! I don't know when her summer starts! What! What did she say? You son of a bitch! I'm glad she wasn't there. Sister's fine. As if you ever cared. Look! Stop calling here! If you call here again, I'm going to put my bulldog and six puppies on your ass. What's that? It's a gun, you stupid motherfucker! Okay! Try me!" Mama slammed the phone down. Sister quietly closed the door and wondered who Mama was talking to. She wondered if she could have been talking to David. Sister decided to ask her. Just as Sister was approaching Mama's room, she heard her add, "That bastard. I can't stand his ass."

"What bastard?"

"Oh shit! Make some noise when you come into someone's room. You scared me."

"Who were you screaming at on the phone just now?" Mama was good at trying to play the dumb role.

"When?"

"*Just now, not two minutes ago. I heard you screaming at someone on the phone. Who were you talking to?*"

"*Oh! Oh, no one you know,*" Mama said as she waved her hand, *wanting me just to drop it.* "*Just a poop butt friend of mine getting on my nerves, trying to borrow money, you know.*" Mama chuckled. *Sister looked Mama in her eyes.*

"*Mama? You must really think I'm stupid. You don't talk to your friends like that. If anything, I've heard you kissing their butts. I thought I heard you mention our names.*"

"*Why would I mention your name to my friend? Stop looking at me like that. And anyway, get out of my room!*"

"*I want you to know I'm not stupid.*"

Sister left Mama's room, thinking You crazy bitch! *Sister didn't know if she wanted to mention any of this to me. Sister looked at her watch and decided it was too late to call me. She knew she wouldn't sleep a wink that night.* Mama's definitely got a secret, *she thought.*

CHAPTER 13

It was a very dreary Saturday morning. I hadn't slept well. I woke up early and couldn't get back to sleep. I felt depression coming on. It was strange how one could feel it, like life didn't have any purpose and everything that troubled you came to the surface. Jamal was out of town. He felt so gone.

I hated my life sometimes. I felt like ending it. But then Sister would be alone with Mama. Maybe Sister and I should just move away and start somewhere fresh. But I'd miss all my friends, and so would she. I remember something my Grammy told me not too long ago:

To live moments means death.
To change worlds means a new life.
To move forward takes effort.
While being pushed backwards.

She also said, "When life deals you a bad hand, **redeal**." I miss Grammy.

"Heeey, girl," Nina said while stretching in her bed.

"Hey," I said.

"You were restless last night, huh?"

"Yeah, I was. I didn't sleep very well at all."

"Missing Jamal already, are you?"

"Well, I don't feel like I miss him, especially enough to lose sleep over. I don't know. I just couldn't get situated last night. I don't know what the problem is."

"Rose, do you know what today is?"

"No, what?"

"Movie day."

"Oh, that's right. We're going to see *Waiting to Exhale*," I said. "Are we going to dinner afterward?"

"Hey, that's a great idea. Sure. Did we decide what showing we're going to?"

"The evening showing. It starts at seven. I'll check to make sure, then I'll call everyone."

Nina and I got up. The movie started at 7:10 p.m. Believe it or not, we were all ready on time.

* * * * *

"I love how Angela Bassett turns away when she sat all his shit on fire. I'm like, you go, girl!"

"Hell, yeah. Oh, girl was bad," Samara added.

"What are you having, Rose?" Nina asked.

"Hmm…everything looks good. I know. I'm going to get the rib basket."

We continued talking even after the food arrived. "But you know, I didn't feel the closeness I felt when I read the book. I mean, of course we could tell they were all friends, but that closeness wasn't quite the same," I said.

"You're right," Kiki said. "But still, it was a good movie." We all agreed. Kiki took a spoon and clanked her water glass a couple of times. "What do you girls think about all of us getting together with our male friends, just hanging out, playing spades, maybe get some beer, wine, and maybe a little crackers and cheese. Maybe some dip and maybe a little bud."

"No…baby," I said. "My honey don't even know I smoke bud."

"You're lying!" Nina said.

"Uh uh, girl. He doesn't know. I never smoked around him, and he has never mentioned it. Besides, I really want to quit soon anyway."

"Do you really?" Samara asked.

"Yes, I do, because I'm looking at the long term of it. I mean, I really like smoking bud, but I don't want it to be a part of my every-day life. You know what I mean?"

"Yes, I can understand where you're coming from. Well, you go ahead, girl," Nina said.

"I didn't say I wanted to quit just yet." They all started to laugh. "But I think that would be a lot of fun. Well, what does everyone think? Think we ought to go for it?" In unison. we all said yes. "When?" I added.

"How about two weeks from tonight?" We all agreed.

Then Kiki said, "Where are we going to do this at? We can't do it at the dorm."

I made a suggestion. "I'll ask Jamal if we can get together in his apartment."

"You think he will?" Kiki asked.

"I don't know. It won't hurt to try. He'll be back tomorrow. I'll ask him about it." We must have talked about this gathering the whole two weeks. Jamal was fine with the idea. He even said not to buy anything. He would take care of everything. What a sweetheart. We also decided to make it a farewell gathering because school was letting out soon.

Jamal was busy getting everything ready, but he said not to worry. He had made arrangements for me to get there. Me and the girls got together and went for a ride so that we could sneak in a couple of joints before the night began. Since Jamal didn't smoke, we were going to respect his house by not lighting up. I wore my hair up and put my makeup on just right. Looking in the mirror, I thought, *Rose, you are a beautiful black woman.*

"Nina? What do you think?"

"Rose, you look gorgeous in that dress," Nina said, smiling.

"I don't know who's picking me up. Jamal said for me to be ready an hour early. Nina, girl, you better hurry up. You know how slow you are."

"I'll be ready. Oh! Someone's knocking. Wait! Let me run in the bathroom," Nina said.

"Girl! Nobody wants to see your dimpled ass."

"Those are beauty marks," Nina responded from the bathroom.

"What man told you that lie?" I said, laughing. "Who's there?"

A voice I didn't recognize said, "I'm here for Rose Sinclair." I opened the door, and there stood a tall handsome gentleman wearing a black and gold chauffeur's uniform. I was flabbergasted.

"I'm Rose Sinclair." The gentleman took off his cap and bowed a little. I told him I would be out in a second. I ran to the bathroom.

"Nina! Guess what? Girl! Jamal sent a limousine for me!"

"You're lying."

"Yes, he did."

"Well, you go, girl! I'll see you there later."

"All right. Bye."

The gentleman took me gently by the arm and escorted me down and properly helped me into a long fabulous white limousine. Cinderella was going to the ball.

Jamal had everything elegantly set up. His dining room table was spectacular! It was filled with all kinds of delectable finger foods, including shrimp and pate. There was a minibar set up in the corner.

"Oh, baby…you look…I can't describe how you look." He took both my hands, pulled me close, and kissed me.

"Thanks, baby"

"For what?"

"For doing this for me."

"You don't have to thank me. I think it's a great way to end the school year. Besides, whatever makes you happy. You never ask me for much, so I really didn't mind."

Kiki and Taylor arrived first. Kiki looked absolutely beautiful. She just had her hair done for the occasion. Her dress hugged her tiny waist fashionably, flaring out at the bottom. Her dress was a few inches above her knees, a gorgeous royal blue with diamond studded spaghetti straps. Taylor was very handsome as well. He wore his hair low cut, very neat. Then came Samara and Robert. Samara always wore her hair down, but tonight it was off to one side with curls. She had very nice legs. Her dress was red, very much like Kiki's dress, except there were no straps. The red was a great complement to her skin tone. Robert was nice looking. He had a small mustache growing, a well-groomed young man. My best friend was last to arrive with her date, Devon. Like me, Nina also wore a black dress that crisscrossed at the shoulders. It was very elegant. She loved wearing ponytails; even tonight, she wore a curly ponytail held together with a diamond studded band. Her ponytail never looked lovelier. Devon was a shock to us all. He was white. Devon's demeanor let us know right away he was no stranger in the company of black folks. I must admit, we all looked like fashion models. It was great. The girls were itching to get me alone. After about an hour, when everyone was comfortable with each other, we all sneaked away to the bathroom.

"Girls," I said, "look at us. We are beautiful."

"Rose," Nina said, "you are so lucky. No! Blessed. Look at this place. It has that romantic flavor. I know you enjoy coming here. And Jamal, um! That man is so fine."

"Nina?" Samara asked, crossing her arms together in a black male stance.

"What's up, girlfriend?" Nina knew it was coming. "What?"

"Are you going with a white man and never told any of us?" Samara asked.

"No, I'm not going with him. He's just my date for the evening."

"Well, what did you do, call an escort service?" Kiki asked.

"No…he's a friend of mine." Nina was getting angry. "Why? Anyone have a problem with me bringing Devon?"

"Oh, girl, you know we're just giving you a hard time. He's cute," Samara said. "And he has a nice ass for a white boy." Everyone agreed.

"What are y'all doing looking at my date's ass? Uh huh! I'm going out here right now and tell on every last one of you," Nina said, laughing. We left the bathroom.

It was so nice to be out having a nice time with a group of handsome men, men who wanted something out of life besides their next drug deal. We did a lot of slow dancing and necking and drinking. We were all quite toasty, not drunk but feeling good. Tonight, I knew I was in love.

"Rose, there's a call for you. You can take it in the bedroom," Jamal said.

"Thanks, honey. Oh, I hope you didn't mind me leaving your number with the switchboard operator."

"No, of course not."

I'd never seen Jamal's bedroom before and thought it'd be all blue. Some men had no sense of color or style when it came to decorating. But I don't know, Jamal was batting a thousand so far. When I entered Jamal's bedroom, I could have fallen through the floor like my mouth did. It was beautiful. His color scheme was white and the most beautiful gray I'd ever seen, with added touches of burgundy wine. His carpeting had to be five to six inches thick, gray with white and burgundy throw rugs. The room was complete with a master king-size waterbed. I enjoyed the walk to the phone, which was sitting on a burgundy pedestal close to his bed. As I sat, I pretended this bed was ours. White comforter and all.

"Hello."

"Rose?" Sister said.

"Oh, hi, sweetie, I was..."

"Grammy died tonight," Sister said abruptly.

"Grammy's dead," I whispered. Everything was silent. There was nothing. I felt as if a ton of bricks had fallen on me without the pain. All I could feel was the impact. My eyes immediately filled up.

"Rose?"

"I'm fine! Sister, I'm fine," I choked.

"Will you be coming home tomorrow?"

"No. When I leave, I'm going straight there. How's Mama?"

"She's fine," Sister said.

"I'll see you soon, Sister. Bye."

As I sat there on Jamal's bed, all of a sudden, I felt like I was being crushed and that my life wasn't going to be the same. I felt incomplete. "Grammy," I whispered. "Grammy. Oh god! Oh god!" I cried. I jumped up and started pacing and pacing. I didn't know Jamal had entered the room. He came rushing toward me. He grabbed me.

"Rose! What's the matter? Rose? Please, baby, what's the matter?" I could tell he was afraid. I opened my eyes. I couldn't see him for the tears. I cried and cried.

"My gra...grandmother just died," I managed to get out.

"Oh, baby!" Jamal said with the deepest sincerity as he wrapped me in his arms. I sobbed and sobbed. "You lay here, baby. I'll send everyone home. I'm sure they'll understand."

"No! Don't leave me!" I screamed.

"I'll be right back," he said.

"Jamal?"

"Yes," he said so sweetly.

"Tell Nina I'll call her tomorrow." He winked and went into the other room. Jamal picked up an empty wineglass and clanked it gently. Everyone turned and looked. He could tell they were wondering where I was. "Rose is not feeling well. Her grandmother just passed away," he said "She asked me to make her apologies." You could tell everyone was quite disturbed by it. Jamal went up to Nina and said, "Nina, Rose asked me to tell you she'll call you tomorrow." I think Nina's feelings were hurt, but she understood later how I might want to be with my man instead of a best friend. After seeing everyone out, Jamal came back into the bedroom, took off his shoes, and climbed into bed with me, clothes and all. I laid my head on his shoulders. He kissed me on the forehead and asked how I was doing. He didn't say another word, nor did I. In his embrace, Jamal rocked me as I cried on and off all night long. One time, I thought I heard him crying with me. Maybe I was dreaming.

CHAPTER 14

Jamal didn't want me to be alone, so he drove me to Mississippi, only he had to leave the next day. I went on and made arrangements to get out of school early. There were only a few weeks left. Jamal decided to drive me to Mississippi. He didn't think I should be alone. Things were quiet on the way down. I just didn't have a whole lot to talk about.

Grammy's house was full of people when Jamal and I arrived Monday evening. It could have been paranoia, but the smell of old people was intense. I felt nauseous. Mama and Sister were in the kitchen, situating all the food that came. The funeral was set for the next morning.

"Mama?" I said softly when I entered the kitchen. Mama turned around and saw me, walked over quickly to me, and gave me a hug and kiss.

"I'm sorry, baby. I know how close you and your grandma was." I saw tears in Mama's eyes. Her and Grammy didn't get along that well, but one thing I know was that Mama loved Grammy.

"Hi, Rose," Sister said as she walked over to me, giving me a hug.

"Hi, sweetie. How are you?"

"I'm fine, Rose. I love you," Sister said, looking at my swollen eyes.

"I love you too," I said. "Oh! I'm sorry. Mama, Sister, this is Jamal. He drove me here."

Mama had one of them funny looks on her face.

"Hi, Jamal. Thanks for driving Rose down," Mama said.

"Hi," Sister said.

"I've wanted to meet you for a while. I'm sorry it's under these circumstances," Jamal said.

One of Grammy's oldest and dearest friends came into the kitchen. She came up to me and tried to remember my name, but of course she couldn't. I didn't feel like trying to make her remember me, so whatever she said, I agreed to. She had to be at least eighty years old. I took Jamal by the hand and whispered in his ear, "Baby, I gotta get out of here. I can't take it. Please, let's go to a hotel and get you set up. I know you're tired."

"That's fine, baby. Whatever you want," he said.

"All right. I'll let Mama know I'm leaving and that I'll be back soon." Sister overheard me.

"You're leaving? But you just got here."

"I know, Sister. I'll be back. We're going to get Jamal set up in a hotel room. I'll be back once some of these people leave. I just can't take their chattering right now." My voice started to tremble, which made Sister and Mama realize I needed to leave just then.

"Rose, we'll take care of everything. You go on."

Jamal rented a suite at the Holiday Inn. When we went into the room, Jamal drew me a bath. I told him about how I prepared for our first date. So when I went into the bathroom, there was a beautiful scented candle burning. I turned to him and smiled. I could tell he was pleased. He returned the smile and walked away to give me privacy. I was exhausted. The bath was great. It seemed as if I was in there for hours. I thought about a lot of things. But one thing was for sure. I needed Jamal in a way I'd never needed him before. At Grammy's house, all I could feel was death. Even the old ladies that were there, I knew they didn't have long for this world. All I could do was see and feel death all around me. I needed to feel alive. I needed to feel the blood coursing through my veins. I needed to feel my heart beating. I needed to feel love, and I knew just what to do.

"Jamal," I called from the bathroom. "Would you please bring my overnight bag in here?" When Jamal came into the bathroom, I stood up and asked him to hand me a towel. I could tell he was more than a little surprised. His manhood introduced himself right away.

"Come here." I motioned with my finger. Jamal came to me, gently wrapped me in the towel, lifted me out of the tub, carried me into the other room, and laid me on the bed. We kissed passionately. With this kiss came the erasure of everything unpleasant in my life. It was totally filling me up with only the love I feel for this man.

When Jamal and I decided to get up, it was late. I called Mama to find out how things were going and to let her know that I would be there shortly. Jamal dropped me off. I told him I would see him later. Mama was still in the kitchen, trying to find a way to store the food to keep it from spoiling. I felt a strange tenseness when I walked in. Everyone was gone except for Mama and Sister. Sister looked at me, but she didn't say anything. But of course, Mama did. "I thought you said you were coming right back." Mama was angry.

"Mama, I was coming right back, but I was exhausted. I lay across the bed and accidentally fell asleep." What was the big deal?

"Did that man accidentally fall asleep with you?" Mama snapped.

"Mama! That is none of your business! Look, I don't feel like going through this with you now. We can talk about it later."

"Rose, in the morning, I want you to go to the funeral home with me and comb your grandmother's hair." I wanted to say no, but then I thought this would be the last chance I get to say goodbye to Grammy. I had a lot to say to her.

"Sure, Mama. Sure, I can do that." Sister and I went upstairs. We hadn't seen each other in a while. We had a lot to talk about too.

"So, Sis, what did you think about Jamal?" I asked her.

"Girl…that man is fine! You and Jamal did the do, didn't you?" Sister asked, anticipating my answer.

"Yes, we did."

"Well…how was it?"

"Everything I imagined and more. Sister, I love him so much. That man did things to me that made me too embarrassed to look at him when we were done."

"I am so happy for you. You deserve this."

"Thanks."

"How about you? How are things between you and yours?" I asked.

"Fine."

"That's all? Just fine?" I asked her. "When am I going to meet him?"

"Who?"

"What do you mean who? Your boyfriend," I said, wondering what world she was in. "Sister, are you having problems with Tweety?"

Sister looked at me and said, "Tweety is not my boyfriend."

"Oh, I thought…"

"That's because I let you think it. I have someone else. A friend I've known for quite a while. This person would look at me all the time. Finally, we started dating," Sister said, holding her head down.

"That's good, isn't it?"

"Yes."

"Sister…you're hiding something. Are you pregnant?" Sister jumped up.

"No! I'm…I'm gay."

"Gay?" Sister looked at me strangely. I laughed a little. I didn't want her to regret telling me, so I pretended it was okay. "I'm only teasing you. Well! Are you happy?"

"I don't know. Sometimes I feel that I am, and other times, I'm not so sure. I mean, I really like Brenda a lot."

"Brenda? I heard you mention her name before. I think you said something about going to the movies with her one Saturday."

"Yes, that's her. Man! I thought you were going to get upset when I told you."

"Upset!" I got up and took a deep breath. "Why should I be upset? I just want the best for you, and if the best for you is being with a woman, who am I to change it? As long as you're happy." I was very convincing.

"Rose?"

"Yeah?"

"I'm thinking about going to a psychiatrist. What do you think?"

"Why?"

"I'm confused about a lot of things."

"So does Mama know about Brenda?"

"Hell no! Mama would have a fit. She still thinks I'm going with Tweety."

"Sister, I'm a little confused myself. You never acted like you were, you know…a lesbian," I stumbled out.

"Well, how does a lesbian act?" Sister asked, looking straight at me.

"I don't know. You never talked about women like you liked them."

"I never was interested until I met Brenda."

"How do you know you're gay? Maybe you think you're gay."

"Rose, that sounds dumb."

"What? I don't think so. If you're confused, then how would you know? Are you attracted to men at all?" I asked Sister. It was a question I really wanted to know the answer to.

"Sometimes," Sister said, not really sounding sure of herself. I worried about Sister a lot. Sometimes I thought she was more affected by our childhood than I was.

"Sister, how are your eating habits? I mean, have you had any more binges?"

"No." She looked away and asked, "Rose, isn't it going to be hard for you to do Grandma's hair?"

"I have to do this. I have to say goodbye," I said, tears filling my eyes again. Thinking about Grammy, I decided to cut the conversation short. "Sister, I'm tired. I'm going to bed. Good night."

"Good night, Rose."

Mama was ready to go first thing in the morning. It didn't matter to me. I barely slept a wink anyway. When we approached the chapel where Grammy's body was, I got a sick feeling in the pit of my stomach. Just for a minute, I was scared. My heart started to beat rapidly. I had to take a minute to relax myself by breathing in and out slowly. I dreaded each step going up to the chapel. It was beautiful. I didn't want to cry, so I tried to control myself. I grabbed onto Sister's hand and went up the steps with her, Mama in front.

The eerie quietness and artificial flowers scattered about told the tale of many deaths. When I went into the room where Grammy was, I didn't know what to expect. I didn't know if I would run out, stand there paralyzed, or cry hysterically. Surprisingly, I did none of the above. When I saw my Grammy lying there, she looked peaceful. All the fear and all the anxiety disappeared. I took a minute then walked over to her. A beautiful white afghan covered her. Her beautiful white hair hung loosely to one side. I opened my bag and pulled out my comb and brush.

"Hi, Grammy. It's me, Ro." I didn't realize how nervous and scared I was until I noticed my hands trembling. I took a deep breath and continued, "I'm going to make you look so beautiful. I love brushing your hair. I hope my hair looks just like yours when I'm older. When I have my children, Grammy, I'm going to tell them all about you and show them pictures of you. I'm going to tell them how good you were to me. I'm going to teach them to have pride in who they are. Grammy, I will never ever lie to them. I will always tell them the truth. I will never ever hurt them like Mama has hurt us. What am I going to do without you? I could always talk to you no matter what." I could feel the tears beginning to form in my eyes. "I've never told you as often as I should how much I love you. I remember when we were kids, you always took special time with me and Sister. You loved us both the same. Thank you, Grammy." As I put my Grammy's hair in its final resting place, I said goodbye.

I dreaded going back to the house with all these people I didn't know. I hated after-funeral gatherings. I wish Jamal could have stayed with me. I missed him. When I went into the house, I saw something that made me cry like a baby.

"Hi, girlfriend," Nina said, smiling. I couldn't stop crying. Every time I raised my head off her shoulders, I would lay it back down and cry again. Finally, the tears I had bottled inside came pouring out. After getting over the shock of Nina being there, I introduced her to Mama and Sister.

"Rose, these flowers came for you a little while ago," Mama said as she fiddled with them a little bit.

"Oh my goodness," Nina said. "I'll bet they're from Jamal. A dozen black roses. How pretty."

"No," I said strangely. "These are not from Jamal."

"How do you know?" Nina asked.

"Because I know."

"Is there a card?"

"No...I don't see one. Something's not right here. I can feel it."

"Maybe it's from someone who just wants to say they're sorry about your grandmother's death," Nina said. "What else could it be? Come on."

"Okay, maybe. Anyway, they are pretty." I didn't care. I could feel it in my gut. And why was there no card?

Nina and I stayed up pretty much all night talking. Sister enjoyed sitting up with me and my friend. My eyes kept wandering over to the black roses I had sitting on the dresser. I felt strange.

We stayed in Mississippi for a few days after Grammy's funeral. We had to go meet with Grammy's lawyer. Grammy didn't have much. She left Mama some personal belongings. She left Sister and I her house and all it contained. When the lawyer read that decision, I saw a fierce look in Mama's eyes. What? Did she want the house? And to Aunt Fannie, she left jewelry that included her wedding rings. Aunt T is going to be so hurt to find out when she gets back that her Mama had died. She went on a cruise and didn't say where. She was always taking off, not telling anyone where she was going, I knew one day we would need her and not be able to get in touch with her. She called it her quiet time—time away from everyone she knew. I was looking forward to seeing her.

I was surprised Grammy left us the house. I didn't know she had a will. I didn't think I could live in that house. I couldn't imagine living in Mississippi. I thought of selling it.

Jamal had left a couple days before, so I decided to ride with Nina back home. She had decided to visit with me a little while longer at Mama's house. It was going to be great having her there for a while.

"Nina, I just can't get the roses off my mind."

"Why not?"

"Because of my father."

Confused, Nina asked, "I don't understand, Rose. Your father's dead, isn't he?"

"I think he is. I was a little girl. The only thing I remember is that all of a sudden, he just wasn't there. I mean, I don't remember a funeral or anything like that, and I can't remember anyone ever talking about it."

Nina had the strangest look on her face when she asked me, "Rose, do you think your father is alive?"

I was quiet for a long time. I really didn't know what to think. He couldn't be. Mama wouldn't have kept that from me. She knew how much I loved him.

"No, Nina, he couldn't be. It's just weird for me to get black roses with no card. Well…I'm not going to worry about it anymore. Maybe someone sent them and just forgot to attach the card."

"I really think that's it," Nina said.

CHAPTER 15

It had been three weeks since Grammy's death, and things were pretty much back to normal. Nina stayed with me a couple of days and then left. I talked to Jamal, but I haven't seen him. Mama still continued to stay out a lot. I wondered what was with her. She must be getting old. She didn't look as attractive as she once did. And my sister started to go downhill. She broke up with Brenda because she said she couldn't trust her. But Brenda assured me that Sister had been slowly changing for the past few months. She started accusing Brenda of all sorts of terrible things. Brenda came to me, and we talked a long time. I could not believe some of the things she was telling me. She accused Brenda of trying to poison her. I decided to drop out of college and finish later when Sister was okay. I got a job at a nearby newspaper office. Sister couldn't hold a job because she thought someone was following her all the time. The more time I spent with Sister, the more I understood what Brenda was talking about. Sister went days without eating. Her excuse was she was fasting. I knew she was still bingeing because I'd find food wrappings stuck way down in the trash barrel, obviously covered with other trash. When I asked about it, she'd say someone else was throwing their trash in our barrel. I hated that Sister wasn't well. Me and Mama…we were going to have a talk tonight.

Sister had a headache, so she went to bed early. That gave me plenty of time to talk to Mama. Mama was watching *Home*

Improvement on television. She should have been watching *Family Improvement*.

"Rose, do you like *Home Improvement*? I love this show."

"It's okay, I guess. Mama, can we talk?"

"Can it wait until this goes off? It'll be off in a minute," she asked without looking at me.

"No, Mama, this is really important."

"What is it then?" she said, still not looking at me.

"It's Sister," I said.

"What is it now, Rose? What about Sister?"

"She's not well. Mama! Look at me! She's not well."

"Girl." Mama chuckled. "Your sister's fine." She waved her hand at me and continued watching television.

"Mama!" I yelled. "Sister is not fine. She's sick and she needs our help."

"Sick how?" Mama asked without taking her eyes off the television. I started looking around for the remote. I found it under some papers Mama had been looking at next to her. I turned off the television. That got her attention.

"You know, Mama, you're pitiful! Your own daughter is about to have a nervous breakdown, and you won't stop watching that stupid show."

"I don't mean to be a bitch, but I do have my own problems."

"So having your own problems mean you can forget about your daughters? Daughters you're supposed to love so dear?" I said. "For once, would you think about someone other than yourself? Mama, please! I'm really concerned about Sister!"

"I can see that, Rose. I'm sorry. What's happening with her?"

"I don't know. It's hard to explain. I think Sister still has that eating disorder. She's paranoid about everything. She barely wants to get out of bed in the mornings. We have to do something. And to top it all off, she thought her friend was trying to poison her." Mama asked me to hand her her purse off the chair next to where I was sitting. She took out her cigarette pack and lit a cigarette. I almost wished I smoked at this point.

"Poison her?" Mama said in disbelief.

"Yes. I think Sister needs to see a doctor."

"A psychiatrist!"

"Yes! A psychiatrist. Sister's having some real emotional problems, Mama. We have to do something."

"Damn! If it's not one thing it's another. Let me think about it for a while, okay? But right now, I have to get ready to go."

"Now see! That's what I mean. You act like this is an everyday occurrence." I was getting angrier. "Where are you going?" I asked her.

"Never you mind. I have plans."

"Yeah, that's just it. You care so much about your plans that Sister and I could fall off the face of the earth and you probably wouldn't notice!" I said. "But that's okay. You go on with your plans. I'll take care of Sister!" I turned my back to Mama and quickly walked out of the room. I heard her calling my name. I ignored her. I didn't see Mama for three days. And as much as I hated to admit, I was worried. Sister and I decided to watch television together. We were both worried about Mama. We called a few of her friends. No one seemed to know where she was. Sister had fallen asleep when I heard the phone ring. I jumped up, hoping it was Mama.

"Hello!"

"Hello, Rose?" It was Mama. She sounded strange.

"Mama, where are you? What's wrong? We've been worried sick."

"I'm fine. I need you to do me a favor," she said. "I need you to bring me some money."

"Bring you some money? For what? Where are you? What's wrong with your voice?"

"I'm at a friend's house. I have some money in my bottom drawer in my bedroom. Rose, get it and bring it to me. There's enough for you to catch a cab and back," she said.

"Why can't you come and get the money and—" Mama cut me off before I had a chance to finish.

"Rose, please! Please, just bring me the money."

"All right! Where are you?" Mama gave me the address." When I arrived, Mama was standing on the porch, waiting. She ran down to meet me in the cab.

"Do you have the money, baby?"

"Yes, who are these people? And why are you sweating like that. It's not hot out here." All of a sudden, I heard someone in the background tell Mama to hurry up.

"Thanks, baby. I can't talk now. We'll talk when I get home," she said as she walked away. Everyone followed Mama inside.

"Mama!"

"I'll see you when I get home!" I heard her say as she closed the door. When I got home, Sister was still sleeping. I won't ever forget the look in Mama's eyes. I'd seen it before. I started to remember this house party me and Nina went to while we were at school.

"Are you going to the party with me, Rose?" Nina had asked me.

"Whose party?"

"A guy in my general psychology class. He says it's going to be the bomb and everyone's going to be there. Come on, go with me. You don't have to change. You can come just like you are. I'm wearing what I have on. Please?"

"All right. I'll go for a little while, okay?" I said. I really didn't feel like going, but I knew Nina didn't want to go alone, so I went. When we arrived, the music was blasting. We were a couple hours late, so most of the guests were already toasted. All the rooms in the house were being used for something. One room was used for playing cards, and another room was used for smoking bud. They had this one room where you hardly ever saw anybody come out, and if they did, they went right back in. What I remember most about that room was the odor that escaped every time the door was opened. I'd never smelled anything like it before. Out of curiosity, me and Nina went in. We saw about five people sitting on the floor around this table. On the table sat this tray full of white stuff separated into little piles.

"What's that?" I asked Nina. She looked at me as if to say, "What planet are you from?"

"Rose, you're kidding me! You don't know what that is?"

"No, what is it?"

"Cocaine," Nina said, not taking her eyes off it.

"Have you ever tried it?" I asked.

"Hell no! That shit ain't nothing nice," she said. "Watch, watch him. He getting ready to take a hit."

"Oh my goodness," I whispered. "How does he hold that in so long? And why is he holding his nose?"

"Well, they say the longer you hold it, the better it is. He holds his nose to keep it all in."

"Wow! Look at his mouth. Why is he moving it all around so funny? They all sound like they have a mouthful of food. Look how they're sweating."

"Um hm," Nina said.

"And they like that?" I asked, wondering how anyone could like what they were doing.

"They're hypes," Nina said, smiling. "They're all hypes. They'll kill they mama for the shit."

"Oh my god! My Mama is a hype. How did this happen? When did this happen?" I didn't want to think anymore. I just wanted to crawl into bed. I woke up Sister and told her to go get in bed. I took a shower, took a couple of Tylenol for the tremendous headache that had formed, and turned my face down into the sheets, cried, and asked God to please help us.

Mama got home at daybreak. When I got up, she was still sleeping. I went into her room about 4:00 p.m. She was still sleeping. I decided to wake her up. I shook the bed a little to get her to stir, but she didn't move. I then used both hands and shook her. She didn't move. I shook her and yelled her name at the same time. She didn't move. I panicked! I picked up the phone and dialed 911. Sister heard me on the phone and came running into Mama's room.

"What's the matter with Mama? What did you do to her?" I couldn't believe what I had just heard. I looked at Sister as if she really was crazy. "Mama! Mama! Wake up! Open your eyes. Mama! Please, wake up!" Sister yelled. Sister continuously shook the bed with no response.

"Yes, ma'am, she's breathing, but she won't respond," I told the operator. "Yes, ma'am, I will. She said the ambulance will be here soon, but keep trying to wake her up."

"Rose, what happened?"

"I don't know. She came in at about four this morning and got in bed. When I came in here just now to wake her, she wouldn't move. Sister, I'm scared!" Sister heard the ambulance in the distance.

"The ambulance is coming. Rose, run and open the door."

Sister and I stood back and watched them work on Mama.

"How long has she been like this?" one of the paramedics asked.

"I don't know. I came in to wake her. She wouldn't move. Is she going to be okay?"

"I hope so, ma'am. Is she taking any drugs?" I told the paramedics my suspicions. He said he could tell by her pupils that her coma was drug induced. Sister and I rode alongside Mama in the ambulance. I told Sister in the ambulance what had happened that night.

"I knew something wasn't right with her staying out all the time. But I never thought…drugs. Rose, what are we going to do?" Sister said. "Our mother is a junkie." We were silent the rest of the way. "Rose? I'm sorry for that comment I made back in Mama's room. I really didn't mean it. I just wasn't thinking straight." I had already forgiven her.

It was different seeing Mama in such a fragile state. I wondered what was going on with her to make her turn to cocaine. I didn't think anything bothered her. Sister sat on the bed and picked up Mama's hand and started to gently rub it. I saw tears in her eyes.

"Rose, look at our mama. What would make her do such a thing? How long do you think Mama's been using drugs?"

"I don't know, Sister. I think probably a long time. When I saw her last night, she didn't look like the same person. Her hair hadn't been combed. Her eyes were big like someone was stretching them open, and she was sweating profusely."

We sat with Mama most of the night. The doctor said he would give us a call if there was any change. The next morning, I called Mama's job to let them know she was ill. But they said she didn't work there anymore. After three days, Mama still wasn't out of the coma. Sister and I would spend most of the day there just in case she came out of it. Mama could be a real bitch sometimes, but I actually felt sorry for her. Sister went to the hospital alone and came back with a strange look on her face. *Oh my god!* I thought. *Mama's dead.*

"Sister, what's wrong? How's Mama?"

"Mama's fine."

"You look like you're ready to faint. What's the matter?"

"Rose, sit down for a minute. I want to ask you something. Do you think I'm crazy? I mean really crazy."

I wasn't quite sure how to answer, so of course I said, "Of course not, Sister. Why?"

"I saw someone today. Since I don't know how to say this, I'm just going to blurt it out." Sister paused for a minute. "I saw Daddy today."

CHAPTER 16

We just sat there and stared at each other. We looked deep into each other's eyes. I knew Sister wasn't lying. Although I found it hard to believe what she was saying.

"What?"

"Just as the cab pulled up in front of the hospital, I saw this man get into his car and…Rose, it was Daddy."

"Did he see you?" I asked.

"No, he was already in his car when I got out of the cab."

"Sister, do you realize what you are saying?"

"Yes, I do," she said with certainty. "Rose, I am not crazy. I know I saw him."

"Sister, I believe you." Sister look surprised.

"What?"

"I believe you. Remember the black roses I got at Grammy's house?"

"Yeah."

"You know how Daddy used to call me his beautiful black rose? I believe he sent those flowers. Whoever sent them didn't put a name on the card. Who else would have taken the time to send black roses?"

"Oh my god, Rose, you think! How can we find out?"

"I don't know." All of a sudden, Sister put her hand up to her mouth.

"What!"

"I just remembered something too," she said.

"What!" I asked.

"A while ago, I heard Mama arguing on the phone with someone."

"Yeah, so?"

"Rose…I got the strangest feeling she was talking to David, but maybe it was Daddy." For a minute I was angry.

"How come you never told me about this?"

"Because I wasn't sure, and I didn't want to start anything."

"What were they arguing about?" I asked.

"I don't remember, but I do remember her calling out our names. I asked her who she was arguing with, but she wouldn't tell me. It was somebody she didn't want us to know about."

"Sister, what if, no, but, what if we're wrong?"

"What if we're not?" There was a long silence. I guess Sister and I had a lot to think about. I couldn't believe Mama would keep this from us. Although Mama never said Daddy was dead, she let us think it.

We sat around a while, not knowing what to say. When I was half asleep, the hospital called to tell us she was coming out of her coma.

When we arrived at the hospital, Mama was still being examined. Sister and I sat on a bench outside of her room. We were discussing whether or not to ask Mama about our father. We decided that this wasn't the right time. We didn't want to upset her.

Mama only stayed in the hospital a week. We didn't see anything more of the man Sister said she thought was our father. We gave Mama a couple of days before we mentioned Daddy to her, but we couldn't wait any longer than that. It was a real quiet sort of day, cloudy. Mama was in her bed, finishing her lunch. Sister and I went in. I sat on the bed, and Sister pulled up her recliner.

"Mama, Sister and I have something we want to ask you."

"I know you want to know about the cocaine," Mama said, holding her head down.

"No, I mean we do, but that's not what we want to ask you about right now," I said. She seemed relieved.

"Well, what is it?" Mama asked.

"The other day, when Sister came to see you, she said she saw a man come out of the hospital that looked like our father," I said, looking Mama directly in her eyes to see any hint of a lie coming. "Now, Mama, I know that you have not always been honest with us in the past, but Mama, if Daddy is alive, Sister and I want to know." Mama kept her head down the whole time I was talking. "Remember the roses I got at the time of Grammy's funeral, Mama? Were those roses from Daddy?" I asked her. Mama raised her head.

"What in the hell are you talking about? I never said anything about your Daddy being dead. It's just that when he wasn't here anymore, I didn't talk about his ass," Mama said. Sister and I just sat there. We could not believe what she was saying to us. We looked at each other.

"What! Mama you knew we thought our father was dead. You knew that!" I said.

"Your father was gone. He was never coming back. I didn't want to hurt you girls."

I was watching Sister. She wasn't saying anything. She just had this look about her. I really couldn't explain it. I was worried. Sister got up, ran to her room, and closed her door—hard!

"I don't believe you, Mama! How much of this do you think I can take? Have you been seeing him? Has he asked about Sister or me? Where does he live? Does he live here? Mama?" All of a sudden, I stopped and said, "I want to see him."

"No!" Mama said.

"Why not!"

I heard the phone ringing in the other room and ran to answer it.

Loudly, I said, "Hello!"

"Rose?"

"Oh, Jamal! I'm sorry."

"What's the matter?"

"Nothing, I'm just talking to Mama. Can I call you back?"

"Rose, we have to talk. Lately you just don't have the time anymore. I think we should talk about it. If there is something wrong, I want to know." He was right. I hadn't had very much time for him.

I never really thought about it until now. And I had to finish this up with Mama.

"Yes, Jamal, you're right. I'll call you later and we can discuss it then, okay?"

"Okay. And, Rose? I love you."

"I love you too. Bye."

That call shook me, and I had to sit down a minute before going back to Mama. When I went back to her room, I saw her hang up the phone quickly.

"Who was that on the phone?" I asked her, thinking she might have been trying to sneak a call in to Daddy.

"No one," she said.

"Mama, listen, I really don't want to argue with you about this. I really don't. So can we for once talk about this like adults? Could you for once stop thinking about yourself?"

"Myself! Myself!"

"Yes! All you do is think about yourself. You never think about the way Sister and I feel, because if you did..." Mama started to say something, but I cut her off quickly. "Because if you did, you would have sat us down like normal people and told us that our daddy was leaving for whatever reason. No, you let us think that our father was dead. How could you do that to children you love? Mama, I don't understand. How could you let two innocent little girls think that one of the most important people in their life was dead?" I think what I was saying started to get to Mama, because I saw a hint of emotion sitting on her eyelids, about to fall.

Mama startled me when she said, "Shut up! You shut up! What do you know? You know nothing about what I was going through!"

"Yeah right! I know that you cared for Sister more than you cared for me because she's half white!" I had been wanting to tell Mama that for a long time. "How could you do that to us? I always thought it was her fault, that she was light and had the most beautiful hair I've ever seen! I thought it was her fault she had all those pretty clothes and I had short sets from K-Mart! I thought it was her fault that people talked about us behind our back because they saw the difference you made with both of us! But it wasn't her fault, and I'm so glad I realized that before our love for each other was destroyed. This is not all about me either. I can't even imagine what Sister has went through. She knew you treated us differently, which made her treat me differently, and I don't think she'll ever get over the pain of that. That's probably why she's losing her mind today, because of you!" I saw such hurt in Mama's eyes when I said that. I wanted to get down on my knees and beg her forgiveness, but I didn't. I wouldn't, couldn't. Mama had a glare in her eyes when she looked at me. She didn't say anything.

"Mama, tell me about the cocaine. How did you get started using? And when?" I handed Mama a Kleenex, but I couldn't allow myself to feel sorry for her. Not yet. Not until I've heard everything. Mama wiped her eyes and began:

"Rose, this is hard for me, okay? I was over at my girlfriend's house."

"Who? That Arlene?" I interrupted.

"No, Marilyn."

"Marilyn. Do I know her?"

"No, I don't think so. Anyway, we were bored, so she called a few of her male friends to come over. We were going to play dominoes and have a beer or two. Everything was going real well. We were having a lot of fun. The phone rang, and it was Marilyn's friend Toot. Toot was tall, dark, and very well groomed. I didn't hear what her and Toot were talking about. The next thing I know, he was knocking on the door, and everyone seemed to be glad he was there because they immediately got up and went into this smaller room. The only thing this room had in it was a round table sitting close to the floor and a few of those really big oversized floor pillows. She pulled from under the table some plates, so I was thinking there was food involved. But then, Toot pulled out a sandwich baggie with white powder in it. Marilyn went to the closet and pulled out a plastic grocery bag with these glass tubes in it. Marilyn explained to me what was going on and that they were getting ready to get high. She said I had to try it, that there was nothing like it. I just watched for a while. Marilyn asked me if I wanted to try it. I didn't say anything. She filled the pipe and got up, brought it over to me, stuck it in my mouth, and said, 'Okay, pull in when you see me light the pipe.' I did, and I have been smoking ever since."

"How long, Mama?"

"Five years."

"Five years! Oh, Mama."

"It didn't start to get bad until about two years ago," Mama said. "I'm sorry for what I've put you girls through, but it's like the cocaine has taken over my life." Mama started to cry. I went to her and put my arms around her. But at that point, I felt nothing.

I went upstairs to check on Sister. Her eyes were swollen from crying. She looked at me. I went to her. She laid her head on my shoulders.

"Rose, Daddy's alive." And together we cried and cried and cried. Mama said she was going to call Daddy later that evening. I was excited. I decided to take a bath. I haven't been in the mood lately for a candlelight bath, so instead I took a shower. I called Nina when I got out of the shower to tell her the good news about my father being alive. Mama arranged for him to come to the house. The closer the time came for Daddy to arrive, the more nervous I became. The last time I saw my daddy, I think I was about ten years old. I wondered what life had been like for him. I wondered id he remarried. Oh my god! I wondered if he had any more children. I probably had another sister or brother somewhere. I wondered what he looked like now. Each question I thought of made me more nervous. Sister was nervous too. She didn't know what she should wear or how to comb her hair. We were a mess.

Sister and I decided to make dinner so that the time would pass faster. We were making a simple dinner of steak, baked potato, corn, and a salad. Daddy was due to arrive in fifteen minutes. Sister and I kept watching the clock.

"Damn!" I said.

"What?"

"We don't have any salad dressing. I'll have to walk to the store real quick and get some. I'll be back in a flash," I said. I grabbed my purse and hurried out the door. Wouldn't you know, Daddy came soon as I left.

When I walked into the house, Sister ran up to me and whispered, "He's here, Rose. Daddy's here." Sister was out of breath from the excitement.

"Sister!" I whispered back. "I'm scared. How does he look?"

"He looks just like Daddy, except older. He looks good. He's in the room with Mama. I can't believe he's here. And when he kissed and hugged me, oh…Rose, I felt so safe. I'll tell him you're back." Sister turned quickly and ran off. I tried to grab a hold of her.

"Sister! Wait! Wait!" Then I waved my hands at her to go ahead. I didn't know why I was stopping her. *Oh Lord! My heart's beating so fast. Maybe I should sit down. Maybe I should act like I'm doing something.* "Shit! Shit!" Oh, Jesus, help me. I ran into the kitchen to get some water to wet my throat. Just as I put the glass up to my mouth and took a sip, I heard my father's voice.

"Rose?"

I looked around and saw him rushing toward me. I had dropped the glass and did not notice.

"Step back. Are you okay?" he asked. I didn't answer. Instead I just looked at him. I looked deep into his eyes. All I could feel was this huge lump in my throat. I couldn't say a word. I smiled, and Daddy knew I was okay. When Daddy put his arms around me, I was ten years old again. I started to sob.

"Come on now," he said. "It's okay. Daddy's here." I could see Sister in the background with this huge grin on her face.

"Okay, okay, let me see you," he said.

I stood back, and we both looked at each other. We laughed. Sister joined us, and we all went into the living room. The first night Daddy was here, Sister and I decided not to make a big deal of anything. We just wanted to enjoy him being there. I was sure he appreciated that. Mama got up and sauntered into the living room where we were. Strangely, the laughing stopped. Mama took a seat next to Sister. The quietness after Mama came in must have gotten on Daddy's nerves because he blurted out, "Girls, do you have any pictures of yourselves when you were younger?"

We had a few pictures sitting on the mantel. I got them and showed them to him. I had a lot of questions I wanted to ask him, but not in front of Mama and Sister. He gave me his phone number to call him when I got a chance. He was still the most handsome man. He didn't have as much hair as he used to, but he was handsome all the same. I got the feeling that Mama and Daddy had been communicating much more than we knew. She looked at him like she was afraid of something he might say. She watched him like a hawk.

He decided not to stay very long. I walked him to his car.

"Rose, I can't believe I'm looking at you. Did you get the roses I sent when your grandmother died?"

"It was you. I had the strongest feeling they were from you, but no one wanted to believe me."

"I sent a card along. Didn't you read the card?"

"There was a card?"

"Yes, there…" He suddenly stopped. We looked at each other, and we knew what happened. Mama had taken the card off the flowers so I wouldn't know who sent them. I wasn't surprised. That seemed like something she would do.

"Rose, call me. Maybe we can get together for lunch and catch up on some things. Okay?" he said. And Sister too. Bye." He gave me a very tight hug, got in his car, and left. I watched him until I could no longer see him. Things were pretty quiet when I went back inside. I helped Sister do the dishes. Neither one of us felt like talking very much. When we were done, Sister went to her room. I went to mine and reflected on the thought of having our father back.

CHAPTER 17

Jamal wanted to come up for a visit, but I didn't feel comfortable having him here. It was just too much happening. I'd have to explain, and I didn't know how. But I had decided to tell him everything. I called him. We were all settled in our own space; the quietness made it perfect for a lovers' chat.

"Hi, Jamal."

"Hey, baby, how doing?" he said, sounding like he'd been asleep for hours. I could tell when Jamal was in a real good sleep mode. His sentences were incomplete.

"Were you sleeping? I can call you in the morning."

"I'm woke, baby. I'm woke. Just give me a second to sit up. It's good to hear your voice. What's the matter, baby? Lately you've been so preoccupied. What's bothering you?" I could tell he really wanted to know. I didn't think I could tell him, not yet. Should I have to tell him that I didn't know who my father was? Would I be wrong if I never mentioned the subject? Could I live with the secret of my mother's shame?

"I'm having some family problems. You know how that can be?"

"No, I don't know, baby. I know families have problems, but I thought we had come to a point in our relationship that we could tell each other anything. I just hate to see you so upset all the time."

I wanted to tell him everything. I tried. Nothing came out. I just wasn't ready.

"You're right! You're right! Really, Jamal, there's nothing to tell. I'm just sensitive sometimes. My sister and I have been arguing lately. It's really nothing. I think I'll apologize to her."

"Okay, baby, if you're sure."

"I'm sure."

Jamal was so sweet and understanding. I could tell him anything, so why did I just lie? I hated myself.

Later that night, I heard Sister come into my room and climb into my bed.

"Sister?" I said. "Sometimes you act like a little girl."

"I know," she said. "But you know you love it."

"Yeah, I do."

"Besides, I want to tell you something. I'm seeing a psychiatrist."

"Sister!" I rose off the bed. I was so happy and surprised. "How? When?"

"Mama said she would put it on Daddy's insurance. That's what we were talking about when you were outside with Daddy just before he left."

Mama didn't say a word about this when we were arguing. I guess she wanted me to feel stupid.

"How's it going? Is it helping you at all?" I asked her. "Do you have a male or female doctor?"

"Female. There is no way I'm talking to a man about my problems. Uh uh, no. Would you go to a session with me sometime?"

I didn't have the heart to say no. Besides, I really wanted to.

"When?"

"I'll let you know." I let Sister sleep in there with me the rest of that night.

When I opened my eyes, Sister was dressed and ready to go.

"Hey. Where are you off to so early this morning? And you look nice too."

"Brenda called me last night and asked to have breakfast with her before she goes to work."

"Are you and Brenda...you know. You know what I'm trying to say."

"Yes, I know what you're trying to say. I don't know. We've been talking a little bit," Sister admitted. "I told her that I'm seeing a psychiatrist. She said she would go to a couple of my sessions with me too."

"That's good, Sister. I'm happy to hear it."

"She'll be here any minute. I'm going to wait out front. Just tell Mama I'll be back soon. Bye."

I called Daddy to see if he was free for lunch. He said yes and to meet him at the Den at 1:00 p.m. I got up and checked on Mama. She was just waking up when I peeped in.

"Good morning, Mama. How are you feeling?"

"I feel really good today. I think I'll get out for a little bit. Rose? Is Sister up yet?"

"Ahh…Sister's been up. She had to run an errand. She said to tell you she'll be back soon."

"She probably went to see that thang." Mama saying that stopped me dead in my tracks.

"What! What thang, Mama? What are you talking about?"

"Don't act like you don't know. I know Sister tells you everything. I know you know about that thang."

"What thang, Mama?" I wasn't sure what Mama was talking about. I sure wasn't going to say anything until I was sure.

"That girl your sister hangs around with. That Brenda girl. When I first met her, I thought there was something fishy about her."

"Sister says she's a real nice girl."

"Uh huh! See! I knew she told you. How come you never told me about this, Rose? You're so quick to run to me with everything else about her."

"Maybe I didn't think this was any of your business, Mama. It's not like you've ever cared about what we were doing."

"Look, Rose! I don't want to argue with you this morning. I just thought you would have mentioned something like this to me."

"When I told you I thought Sister needed a psychiatric evaluation, you didn't do anything."

"She's getting treatments now, isn't she? Damn, Rose! Give me some credit."

"Give you some credit? Oh…now I know why you changed your mind. Everything was fine until you found out that your precious daughter might be gay…"

"Stop it! Stop saying that! Sister is not gay! She's not! She's going to marry and have children like everyone else."

"Face it, Mama! Sister is a lesbian!"

Mama grabbed her temples and bent over almost to the floor, yelling, "No, she's not!"

"And I say more power to her."

"You get out of here! Get out of my room! She's not!"

I didn't know how I felt about Sister being gay, but I was intensely curious about it all. So of course I pumped her for a description of her brunch with Brenda.

"Can I help you?" the waiter asked.

"Yes. Brenda Morgan's table please."

"Sure," the waiter said. "Right this way please."

"Can I start you ladies off with some coffee this morning?"

"Yes, make one a tall glass of orange juice," Brenda said, then turned to Sister. "Hi, baby. How are you this fine morning?"

"Yes, it is a fine morning, and I'm doing great!"

"You don't sound great."

"How do you expect me to sound, Brenda? You just stopped calling me. Why?"

"I didn't know what was going on with you."

"What do you mean?"

"I mean, I didn't know where you were coming from. I know who I am. I know what I want. You don't seem to know that. And until you do, things are not going to work out between us. And it's other things too."

"Like what?"

"Like when you thought I was cheating on you, and I wasn't. Like when you thought I had put something in your food, and I didn't. I don't know, Sister. You had me going there for a while. I thought it was best we break it off. The only thing is, I still love you." Brenda smiled.

"That's why I'm seeing a psychiatrist, Brenda. Because I love you and I want this to work."

"How's it going with her?"

"I think it's going okay."

"How many sessions do you have with her?"

"I can continue to see her for as long as I like."

"Have you told her you were a lesbian?"

"Yes, I have."

"What did she say about it?"

"You know psychiatrists. They don't say much of anything."

"Well, did she look funny when you told her?"

"As a matter of fact, she didn't. She just sat back in that big chair of hers and asked me how I feel about it. If I didn't know any better, I would have sworn she already knew."

"What did you say?"

"I said I wasn't sure. I told her that you're the best thing that's happened to me. She then asked me if I thought a man could make me feel the same way. I told her I suppose a man could, but that's not what I want.

"Then..."

"She asked me why. And I told her it's not what I want because I'm in love with you." Brenda reached out for Sister's hand. They sat in that restaurant for hours, talking.

I heard Brenda's car pull into the driveway. Mama was taking a shower. I wanted to talk to Sister before Mama knew she was home. When Sister got out of the car, I went out, took her arm, and said, "Let's go for a walk. I want to tell you something." Sister looked at me strangely.

"What?"

"Mama knows."

"Know what?" Sister said, pulling away from my arm.

"About Brenda. Don't ask me how. She just does."

"What?"

"She said she knew I knew and asked why hadn't told her about it."

"What did you say?"

"I told her it was none of her business."

"Oh my god, Rose! What am I going to say to her?"

"Sister, let me tell you something. Don't be afraid of what Mama might think. What can she do? If you want to see Brenda, see her. It's not a damn thing she can do about it. That's why she finally decided to let you see a psychiatrist. She's hoping she'll change your mind about being gay."

"Mama has discussed this with my psychiatrist?"

"No, I don't think so. But she knows it's going to be discussed."

"You know what, Rose, I don't care that Mama knows about Brenda. She needs to know. It's time I stood up to her anyway. At least you'll be there."

"No, I won't. I called Daddy and got him to buy me lunch. I'm getting ready to leave in a little bit."

"Well…that's okay. I'm not afraid."

"See! You go, girl! That's what I like to hear. So…how is Brenda? Did you work it out or what? And when am I going to meet her?"

"She's having a card party Saturday. Do you want to come?"

"Are the people…how can I say this? Is this a gay card party?" Sister chuckled.

"Yes, kind of sort of."

"Sort of kind of." We laughed. "No offense, Sister, but I think I'll pass this time, okay?"

Sister laughed again and replied, "I understand. Tell Daddy I said hello."

"I will. Bye."

CHAPTER 18

I saw Daddy sitting across the room. He was as handsome as I remember.

"Hi, Daddy," I said happily. "Have you been waiting long?"

"No, I just arrived."

"Daddy! I didn't know you smoked."

"I've always smoked. You were just too young to remember."

"Daddy! Did you marry again?"

"Yes, I did. Her name was Beverly. You'd have liked her. She was very high-spirited."

"Was?"

"She died five years ago in a car accident."

"Oh…Daddy, I'm sorry."

"No, it's okay, baby. I've dealt with that and it's done. I've gotten on with my life."

"Did you have any children with her?"

"Yes, I have a daughter in Long Beach. She's twelve. When her mother died, she went to live with her grandmother. I haven't seen her. It's been two years now."

"Why not?"

"Well, her grandmother is overprotective. She blames me for her daughter's death. The brakes went out on the car that killed Beverly. She feels like I should have known the brakes were going out. The auto mechanic assured me there was no way of knowing. So I've put it behind me."

"Daddy, did you say she was twelve?" Daddy knew where I was going with that, so he interrupted me.

"Rose, your mom and I was having a lot of problems. The relationship was over a long time before we actually split up."

"You cheated on Mom?"

"Your mom was in another relationship as well. We stayed together for you and your sister. But I couldn't take it anymore. Rose, I had to leave."

Daddy changed the subject in a hurry. I wasn't upset. Actually, Daddy didn't realize I understood better than he thought.

"Your mother tells me you dropped out of college. Why?"

"I plan to go back. I'm just not sure when. Daddy, did you ever try to get in touch with Sister and me?"

"Your mother and I wasn't getting along very well at all. She told me never to call or come by or ask about you girls. Of course, I did anyway without her knowing. I'd drive by the house and see you girls playing outside. Your mother didn't like it. She called the police, so I stopped. I started going to your school. But it was getting to be too much for me. I stopped and decided to go on with my life. I thought when you and Sister got older, your mom would stop this foolishness, but she didn't."

"So Mama wouldn't let you see us?"

"No."

"That bitch!"

"No, Rose. Don't call your mother that."

"Why not? That's what she is."

"Rose, your mother did what she thought was right at the time."

"But she let us think you were dead."

"Is that what she told you?"

"No, but she knew that's what we thought."

"I tried to call you at college, just before your grandmother passed away."

"I remember! My girlfriend told me I had received a call from someone. It was you. I knew it."

"Baby, is there a man in your life?"

"Yes. His name is Jamal David."

"How did you meet him?"

"At a college party."

"I know about those college parties."

"This was a really nice party. Jamal is so sweet to me. He doesn't do drugs. He doesn't drink very much, and he loves me. As a matter of fact, I'm going to go and see him this weekend."

"Where does he live?"

"Just a couple hours from here. I know you'll like him."

"What does your mother think about him?"

"I really don't care what she thinks."

* * * * *

"Sister? Is that you? Come in here, please," Mama said.

"Did you call me?" Sister said.

"Yes, how are your sessions going with Dr. Prescott?"

"Fine."

"Do you think it's helping you at all?"

"Yes, I think so."

"What do you two talk about?"

"We talk about a lot of things, Mama." Sister was becoming irritated.

"I know, but anything in particular?"

"Mama, what is it? What is it you're trying to find out?"

"You know what I'm trying to find out. How come you didn't tell me?"

"Tell you what?"

"About that girl. That girl that used to always spend the night. What's her name?"

"Who, Betty?"

"No."

"Karen?"

"No! Sister, you know damn well who I'm talking about."

"Yes, I know! I didn't want to tell you because I knew you wouldn't like it or her."

"You damn skippy. I don't like her! Sister, you're not that way. You just think you are. Talk to the doctor, honey. Tell her about it. She might be able to help you."

"Help me, Mama? I don't need any help. I love Brenda." When Sister said that, Mama hit the roof.

"No! No! You don't! You just think you do!"

"Yes, I do!"

"Stop it, Sister. You're trying to punish me, aren't you? You don't really like girls. You're trying to get back at me for something. Okay, Sister, maybe I was a bad mother. You don't have to go to this extreme. I'm sorry! I'm sorry! Is that what you want to hear? Now tell me, Sister, you don't like girls." Mama started to cry.

"Mama, don't flatter yourself! Stop yelling and answer the phone!"

"Hello!"

"Hello…ah…may I speak to Sister, please?"

"No! Hell no! Don't call here. Don't ever call here again with your sickness."

"Mama, is that Brenda?"

"She doesn't want to talk to you." Sister snatched the phone from Mama's hand.

"Brenda? I'm sorry."

"What's going on? Did you tell her? Listen to her. I can hear her. Baby! Are you okay? Should I come over?"

"No, she found out herself. But I'm fine. For once, I'm really fine. Don't worry. But this is not a good time, so I'll call you back, okay?"

"All right, baby, if you're sure."

"What is wrong with you, Mama? You kept secrets from us for years! Why does my being gay bother you so much, Mama? Huh? Is it because I know longer fit that perfect image of a perfect half-white child? How did you find out about us anyway?"

"None of your business," Mama said as she reached for a tissue from the box sitting on the table.

"I know how you found out. You read my letter I had laying on the dresser. I'm not stupid, Mama. I know how I leave my things. But that's okay because Brenda asked me to move in with her, and I might just take her up on it." Sister walked swiftly out of Mama's room. Sister could not believe what she had just done. It felt great!

"Daddy? Lunch was great. Thanks. Have you been living here all this time?"

"I don't live her, sweetie. I come here a lot on business."

"Where do you live?"

"Los Angeles."

"I've always wanted to go there. Can I come and visit you sometimes?"

"Sure. You and your sister are both welcome anytime. As a matter of fact, I'm leaving next weekend and driving back. You girls are more than welcome to come up. There's more than enough room. We'll have a pizza party."

"Great. I'll talk to Sister."

When Daddy dropped me off, the mailman was just approaching the house.

"Hi, Rose. How are you this afternoon?"

"I'm fine, Smitty. How are you?" Smitty had been our mailman for a long as I could remember. He was black, tall, and once upon a time very handsome.

"Good, good. How's your mom? I hear she's been sick."

"She's fine."

"I have a certified letter for you. Just sign here by the *x*."

"For me?"

"Yes, ma'am."

"Thanks, Smitty. Tell your wife I said hello."

"I will. Bye," Smitty said as he continued on his way.

"Rose?" Mama called. "Did I get any mail? I saw the mailman leaving."

"No, but I got a certified letter from Grammy's lawyer, asking me to come down there next month."

"Why?"

"It says I need to complete some forms. It's probably about the house. Mama, I'm thinking about going out of town this weekend to see Jamal."

"What are you telling me for? You girls don't give a shit about what I think. Go ahead and have a nice time," she said sarcastically.

"Mama, where is this coming from?"

"What?"

"This attitude."

"You're going out of town and you're just now telling me. And Sister's moving in with that girl. I don't care what either of you do."

"Mama, I'm telling you now. Wait a minute, what did you just say? Sister's doing what?"

"She's moving in with that girl."

"Who says? When?"

"Ask her. She just told me," Mama said. I could not believe what Mama had just told me. I ran to Sister's room to see what this was all about.

"Sister?"

"What's the matter, Rose? You're out of breath."

"Mama said you're moving out. Are you?"

"She sure didn't waste any time telling you, did she? I wanted to tell you myself."

"So it's true! You're leaving? You're leaving?"

"Well, gee, Rose! Don't make it seem like I'm leaving the state. I'm just moving in with Brenda. Stop looking at me like that. What?"

"I don't understand, Sister. Why do you want to move?" I was hurt.

"I'm tired, Rose. I need to get away from here for a while. You said you liked Brenda."

"Yes, I do. But I didn't think you'd go and live with her. When are you moving?"

"Tomorrow."

"Tomorrow!"

"Rose? Look at you, you have tears in your eyes. Listen, sometimes a person has to do what's best. And for me, living with Brenda is best. I've learned a lot of things from her."

"Yes, you have," I said. "This conversation proves that. I can tell you've grown a lot."

"Well, what this conversation is about, I didn't learn from Brenda. I learned from you. I stood up to Mama today, and it felt great! Why don't you come over to Brenda's this weekend? We'd love to have you."

"I would, but I'm going to see Jamal. I miss him."

"I'm sure you do. Rose, don't worry about me. I'm fine. Can I have a hug?"

"Of course." I wiped my eyes and gave my sister a hug as she came into her own.

Later that evening, I called Jamal to find out what his weekend was looking like.

"Hello…Jamal?"

"Hey, baby, I was just thinking about you."

"Oh yeah? What about me?"

"I miss you. I need to see you."

"My, what a coincidence. I was telling my sister how much I miss too. I told her I was thinking about coming up this week-end. How about it?"

"How about it? How about it? It's great. I'll rent some movies. What do you want to eat? I'll buy some wine. The best wine!"

"Jamal? Jamal? Calm down, baby. I love you too."

"I'm sorry, Rose. I'm just so excited you're coming. I love you."

"I love you too. I'll call you later to let you know what time the bus gets in, okay? Bye."

* * * * *

"Come in, Sister," I said.

"What are you doing?"

"Nothing. I just called the bus station to find out what bus I can catch. There's a bus at seven p.m. I think I'll take Friday night."

"Rose? What do you think Daddy will say?"

"About what?"

"You know, about me and Brenda."

"I don't know, Sister. Does it really matter? I mean, it's not like he was here for us. If he doesn't like it, it's just too bad."

"I know, but I'm scared to tell him. I don't want him to look at me funny. Rose, would you tell him for me?"

"Yes, I'll tell him. But it'll have to wait until I get back from visiting Jamal."

"That's fine. Believe me, I'm in no rush for him to know. What if Mama tells him first?"

"She won't."

"How do you know?"

"Believe me. Mama's not going to tell anyone her daughter is gay. Anyway, I gotta get out of here. See you when I get home from work. Maybe I'll help you pack, okay? All right. See you later."

I enjoyed the bus ride to see Jamal. It was nice and quiet and gave me time to relax and get my thoughts together, especially after helping Sister move into Brenda's.

Brenda was a very attractive dark-skinned female, very feminine. She had a really nice two-bedroom apartment. There wasn't a lot of furniture, but she had the essentials. I felt comfortable talking with Brenda. Although I had spoken with her before, we had never met. She assured me that she would take good care of Sister and would call me if she ever felt the need. I was comfortable with that. I gave Sister a hug and told her I'd call when I got back.

When I arrived, Jamal had a dozen roses waiting for me in the back seat of his car, along with a bottle of my favorite cologne.

"Hi, baby. How was your ride?"

"It was fine, but I am glad to be here. Hi, baby."

"Are you tired?"

"Yes…a little bit. I helped my sister move before I came. That tired me out."

"Well, let's go," he said.

It felt good to be back in Jamal's apartment. I didn't realize how much I missed being there, though being there reminded me of Grammy.

"How about a glass of wine?"

"I'd love some. I think I'll take a shower." I took a bath instead. I needed time to think about how I was going to tell Jamal I was the product of a rape. Maybe I would say, "Jamal, sweetie, I love you and guess what, I don't know who my real father is. Ahh…Jamal, I've been meaning to tell you. My real father is a rapist." Nope! That wouldn't work.

I must have sat in the bathtub for a long time because my skin had started to wrinkle, and I heard Jamal say, "Rose, honey, are you okay? You didn't slip through the drain, did you?" I laughed.

"No, baby, I'm fine. I'm coming out now."

"Are you hungry? I ordered Chinese," he said.

"Yes, Chinese is fine."

"That was delicious," he said after wiping his mouth. "How was your fried rice?"

"It was excellent."

"Rose, put your fork down. What's the matter? You've haven't been talking very much. It's the same when I call. What is it? I thought you and your sister had made up."

I just held my head down. I lied, and there was no way around it except to admit it.

"I'd like to have another glass of wine first," I said. I got up and walked into the bedroom and started to pull the covers down on the bed. When Jamal handed me a glass of wine, I took a sip and put both arms around him and hugged him as tight as I could.

"It feels like you're trying to squeeze the life out of me. Rose, what is wrong?" I climbed into bed and reached both arms out to him.

"It's nothing serious, but before I tell you, I want you to make love to me." Jamal started to kiss me and kiss me, but my mind kept thinking about how I was going to tell him. I tried hard to concentrate on what he was doing, but I couldn't. Jamal slowly laid me down on the bed and removed my robe. He started to kiss my forehead, then my nose, my lips, my breasts, my stomach, my navel, my...ooooooh la la. What a way to forget.

"Rose, I'm sorry. Did I hurt you?"

"No, it was great!"

"Then why are you crying?"

"I love you so much. If I were to ever lose you..."

"Lose me? Honey, you're stuck with me forever."

I should have had something to say to that, but I didn't. We lay there silently, a little tense.

"What did you want to tell me?" he asked.

"Hold me," I said. "Remember the night I was here at the apartment? We were talking about the black rose that was on the table, and I was telling you that Mama never really did say that my father was dead?"

"Yes."

"Well, recently, I found out that he is alive, and he came to see me and my sister."

"That's good, isn't it?"

"Yes, I mean, we were glad to find out he was alive and even happier to see him." Jamal kissed me on my cheek.

"I'm happy for you, baby."

"But…"

"But what?"

"He's not my biological father."

"So what?"

"My biological father is a rapist."

"Oh, baby, I'm sorry to hear that."

"Wait, let me finish before I lose my nerve. You've met Sister. Didn't you think it was strange that we look so different?"

"Maybe. But siblings look different all the time."

"The man we both know as our father is white. One day, I confronted Mama, and I asked her why my sister and I looked so different. She said it was because she'd been raped. I'm the product of that rape." As Jamal held me tighter, I started to sob. He didn't say anything. I left it alone.

The next morning, I was awoken by the smell of sausage cooking, coffee brewing, and a kiss from the man I loved.

"Good morning, love," he said.

"Good morning. Are you cooking?"

"Yes, ma'am. Are you hungry?"

"Starving."

"Okay, come on. It'll be ready in a minute."

"Jamal, wait! You didn't say anything last night. Why?"

"Honestly, Rose, I didn't know what to say. So I thought it would be best not to say anything."

CHAPTER 19

"Dr. Prescott, this is my friend, Brenda."

"Hi, Brenda. Sister told me you would be sitting in on her session today. I'm glad you could make it."

"Sure. Anything I can do to help."

"Why don't you ladies have a seat over here? Is there anything in particular you ladies would like to discuss today?" Dr. Prescott asked.

"No, not really," Sister responded.

"Okay then, let's continue where we left off last week. Do you remember what we were talking about?"

"Yes. You asked me how I feel about my father being back."

"And how do you feel?" she asked Sister.

"The very first emotion I felt was extreme happiness, disbelief, fear, and concern."

"Have you broken it down?"

"Yes, I have. The thought of having my father back after years of thinking he was dead, of course, I was extremely happy. But it's hard to believe he's really alive. After realizing this wasn't a dream and my father was actually alive, I became afraid."

"Afraid of what?"

"Afraid I hadn't lived up to his expectations of me, afraid that I might not love him like I once did, and maybe he doesn't love me the same. Afraid of what all this means." Sister looked up at Dr. Prescott.

"Why does it have to mean anything? Why can't it just mean your father's back?"

"But why now? It seems strange to me."

"Does anyone else in your family feel this way?"

"I'm not sure. We don't seem to talk much about it."

Brenda was feeling uneasy with Dr. Prescott. Although they had decided not to talk about anything in particular, Brenda changed the subject.

"Excuse me," Brenda interrupted.

"Yes, Brenda."

"I would like to ask a question, if that's okay?"

"Certainly. We encourage all of our clients' guests to participate."

"I know Sister told you that we are lesbians."

"Yes, she did."

"If you're going to be counseling Sister on this, I want to know how you feel about lesbians."

"I don't feel any way at all. It's just a sexual preference. People are free to be and do whatever they want." Brenda looked at Dr. Prescott.

"Uh huh! I think our hour is up. Sister, are you ready?"

Dr. Prescott's secretary knocked on the door to tell her she had a call.

"Okay, Betty. Put it on line one, please."

"Man!" Sister said. "That went fast. Goodbye, Doctor. I'll see you next week."

"Hello? This is Dr. Prescott."

"Well, how did it go?"

"It went fairly well."

"What do you mean it went fairly well?"

"Did you know she was bringing Brenda with her?"

"What! She brought that girl with her? What did she say?"

"She wanted to know how I felt about lesbians."

"What did you say?"

"I made her think I was okay with it."

"Good! Keep me in touch."

"I will," Dr. Prescott said. "Oh, by the way, your check is late."

"I just dropped it in the mail. You should have it tomorrow."

Mama was doing good not smoking any cocaine. I was really proud of her. But Mama had not learned to disassociate herself from the people who still smoked.

"Hello?"

"Hey, girl! How are you doing?"

"Marilyn? Where have you been? I've been calling you for the past couple of weeks," Mama said.

"Girl, you know that nigger I was telling you about? You know that nigger with the pretty teeth?"

"Why do you have to say nigger all the time? That sounds awful."

"Anyway, can you get away?"

"Why, what's up?"

"That's where I was. Me and a friend drove up the coast. I got that shit you've been waiting months for," Marilyn said. *"I haven't even done any yet, so how about it?"*

"I don't know. You know I've been trying to get off that shit!"

"Come on, girl. One more for old time's sake."

"All right! I'll be there in twenty minutes."

"Okay. You should be here by the time I get out of the bathroom. Bye," Marilyn said. *"Oh, and pick up a bottle of grain alcohol."*

* * * * *

It was hard leaving Jamal again. It was hard for him too. He watched the bus I was on until it was no longer in view. "Bye, baby," I whispered. I did not want to go home and deal with Sister or Mama.

"Hello, Sister," I said.

"Rose, hi! When did you get back?"

"About an hour ago."

"How's Jamal? Did you tell him I said hello?"

"Yes, I did. Have you heard from Daddy?"

"No, as a matter of fact, I haven't. You are still going to talk to him for me, aren't you?"

"Yes, I think I'll call him now. Maybe I can see him later today. Are you sure you don't want to come with me?"

"Yes, I'm sure. Call me after you talk to him."

"All right. Tell Brenda I said hello."

I wondered if Daddy knew anything about David. What might Mama have told him? I called and asked him to come over. I wasn't quite sure how to mention the subject of David. I just knew I had to. Daddy came around dinnertime and brought a bucket of KFC.

"You know, Rose, you were very special to me, and you still are. I know I've been gone a long time. But I can tell you have something on your mind. How do you and your mother get along?"

"It's strange you asked that, Daddy," I said.

"Well, your mother was going through some changes when you girls were small."

"I really don't know how to start. It seemed like after you were gone, Mama changed. This is hard, Daddy."

"Just take your time, sweetie." Daddy sat straight up on the couch and clasped his hands together as if he knew what I was about to say.

"Were you going to tell me that you are not my real father?" Daddy almost choked on the orange soda he was drinking.

"I...I..."

"I'm sorry, Daddy," I said, handing him a napkin. "I didn't mean to startle you. It's just that I had to get it out before I lost my nerve."

"How did you find out about that?"

"One day I confronted Mama about my looking so different, and she had to tell me."

"Exactly what did she tell you?"

"She told me that the reason I look so different is because she had been raped. I asked her if she knew his whereabouts. She would only tell me his name, David. Daddy, did you know about this?"

"I'm sorry, Rose, what?"

"Did you know about this?"

"Yes, I did."

"What? You knew about this and you weren't going to tell me?"

"Baby, I..." I was heading for the door when Daddy grabbed my arm. "Wait! Rose, you must remember that you were only ten years old when I left."

"Why did you leave? Was it because of David?"

"It was because of a lot of things, but the rape wasn't one of them."

"How did you find out?"

"Your mother was brought into Mt. Mercy. I was an intern there at the time, working in the emergency room when she was brought in. She had scrapes and bruises and was out of control. I administered a mild sedative so that I could get more information from her. I fell in love with your mother on sight. She was so young and beautiful. I checked on her every day. I went by the house after she was released. We dated and eventually got married."

"Then Mama got pregnant with Sister?"

"Yes, and that's it in a nutshell."

"So you knew about me from the very beginning? I was so worried you left because you found out Mama had been raped or you didn't love Sister and me anymore. Why did Mama call the police when you'd try to see us?"

"I don't know if she knew I'd never harm either of you. I can't remember. Your mother was going through some changes back then. Us staying together just made it worse."

"What kind of changes?"

"I don't know, baby. Just changes." I didn't say anything for a while, nor did Daddy. He was hiding something. "I have some calls I need to make, so I'll need to leave."

"Oh, Daddy, there is something else I need to talk to you about before you leave. Actually, Sister wanted me to talk to you."

"About what?"

"She moved out a few days ago into an apartment with a friend of hers."

"A boyfriend? Is it serious?"

"Yes…it's serious…but it's not a boyfriend. It's a girlfriend."

"Someone she grew up with? But Sister's not working. How can she afford her share of the rent?" Poor thing. He had no idea what I was about to tell him.

"Daddy…Sister's gay." Daddy reached one arm behind him, looking for the arm of the chair to sit down.

"What?"

"Daddy? It's not so bad. I mean, this is the nineties, right?" Daddy was in a daze. He gave me a hug and walked out the door. I went upstairs to my room and lay across the bed. I needed a friend.

"Hello, Nina?" When Nina heard my voice, we both laughed and laughed.

"Hey, girl! What have you been up to?"

"Not much."

"Where's Sister?"

"That's right, I haven't talked to you in a while. Girl, Sister moved out a few days ago."

"I'll bet your mom had a fit."

"Yes, she did, but it was nothing she could do."

"So what's been going on? How's Jamal?"

"He's fine."

"Listen at you sounding like a girl in love."

"Nina? I am. That man is so good to me."

"Hey, that's what I want to hear."

"What about you?" I asked. "Are you seeing anybody yet?"

"No, not seriously anyway. I just date a lot. I went out with this one guy one night, girl. That motherfucker tried to tear my clothes off. And when I wouldn't let him, the bastard made me walk home. The bad thing was, I didn't know where the hell I was. That's why I quit smoking bud. Stop laughing!"

"I can't help it! Okay, okay, have you heard from any of the gang? What's Kiki up to?"

"Guess what? Kiki has to go for a biopsy."

"Oh no. Why?"

"She found a small lump in her breast. Well, actually, her boyfriend found it while they were making love."

"Really? How is she?"

"I haven't talked to her. Me and Samara's been keeping in touch," Nina said. "You know what we ought to do?"

"What?"

"We should all get together and go see her. Kiki wants us to come down anyway."

"Okay," I said. "Let's do that then. You call everyone, set something up, and call me back."

"Oh, wait a minute. I won't be able to go for a few weeks. I told my dad I'd come and spend a couple of weeks with him. But we can go right after that, okay?"

"Fine," I said. "And, Nina, I miss you."

"I miss you too, sweetie. Later."

Brenda called me a couple of weeks later and said she needed to talk to me. She said Sister's jealousy was getting out of hand.

"What's the matter, Brenda? What is Sister doing?"

"I don't know, Rose. Your sister is something else. I'm trying. I really am."

"What's going on?"

"Sister is freaking. Whenever I come home late from work, she trips."

"What do you mean she trips?" I was becoming agitated.

"She starts yelling and throwing things at me. When I'm talking business on the phone, she'll pick up the receiver to make sure it's business, and she had the nerve to ask the person I was talking to if they worked with me. I was so embarrassed. I'm trying, Rose. I really am. But if this keeps up, I'm going to ask Sister to move back home. I can't take it. And then all hell will break loose."

"I'll talk to her."

"Would you, Rose? Although I really don't think it's going to do any good."

"Where is she right now?"

"At home."

"All right. I'll give her a call right now." It was 3:00 p.m. when I got to Sister's apartment. Sister was still in her nightclothes. She spotted me outside her window. I saw her make a move toward the front door.

"Hey, Rose, what are you doing here? Why didn't you call?"

"I was going to call and chitchat, but then I thought I haven't seen you in a while, so I just decided to come over. I hope that was all right?" I said as my eyes glanced around the apartment.

"Yeah, sure. That's fine, but I would have gotten dressed."

"As a matter of fact, Sister, why aren't you dressed? It's after three."

"I don't know. I've been feeling sluggish all day. I was just getting up when I saw you from my window."

"Maybe you're pregnant," I said as I broke into a smile.

"Funny, Rose, ha, ha. So how's Mama?"

"She's fine. I really don't see her that much anymore. She's gotten her job back."

"Oh really! When did she start back?" Sister inquired.

"Last week. How are things going with you and Brenda?"

"Why do you ask?"

"Are you happy?"

"What do you mean am I happy? Of course I'm happy, or I wouldn't be here." Sister went over to the easy chair, slumped down, and put her hand over her face and started to cry.

"Sister, what's the matter, honey? I knew something was wrong when I found you still in your nightclothes. You know you can't hide anything from me. We're like two peas in a pod. I know when something is wrong. Tell me, Sister, what is it?" I knelt down beside her and moved her hands from her face. "Sister!" I said firmly. "What is wrong?"

"It's Brenda," she whined. "She's cheating on me." It was hard, but I had to act surprised.

"I don't believe that, Sister. Brenda loves you." All of a sudden, Sister became irate. I stood back.

"So what are you saying? You think I'm making this up? You do! You think I'm making this up! You think I'm crazy! That's all right. You and Brenda can kiss my ass!"

"Sister! You know what? Uh uh! I'm not even going there! Yes, I am! Maybe you should not have quit your sessions so soon."

"What? How did you know about that?" Sister started pacing the floor. I knew things were about to get serious. I really wasn't sure how to handle this. Sister was not the Sister I knew. "Oh my god! You've been talking to Brenda, haven't you? Haven't you?" she bellowed. I just stood there in a daze, watching the devil rape my sister's mind. I was afraid. I didn't know how to fight the demon that was hovering over her, but then I looked deep into her eyes and saw my sister was still there. I put that fear behind me and ran to her, grabbed her, and held her as tight as I could.

"I love you, Sister! I love you. It's me, Rose! Why are we yelling at each other like this?" When Sister noticed my tears, I saw her come back to me. We calmly talked after that. She told me that Brenda had asked her to find another psychiatrist, one that she could trust and that she'd pay for it. We talked about a lot of things, but most of them didn't make sense to me then.

* * * * *

Daddy was getting ready to go home, so he invited us all out to dinner. I didn't know what to think about him leaving. I was afraid. I had forgotten he had a life somewhere else. All I knew was that I didn't want to give him up…not yet. It was a little awkward at first, especially Daddy knowing about Sister being gay. But he seemed to put it behind him. Even so, I had to kick him a couple of times to keep him from staring at her. He got the hint, and everything was okay. At dinner, we were all having a really nice time, even Mama. We were laughing and talking. I felt like a little girl again, wishing my parents were back together.

"Rose? What's the matter? What are you thinking about?" Mama asked.

"Oh…just a private thought, Mama." Then I smiled.

"So…Daddy, when can Sister and I come for a visit?"

"Anytime you want. Just call first because I'm out of town a lot." We enjoyed the rest of that evening, Daddy, Mama, Sister, and me.

I knew there was no chance of Mama and Daddy getting back together. I didn't want that for them, and I know they didn't want it for themselves. I was glad knowing he was alive and well. Daddy left a few days after that.

CHAPTER 20

Nina was on her way to pick me up. It was going to be a lot of fun seeing the old gang again, despite the fact that I hated the reason for this gathering. I hoped Kiki would be okay.

"Mama? Nina's going to be here any minute. If Jamal calls, tell him I'll call him later on tonight. Okay, Mama?"

"Yes, Rose. How long will you be gone?"

"I took a week off from work. I'm not sure, probably the whole week. I didn't get a chance to call Sister either. Tell her I love her, will you?"

"All right, I will. I hear a horn blowing. Isn't she coming in?"

"No, we want to get there before dark. She did tell me to tell you hello when she called this morning. All right, Mama. I'm leaving. I'll call you later. Bye."

"Bye, baby. You girls drive safely."

It was a beautiful day for a long drive. I was glad to be leaving for a while.

"Hey, girl. What's up?" Nina hollered from the car.

"You are what's up. Whose car is this?" I asked.

"What do you mean, whose car is this? It's mine." Nina was grinning from ear to ear.

"Girl, it's bad! When did you get it?"

"A couple of weeks ago. My old man said he would pay the down payment if I would keep up the payments. I said *hell yes!* Of course, I didn't say it like that, but you know what I mean."

"That was sweet of him," I told her.

"Sweet hell! I haven't seen him since I was about fifteen years old. Hm! He owes me this and a whole lot more," Nina said, rolling her eyes.

"It was still sweet."

"So how is Jamal?"

"He's fine. I went to visit him a few weeks ago. I told him about my daddy and about my biological father being a rapist."

"No, you didn't! What did he say?"

"You know, he didn't have a whole lot to say, only that he didn't care about any of that and he loves me for me."

"Well…that's good, isn't it?"

"I guess so, but—"

"But what?" Nina interrupted.

"I don't know, Nina. Nothing seems to bother this man. I mean, he never gets angry or upset about anything. It makes me just a tad uncomfortable. You know what I mean?" Nina looked at me as if to say, "What is wrong with this fool?"

"No…as a matter of fact, I don't know what you mean. Look, Rose, we are always complaining when we don't have a good man like Jamal and still complain when we do. Girl, you should count your lucky stars. It's a whole lot of women who'd give any and everything to have your man, honey." I was a fool. Why was I complaining?

"You are so right. I didn't realize I was complaining so much, and you know what? I'm going to stop before the Lord takes my man from me," I said as I looked up.

"I heard that!" Nina responded.

"So, girlfriend! What's up with Kiki?"

"Well, Saturday she'll go up for her biopsy."

"I am so afraid for her. You know how proud she was always about her breasts. It would kill her if she had to have them removed."

"I know. When will Samara get in?"

"Later tonight." Nina and I didn't say anything for a long time. I guess we were both thinking…what if that were us?

Kiki had planned a barbecue for us and told us not to worry about a thing. She would take care of everything.

"Rose? How is Sister?"

"Oh, girl, let's not even go there." Nina turned and looked at me.

"Why?"

"I'm so worried about that girl. I think she is losing her mind."

"What?"

"She keeps accusing Brenda of sleeping around."

"Brenda! Who the hell is Brenda?"

"Ooops, I didn't tell you, did I? Sister is gay." All of a sudden, I heard the car shriek.

"Get the hell out of Dodge!" Nina responded.

"Girl, drive this car."

"She follows her sometimes, and lately she's been throwing these temper tantrums. For a minute, I didn't know who she was. Nina, it scared the shit out of me. She thought Brenda and I was in cahoots. It was bad. I didn't know what to do."

"Have you told your mother?"

"No, because I don't know. Mama seems to be off into her own world these days. But I am going to tell her. Maybe when I get back. I'm not sure yet."

Kiki had a real nice apartment. It was small but just right for her. When we arrived, Kiki was standing there like she knew we would be driving up any minute.

"Look at you still wearing those short dresses. Hey, girl, how are you doing?" I asked as I gave her a hug. We hugged each other like we hadn't seen each other in ten years.

I'm fine. A little scared about the surgery, but I'm okay." Kiki grabbed us both.

"God! I'm so glad everyone could come up."

"What time is Samara getting here?" Just as I said that, a figure appeared in her doorway.

"Who's the finest one here?" Nina and I looked up and saw Samara standing in the doorway. We all screamed. We were laughing and jumping. Anyone passing would have thought we were a bunch of kids.

Then Nina asked, "When did you get here?"

"About eleven o'clock last night."

"I heard someone lightly pecking on my door. I thought it was my neighbor wanting to borrow something again. I almost didn't answer until I looked out the window and saw her car," Kiki said.

"Where is your car?" I asked Kiki.

"I sent a neighbor to get some beer because we didn't want to miss you all," Kiki said. "So what should we do tonight?"

"Well," I said, "I'm tired. I say we get a movie, some munchies, and call it a night."

"Look, heifer, you've been here resting all day. I'm a little tired too," Nina said.

"Okay, okay! You did have a long drive. I'm game for a movie. What should we get?"

"Get?" Samara said. "Come here, y'all. Look at this." Samara opened the doors to Kiki's built-in cabinets. Kiki must have had a couple hundred movies in there.

"Where did you get all these videotapes from?" Nina asked.

"I taped them. I know, I go overboard sometimes. I can't help it. I love my video collection," she said proudly. "Hey! Let's watch *Bridges of Madison County*."

"Um um! I don't want to see that soapy shit. How about...I heard *Devil in a Blue Dress* is good. It's got my baby Denzel in it! Whew! Everybody agree?" We did.

That evening, we were all stuffed on ribs, chicken potato salad, and coleslaw. Although we were all having a good time, we could tell Kiki was putting on the performance of life. After the fun and music had quieted down, we all sat down with a wine cooler.

"Girls," I said. "Remember when we were last together like this?"

"Yes...it was when we were at school. Didn't somebody get raped or something?" Samara asked.

"Um hm," I said as I took a swallow from my glass. "She was almost raped."

"Oh, that's right," Nina added. "She never returned to school."

"Rose?"

"Yeah, Nina?"

"Are you going back to school?"

"Yes, I plan to go back. I just don't know when. What about the rest of you? Samara? Kiki?

"I'm not sure yet about when."

"This is a damn shame," Nina said. "One of us has got to finish college."

"Take your ass back and finish," Kiki said, laughing.

Nina turned her backside toward Kiki and added, "Not until you kiss it." We all laughed.

"No, seriously," Nina said. "I am going back to school. I got to have a job paying more than seven dollars an hour." Samara then pulled out a joint.

"Hell, no," I said. "You're not going back to school."

We all got a surprise when Nina said, "Come on. We don't need that mess." Everyone was amazed when they heard those words come from Nina's mouth. She was the biggest weed smoker on campus.

"What?" Samara said.

"I'm serious. If we keep smoking marijuana, we are not going to finish school. None of us have a lot of money to really afford to buy it. I mean, think about it. How many people do you know have wasted their lives because of drugs, any kind of drugs? I know people say reefer is not that bad. But it is."

"Where is this coming from, Nina?" I asked.

"I realized a few months ago that I didn't want drugs of any kind to be a part of my life."

"Why?" Kiki wanted to know.

"Because…it's just no good. How many of us have smoked a joint and tried to have a conversation and forget what it is we want to say? See, I take that serious. I mean, if all of a sudden you lose your thought, something is not right."

"No, Nina. It's something else. Spill it," I insisted.

"All right! I had a bad experience."

"Nina?" I said. "You never told me about that."

"Because I wasn't proud of it. I should have known better. But I wasn't thinking right because of the weed and alcohol."

"What happened?" Samara asked. Nina had our full attention.

"Well, this guy I'd known for a long time picked me up for a date. We were just going to his house to kick it, you know. Nothing special. He said he had a twenty sack and some beer. I said okay. No harm in that, right? So I got there, and he played some music and handed me a beer. About an hour later, he pulled a twenty sack out of his pocket. He rolled a couple. It was the best. Things were still going okay. But then a couple of his friends came over, and they had bud too. They rolled a few more joints up, and we were all smoking, you know, having a good time. But their weed was different and more potent. This one guy asked me to dance. I said okay. After he danced with me, his friends wanted to dance with me too. I didn't mind. All of a sudden, I became dizzy. I told them I needed to sit down. I fell asleep. I mean, I was out. I don't know how much time had gone by, probably not much, but I started dreaming that I was being raped by three dudes. Somebody knocked over a lamp. It scared me and woke me up. Girl, when I woke up, everybody had their clothes off, gazing at me. Even my friend. I jumped up! And I told him to take me home. Then I noticed my blouse was off. Do you know that bastard wouldn't take me home? I grabbed my blouse and ran out of there. I didn't even know where I was. Finally, I saw a cab. Girl, I said I would never, ever smoke again." All of our eyes were fixed on her. We couldn't believe what she had just told us. "And I know that you all are not going to stop smoking right now. But I just think it's something you should really think about. It's just no good. There is no positivity in marijuana smoking. It took me a long time to realize that. But I am so glad I did." Then something extraordinary happened. We all stood up. Samara went into the bathroom. We followed her, looked at the joint long and hard, and flushed it down the toilet. We turned to Nina and hugged her and told her we were glad nothing happened to her.

We went back into the living room. Kiki lifted a glass and clanged on the side with a spoon to get our attention. "I want to thank all my dear friends for coming down to be with me."

"How are you really doing, Kiki?" Nina asked.

"I'm fine. Scared! But…" All of a sudden, Kiki's whole demeanor changed. "Okay, I just don't understand. Why me? Why me?" No one said a word.

"So what!" Samara said. "Kiki, you have a lot going for you. You're attractive, and you have the best legs in town and you're smart. We still have a lot to be thankful for. At least none of us stopped going to school because of pregnancy." Nina looked at me from the corner of her eye. None of the other girls knew she had been pregnant before. "So negative or positive, Kiki, don't let this destroy your life, sweetie. We are all here for you." Kiki just held her head down. "Come on, Kiki. Hold your head up," I said.

Kiki held her head and started to speak. "I have something I need to tell you all. I had my biopsy two weeks ago," she said. We all stood up. But as we did, Kiki sat down and started to sob. Between sobs, she cried, "Tomorrow I go for a mastectomy on my left breast." Samara dropped her glass and stared at Kiki for a moment and ran out of the room. The rest of us were silent.

A sinking feeling overcame me. If the ground had opened up, I would have fallen right in. I looked at Nina. She had one hand on her face and the other on her chest. We must have had the same thought because we both stepped at the same time, rushing over to Kiki. As we sat on each side of her, we closed her in with our embrace. It was as if we were trying to shield her from anymore hurt. "Where's Samara?" Kiki asked between sobs. "She hates me now. I should have told her. I don't know why I didn't. Find her!" Kiki cried. We all sobbed together. As bad as I was feeling for Kiki, I worried about Samara too. She was as close to Kiki as I was to Nina. I broke the embrace and went to find her.

I heard crying. I knew it wasn't Kiki. "Samara!" I screamed. "Samara!" I saw blood. I didn't quite know where it was coming from. I froze. I could hear footsteps running toward Samara and me.

"What's the…oh my god! Samara!" Nina screamed. As I stood there, both hands on my face, Nina ran over to her and examined her real quick. "Rose, get the car!" But I couldn't move. Nina yelled at me again, startling me. "Rose, get the car!"

Samara had blood on her face and hands. We realized it looked a lot worse than it actually was. Samara had been hitting her hand against the wall of Kiki's apartment building and putting her hands on her face. She broke some bones in her hand. When we arrived at the hospital, the doctor asked us if there were any drugs involved. We all looked at Nina and proudly said no. Samara was so upset. She was given a light sedative to calm her down before the hospital would release her.

"This is all my fault," Kiki said. "I should have told her. I want to talk to her." Kiki went in to where Samara was lying.

"Hey, sweetie. What are you trying to do, steal the show?" Samara started to cry again. She did not think it was funny. "I'm sorry, Samara. Look! I'm going to be fine. I mean, it's not the end of the world, right?"

Samara suddenly pushed Kiki away from her. "Why didn't you tell me? Why didn't you tell me?" she yelled.

"Is that what this is about? Because I didn't tell you? You almost broke every bone in your hand because I didn't tell you?" Kiki yelled back.

"I thought we could tell each other anything. And it's not so much you didn't tell me. It's that you went through this alone. I just don't understand, Kiki."

"Right! You don't understand! I had just been told I wouldn't have any titties. You think I wanted to spread that news right away? You didn't understand? *I didn't understand.* But if I had known you would beat up your hand, I would have told you." They both started to cry again.

"It's not that. I mean, that's not the reason I was doing that. Actually, I don't know why I did it. It just happened. I wasn't trying to."

"Come on, Samara. Don't start again. I'm tired of crying. I've been doing a lot of it lately."

"I know. But when I first found out about your lump, it almost felt as if it was happening to me. I cried for days. Don't think I'm funny or anything, but I love you and I always will. We've always been able to tell each other any and everything, and it hurts me that you kept this from me. Do you know what I mean, Kiki?" Kiki could only nod. "I didn't mean to run out and cause damage to my hand, but I had to hit something. Kiki, I really can't explain it."

"Well, couldn't you have found a pillow or something?" Samara shrugged her shoulders. They then hugged and rocked each other gently.

I peeped in to see how things were going. "The doctor said we can go now. Are you ready?" I asked them both.

All of our eyes were so swollen, we could have taken a trip without packing any bags. We were exhausted. Kiki had a king-size bed that came with her apartment. Samara lay down, properly positioning her hand as to not hurt it anymore. Kiki then lay down next to Samara, followed by Nina, then myself. If anyone had come in, they would have definitely got the wrong idea. But we didn't care. When I closed my eyes for a second and opened them again, I could have sworn there was someone there, but it didn't scare me. I also knew there was no one there. I prayed silently.

Dear God,

I pray that Kiki will be okay. Let her come through her surgery okay. Watch over her and keep her safe. Guide each and every move the doctor makes as if you were doing the surgery yourself. Help her to keep a positive mind and to know she is important no matter what. Please, God, don't let this destroy her life. She is a beautiful, vibrant woman. Help her to know that she has a purpose and we are all here for her. God, please help Samara get through this. Her and Kiki are so close as we all are. Give us the strength to endure whatever life throws our way. God, I also pray that Nina finds the love she is looking for. Help her to keep a strong mind and not be anxious and know that when the time is right, you will send her someone.

A strange thing happened. Nina squeezed my hand as if she heard me praying.

> *I love you, God. I believe in miracles as I*
> *believe in you. Amen.*

We all were up very early the next morning. Kiki had to be at the hospital at 8:00 a.m. When we arrived they, were ready for her. We each gave her a kiss and hug before the nurse wheeled her off.

"Don't worry, Kiki. We'll be right here, hon," I said. We watched the nurse wheel Kiki down the hall. We all took a deep breath.

"Don't worry, Kiki. We'll be right here!" Samara yelled down the hall.

"Anyone want coffee?" Nina asked. As we sat in the hospital cafeteria, there was an eerie quietness.

"Come on, you all. Kiki's going to be okay," I said.

"I know," Samara said. "But you have to admit, this is a scary thing. I mean, it's easy for us to sit here and say Kiki is going to be okay because we want her to be. But what scares me the most is what to say to her when she comes out of surgery without her thinking I'm pitying her. You know what I mean? Because if it were me, I'm not so sure I could handle it."

"You know what?" I said. "I think we should all say a prayer for her right now."

"Right here? In the cafeteria?" Samara asked.

"Yes! Right here. My Grammy used to say if you are embarrassed to pray in front of people, you are embarrassed to know the Lord. I know I don't go to church as much as I should, but I still know the Lord. I know he is there and with me when times get hard. I know he is able. I know that I can count on him no matter what. So how about it?" We all looked at each other and stood up. We took each other's hand and formed a small circle. At first no one would say anything. But I was willing to stand in the gap for my friend. I started the prayer off by asking the Lord to take care of her and any and everything that I could think of in the way of praying for those who needed it. When I opened my eyes, I saw the Lord taking control, because as soon as I said *amen*, Nina took over. I heard someone crying in the far corner of the cafeteria. I knew the Lord was having his way. When we finished, we opened our eyes and noticed everyone in the cafeteria standing with their eyes closed, clapping and crying as well as some doctors and nurses. I felt refreshed. A doctor came over and said whoever we were praying for was blessed to have friends like us. We nodded and thanked him. When we sat down and cleaned our faces of tears, we, for a moment, put Kiki out of our thoughts and started discussing something else. After a couple of hours of sitting in the cafeteria, we all decided to go back upstairs to ask about Kiki. We went to the nurses' station to inquire about how Kiki was doing. The nurse said we were just in time. The doctor was looking for us. She then told us to have a seat in the waiting room while she paged him. We were all so anxious when the doctor came in.

"Samara?" the doctor called. Of course, we all stood up and went over to him.

"How is she?" we said.

"She's fine. As a matter of fact, more than fine. We could not find any evidence of cancer anywhere. I don't really understand it. We checked and double-checked, but when I went in there, no sign of cancer cells anywhere. Only lumps of fatty tissue, which is also unusual given her size." I quietly walked away and sat in a corner and gave my personal thanks to God.

"We are going to keep her here for a few more hours to make sure her incisions are okay. You can go up and see her now. She's waiting for you all." When the doctor left the room, we all jumped and screamed so loud the nurse had to come and remind us that we were in a hospital.

Nina and I stayed a couple of days longer. Samara, of course, stayed a few days longer than we did. When we got back, Nina spent one night at home with me and left early the next morning. I hated seeing her leave.

CHAPTER 21

It was three months since Kiki's ordeal, and all I could think about since then was what I was going to do with my life. I hadn't been writing much lately, or anything else. I had just sat down when I heard the phone ringing.

"Hello?" I heard a lot of yelling.

"Hello, Rose. Come and get her. I can't do anything with her. She's freaking!" Brenda shouted.

"What's going on over there?" I shouted. Brenda didn't answer. I slammed the phone down and hollered for Mama.

"Mama? Mama? Where are you?" I screamed, grabbing my purse.

"I'm in the basement, Rose. What's all the screaming about?"

"Come up here," I said. "Sister's in trouble. We have to get over there now!"

"What?" Mama said as I heard her running up the stairs.

"Brenda said Sister was freaking. She didn't say what was going on. Just for me to get over there. Mama, I don't want to go by myself. Come with me."

"Grab my keys. Let's go!" Mama said.

"Brenda didn't say anything?" Mama asked again.

"She didn't."

"See, I knew this would happen. I knew that girl would destroy Sister! I knew it," Mama said.

"I can't believe you, Mama. Brenda has done nothing but try to help Sister."

"That's your problem, Rose. You think people are always trying to be helpful. She was just using Sister."

"You don't even know what you're talking about, Mama! Brenda is a very nice person."

"Yes, and she turned your sister into one of them things. And if Dr. Prescott had done what I paid…"

"What? Mama, what? What about Dr. Prescott? Oh my god! You hired her to somehow stop Sister from being gay? I don't believe you!" I said angrily.

"You or your father didn't care. I had to do something!" Mama shouted.

"Yes, you did something, all right. Mama, you just can't stop a person from being gay just like that. Mama, how could you?"

"If it wasn't for that girl, Sister would not be like that. Now look at what's happening."

"Mama, you don't know anything. You have a lot of nerve. Sister's been having problems for a long time. You never took the time to realize it. This is not the first time Brenda has had problems with Sister. I just never said anything."

"Why not?"

"Because all you would have done is blame Brenda like you're doing now. Brenda has nothing to do with the way Sister is. I'm surprised she's been with her this long. She cares about Sister."

"Yeah, she cares, all right. She cares about lickin' and lapping," Mama said.

"Mama, that was unnecessary!"

"Okay, I'm sorry, but I just don't understand what makes a person that way." As we pulled into the parking lot, Brenda was standing outside of the building, waiting for us. We immediately rushed over to her.

"Brenda?" I called.

"What's going on here?" Mama interrupted.

"When I came home, Sister was sitting in the bedroom in the dark. I asked her what was wrong, why was she sitting in the dark since it was a nice sunny day. Sister didn't say anything. So I walked over to open the blinds and Sister jumped up and said, 'Shut the blinds,' but I continued to open them anyway and told her it's a beautiful day outside. Then Sister said, 'I said shut the blinds, bitch.' Her voice was a lot lower. It scared me. Sister looked at me as if she was going to kill me. So I closed the blinds back. I stepped back a little bit and asked her what was wrong again. She had her head down but cocked her eyes up at me. I was afraid. I mean, I'd never seen Sister look like that before. Sister asked me where I had been. I told her I had to go by the post office and mail off some documents before it closes to meet a deadline. She then called me a liar and said that I was over some woman's house."

"And were…you?" Brenda was surprised by Mama's question. She looked at me. I waved my hands at her to continue. Then I looked at Mama to let her know she just needed to shut up.

"I told her I was not and where did she get such an idea. She said never mind how she knew and started calling me all sorts of names. I told her I wasn't going to listen to it anymore and started to leave the room. Sister pulled out a knife." Mama and I gasped. "A big butcher knife. Sister said she was going to kill me and that she hated me and I was using her."

"Um hm," Mama responded.

"Shut up, Mama. This is totally different," I said, looking at Mama.

Brenda said, "Well, anyway, we struggled for a while. I was finally able to get out and lock Sister in the bathroom."

"You locked Sister in the bathroom?" Mama yelled.

"Look! I didn't know what else to do. I believe Sister would have actually tried to kill me. I can't take it anymore. I've had enough. I have tried and tried with Sister. Something is wrong with her. She needs some help."

Mama ran into the apartment, calling Sister's name.

"Sister? Sister? It's Mama."

"Wait a minute, Mama!" I said.

"What?"

"Just wait. We have to do this easy. Brenda and I have seen how Sister gets. You haven't, so just wait." Mama looked at me strangely and did not say another word.

"Sister? Sister? It's me, honey. It's Rose. Are you okay?" My heart was beating fast.

"Rose, is that you?" She whimpered.

"Yes, sweetie, it's me. Are you okay?"

"I'm okay, but I'm locked in. Can you let me out?"

"Yes, sweetie, I can let you out. But what did you do with the knife?"

"I put it in the cabinet, Rose. Please let me out. It's hot in here." From the corner of my eye, I saw Brenda stand back when I started to open the door. I turned the knob. All of a sudden, we heard Sister scream as she ran toward me with the knife. She tried to stab Brenda. Then Sister was still.

"Sister? Sister?" I was scared.

"What's wrong with her, Rose?" Mama asked. Sister had a blank stare on her face.

"I don't know! Call 911."

The paramedics arrived within minutes.

"Oh, Jesus, what's wrong with my baby!" Mama cried. Brenda just stood back with this look of disbelief on her face. The paramedics tested all of Sister's vital signs.

"Does she use drugs?" one of the paramedics asked.

"No, she does not," Brenda said. "But she was locked in the bathroom about a half hour." I jumped up and ran into the bathroom to see if there was any evidence that Sister might have taken. I found an empty bottle of Valium.

"Brenda? Was there anything in this bottle marked Valium?"

"Yes, there were like twenty or thirty Valium in there." The paramedics immediately started rummaging through their equipment and proceeded to pump her stomach right there on the spot. We all went to the hospital. Sister was fine after a few hours, but Brenda decided Sister should not come back to her place. The doctor suggested Sister stay in the hospital to make sure there weren't any aftereffects from the tremendous amount of Valium she had taken.

CHAPTER 22

I thought about Sister aloud until I saw people looking at me as they passed. For a minute, I felt as crazy as my sister. I saw a bus coming and got on it and went home. I felt a desperate need to see Jamal. I was crying on the way home. All I could think of was that bastard father of mine. If it wasn't for him, maybe none of this would be happening. Mama probably would have never used drugs. Sister probably would be a model somewhere in New York, and I would probably be on my first book by now. I hate him! I hate him! I hate him! I was lying on the sofa when Mama came in the door. I could tell she had been crying as much as I had.

"Rose?"

"I'm here on the sofa." Mama sat down and put both her hands to her face. I put my hand on Mama's back, gently rubbing her.

"What have I done, Rose? What have I done to my baby? If I could take it all back, I would."

"Take what back, Mama? What are you talking about?"

"Nothing. I'm going to lay down. Anyone calls, tell them I'm out, okay?"

"Okay, Mama. I will."

As Mama got up, I asked her, "Mama, was Grammy mean? I mean, strict?" Mama sat back down.

"I'm sure to people outside looking in, Mama might have seemed mean. It took me a long time to realize Mama did what she had to do to protect me and your Aunt Fannie. I'm not ashamed to say your auntie and me, we were fast. We were hot tailed, pissy tailed little girls. We thought we were all that and then some. I remember your Aunt Fannie and a couple of other girls and me wanted to go to the movies with these boys. Well, we knew Mama wasn't going to let us go. We were too young to date. So we had gotten together and told these little boys we would meet them downtown. Your aunt and me had a pair of lavender wide-legged pants with zippers. The zipper started at the foot and zipped all the way up to the waist. I remember it well. Mama said we could only zip the pants up so far. Well, of course, when Mama wasn't around, we zipped a lot higher. Anyway, for some reason, one of the boys called and asked what time we were leaving and if we were still going to meet them downtown. I quickly said yes and hung up the phone. I wasn't aware at the time, but Mama had picked up the other phone until I glanced in the other room."

"How did you know?" I said, smiling.

"Mama loved mirrors. She had mirrors in every room in the house. In the living room, the whole wall was mirror tiled. She used to tell us, 'I can see everything you do.' You know how she talked. I saw her hang up the phone."

"What did she say to you?"

"Nothing. She acted as if she didn't hear anything. So I played it off like I didn't know she heard and went on to the movies. When your auntie and I got out of Mama's view, we zipped our pants all the way up. girl!" We both laughed. "We thought we were really getting away with something. But late that night, when your auntie and I were sleeping, Mama came into our room with the ironing cord and whooped our asses. We never did that again. Your Grammy didn't take any shit. She was going to make sure we did right. I think it was because your Grammy was kind of hot herself back in the day. Her mama used to pull a gun out on her."

"What? Um hm, wasn't that child abuse?"

"Not the way she did it."

"Why did her mama pull a gun on her?"

"Your Grammy used to go away and stay out for days at a time. Lula, that was my grandmother's name, got tired of it. So when your

Grammy came home one day, she was sitting on the sofa. It was a let-out bed that Grammy used to sleep on. You know the kind that fold up?"

"Yeah."

"Well, the let-out bed was folded up sitting in front of Grammy, and Lula came in to the room with something hidden behind her back. Lula came, slowly walking into the room, and said, 'So you wanna be grown, huh? You wanna be grown?' Then Lula pulled out a gun and pointed at your Grammy. Your Grammy's eyes got wide, and she started inching behind the let-out bed. Grammy started begging...girl. She was saying, 'Mama, please...don't shoot me. Please... don't shoot me.' She never had trouble out of your Grammy again. It wasn't until Grammy was out of Mama's house that she found out that the gun was never loaded. Lula said that's what she had to do because Grammy was getting too wild. And you know what? Grammy appreciated that. She had the best mother in the world, and she wouldn't have traded her for anything. She said she don't know where she might have ended up if it hadn't been for her mother."

"Mama? Did you and your grandmother get along well?"

"As a matter of fact, we did. I loved my grandmother. She used to take me to the store with her. It was this one store around the corner, man! What is the name of that store? Oh! I know it was Del farm, but she used to call it Hi & Low, and across the street from it they had this little hamburger joint. We would go there whenever we walked to the store. And Lula used to get up early on Sunday mornings and make red-eye gravy. Um um! I loved it. She never missed a Sunday at church unless she wasn't feeling well."

"Did you ever go with her to church?"

"Sometimes. Not very often though."

"Mama? Did you give Grammy a lot of trouble when you were a teenager?"

"You know what, Rose? I did. I wouldn't have admitted that a year ago or even last week maybe." Mama had her legs crossed. As she talked, she was swinging the one on top. I saw her eyes start to fill up. "Yes, I did. I've done a lot of things I regret now. I regret not being a better mother to you girls."

"Mama? Are you still using cocaine?" I shocked Mama with that question. She wasn't expecting it. It took her a couple of seconds to answer. She dropped her head.

"Yes."

"Oh, Mama!" I said, getting up.

"But I don't do it as much as I used to. Sit down! Where are you going? You asked me. I assumed you wanted the truth. I know I shouldn't still be smoking, and I'm trying to quit. It's just not that easy. I haven't bought any in a long time. But some people I still associate with call me sometimes. I want to say no, but I can't. It's hard. It's like a deeper force inside me says yes before I even have a chance to think about it."

"But, Mama, if you feel that way, how are you ever going to quit?"

"I don't know, baby. I don't know… Answer the phone, Rose."

"Hello?"

"Hi, Rose."

"Sister! How are you feeling?"

"Fine. I want to come home. When are they going to let me out of here?"

"I think…I'm not sure. You want to talk to Mama?"

"Hey, baby! How are you?" Mama asked.

"I'm fine. Did the doctor say when I can come home?"

"No, not yet. But I'll be there early tomorrow morning."

"What time tomorrow?"

"Nine sharp."

"All right, Mama. See you tomorrow." Mama went to her room and closed the door. I actually felt sorry for her. And Sister too.

CHAPTER 23

"Hello, Daddy."

"Hi, baby! How are you? Boy! This is a pleasure. I had just stepped in the door when I heard the phone ringing. How's your mama and sister doing?"

"That's why I called. Sister is in the hospital."

"What happened? Is she okay?"

"I don't know. I mean, I guess so."

"What do you mean? Come on, Rose. What's wrong?"

"Sister is losing her mind. She tried to kill Brenda."

"Who?"

"You know, her girlfriend." There was a pause. "Anyway, Sister pulled out a butcher knife. We had to take her to the emergency room by ambulance."

"Oh my god!"

"She had taken over twenty Valiums."

"Oh my god! Oh my god!"

"Calm down, Daddy. She's fine."

"That's good. How did this happen?"

"Daddy, I wish I knew."

"I'm sorry, baby. I just don't know what to say. Where's your mother?"

"In her room."

"Let me talk to her."

"Can you call her back later, Daddy? I don't want her to know I called you."

"Why not?"

"I don't know. I just think you should call her back later. Okay, Daddy? Besides, I think she's sleeping anyway."

"All right. I'll call her tomorrow. Look, if you need anything, call me."

"I will, Daddy. I love you."

"Bye, baby. Tell Sister I said hello."

"I will. Oh! Daddy, can I borrow some money? I got fired from my job."

"Oh, Rose. I'm sorry. Why?"

"They fired me for taking too many days off."

"I know how you loved that job. How much do you need?"

"I need a hundred dollars."

"Say no more. Go to the nearest Western Union tomorrow when you get up. It'll be there."

"Thanks, Daddy. I love you."

"I love you too, baby. Bye."

CHAPTER 24

Sister was released from the hospital a few days later. She didn't say much of anything. She just sat in her room all day…alone. I couldn't stand it anymore, so I went in to talk to her to try to get her to go out. Sister stared out of her window as if I wasn't there.

"Sister? Are you hungry?" I asked, trying to sound as pleasant as I could. "How about going for a walk with me? Would you like that?" Sister gave me no response until I mentioned painting. Sister used to paint a lot when she was younger. She loved it and was really quite good. She stopped because she couldn't make the people she painted look lifelike. I went to her closet to dig out some of her oil paints, hoping this would cause more of a stir. Sister had a large closet with a door inside that led to a smaller closet. It reminded me of an old movie, except it was very small. I knew she sometimes kept her oils and easels in there. I noticed a blanket covering something. I lifted the blanket to get a better look, but it was dark. I pulled out a clothes basket full of paints. I asked her if she felt like painting. She simply nodded yes but didn't move. I sat the basket down beside her, gave her a kiss, and left. I peeped in to see if Sister would do anything. She picked up one of the jars of paint and looked at it strangely as if it were talking to her. She went to the closet and pulled out an easel. I smiled and quietly closed the door.

Sister did a lot of painting after that. Months had passed. She never mentioned Brenda once. We all went about our lives as normal…as normal as we could until we received a telegram from Aunt Fannie saying she was coming to visit for the holidays. I was glad. I hadn't seen my aunt in years. Sister and I were really looking forward to it. Mama, on the other hand, wasn't so happy about it.

CHAPTER 25

Thanksgiving was in one week. Jamal and Daddy were coming to share it with us. How happy I was knowing Daddy would finally meet Jamal. I was busy planning and putting up Christmas decorations. Although I usually put the Christmas decorations up after Thanksgiving, this was a special occasion. I wanted the house to really look nice and festive, hoping this would put everyone in a joyful mood. Sister was happier than I've seen her in a long time. She helped me plan the menu for Thanksgiving dinner. We were all anxiously awaiting Aunt Fannie's arrival. Mama was in her room, trying to make herself look less like a dope fiend, especially since she had lost so much weight. When the doorbell rang, Sister and I went running to the door.

"Oh my god! Rose? Sister? Let me put my luggage down. Give me a hug! Look at you girls. How big and pretty you are. Oh my goodness!"

"Hi, Auntie. You still look the same," I said. "I'm so glad to see you!" I hugged her again.

"What have you girls been doing with yourselves?" Aunt Fannie asked.

"Nothing much," Sister said.

"Where's your mama?" Auntie said as she walked around, looking at the house.

"In her room. I'll get her." I ran upstairs to get Mama.

"Sister? Girl, you look just like your daddy."

"He's going to be here tomorrow."

"What?" Auntie looked at Sister curiously. "Steven is coming here?"

"Yes. He was here a few months ago."

"But I thought..."

"It's a long story. We'll tell you all about it later," Sister whispered as she heard me and Mama coming down the stairs. When Mama and Aunt Fannie spotted each other, they screamed with joy. Mama hadn't seen Aunt Fannie in many years.

"Hey, sis!" Mama said as she walked over to Aunt Fannie, giving her a hug. "How are you? Girl, look at you. You look good!"

"Thanks," Aunt Fannie responded, looking at Mama strangely. "Girl, look at me! Look at you. Are you on drugs or something? I've never seen you this small." Sister and I gave a quick look at each other and watched.

"I was never a big eater," Mama retorted quickly. "It's so good to see you. You know about Mama, don't you?" I saw Auntie's expression change.

"Yes. I found out three weeks later. I'll never forgive myself for being gone."

"You didn't know this would happen," Mama stated.

"I know. That's not the point. I didn't get a chance to say goodbye. I don't think I'll ever forgive myself for that." Mama walked over to Auntie and gave her a hug. Auntie then looked up at Mama suspiciously. "So Steven's coming up for Thanksgiving?"

"Um hm" was all Mama said.

CHAPTER 26

There was a certain tension in the air. I wasn't exactly sure why. Mama and Auntie seemed to have lots to talk about. There were even times when I would enter a room where they were talking, and an immediate silence took place. I didn't care though. I was nervous enough knowing Jamal would meet my entire family. Daddy was already in town but decided not to come over until Thanksgiving Day.

All of us women were up all night preparing tomorrow's feast. The aroma permeating through the house reminded me of Grammy. She always took charge when it came to Thanksgiving and Christmas. No one was allowed to eat or open any gifts until everyone was present and accounted for.

Sister and I set the table beautifully. The china plates were beautifully trimmed in gold, with a gold rose in the middle. Daddy gave them to Mama a few days after I was born, along with gold stemware. The crystal glasses used were also trimmed in gold. As I stood back and admired the table, the doorbell rang. It was Jamal. Before I opened the door, I quickly glanced at myself in the mirror to make sure every hair was in place.

"Hi, baby!" I said happily as I gave him a passionate hug. When I turned around, all eyes were on us.

Jamal moved a little closer and whispered, "I'm nervous." I didn't say anything. I took his hand and squeezed it gently.

"He's a little old for her, isn't he?" I heard Aunt Fannie whisper to Mama as she got up.

"Jamal, this is my Aunt Fannie." Aunt Fannie reached for his hand.

"Hi, Jamal."

"Hello."

"I think you know everyone else," I said.

"Hi," Mama and Sister added.

Sister heard a car door and hurried to look out of the window. "Daddy's here."

"Hi, Daddy!" Sister said, smiling and giving him a hug.

"Hi...baby, how are you?" he said, slowly walking in. He noticed Aunt Fannie right away. She stood up.

"Well, hello...Steven."

"Hello, Fannie. I haven't seen you for quite a long time. How are you?"

"Fine. Just fine," Auntie responded with a certain sarcasm.

"Daddy?" I said. "This is my boyfriend, Jamal." Daddy looked at Jamal for a minute before acknowledging. He then stretched out his hand to him.

"Hello, Jamal."

"Hello, Mr. Sinclair. I'm glad to meet you, sir. Rose has told me a lot about you."

"Likewise." Then Mama interrupted.

"There are drinks in the dining room, if anyone's interested." Daddy stood up immediately and proceeded to the dining room to make a martini. Sister had been sipping unnoticeably on wine all evening. I would not have said anything until I noticed that she was picking up her glass more and more. She kept it sitting among some other used glasses.

"Sister," I said. "Don't you think you've had enough?" Sister looked up at me, surprised.

"What? What are you talking about?"

I leaned closer to her ear. "I see your glass sitting among the other glasses. I've seen you drinking from that glass when no one's looking, but I think you're drinking too much."

"No, I'm not," she slightly slurred.

"Yes, you are. And if you don't stop, I'm going to tell Mama."

"Tell Mama! I don't care. What can she do?" Sister turned away from me, walked over to where her glass was hidden, looked at me, picked the glass up, and took another sip. I said, "Okay" under my breath and went and sat next to Jamal.

"Rose?" Mama called from the kitchen. "Would you come and help me set the dinner out?"

"Sure," I said, quickly getting up and going toward the kitchen. I wanted dinner to be over.

Daddy sat at the head of the table, followed by me and Jamal. Mama sat at the other end, followed by Sister and Auntie. Daddy clanged his glass with a spoon. He then stood up and offered to say grace.

"Lord, bless this food for the nourishment of our bodies. Bless everyone that's gathered here today." Daddy then looked up at me and continued speaking. "You know it's been a long time since I sat around a dining room table, sharing a home-cooked meal with my daughters, two beautiful daughters, I thought I would never see again. I feel so blessed to have you girls back in my life."

"In Rose's life," Sister mumbled. I looked up and gave Sister a light kick. Everyone nodded in agreement except for Sister. Daddy cut the turkey.

After dinner, Auntie noticed Sister drinking. She walked over to Mama and whispered, "I think Sister is drinking."

"What!"

"Look at her." I saw Mama look at Sister. She was angry.

"Sister! What's the matter with you? Are you drinking?"

"What? Drinking?"

"Sister? That's enough. Go upstairs!" Mama said as she looked around to see if anyone was watching.

"I only had one glass of wine."

"I don't care. You know I don't allow you to drink. What's the matter with you?" Daddy noticed Mama's anger and walked over to them.

"What's the matter? Is there something wrong?"

"Look at her, Steven. She's been drinking."

"So! So what if I have? You've never cared about anything else."

"Sister! Please, not now," Mama said, looking around.

"Why not now? You don't give a shit about me." Sister reached for her glass. Mama snatched the glass from Sister's hand, spilling it. By this time, everyone noticed what was going on. I got up and went over to where they were standing.

"Does she, Rose?" Sister said, looking at me.

"Sister," I said, "let's go upstairs." I reached for Sister's arm. She pulled away from me.

"Don't touch me!" Sister snarled. "You're on their side. You just want to get rid of me."

"What? Sister, what are you talking about?"

"You think I don't know. I heard you. I heard all of you talking about me."

We were all very confused at what Sister was saying.

"It's the wine, Sister," I added. I looked over at Daddy. He was biting his lip. He then went over to Sister, picked her up, and put her over his shoulders. Sister was screaming loudly.

"You don't love me! Put me down!" she said, trying desperately to squirm loose from him. "Put me down! I hate all of you!" Sister's voice slightly faded as Daddy carried Sister into a room and closed the door. I looked at Jamal. He was in awe. I was embarrassed. I went over to him, and Mama went over to Auntie.

I heard Auntie ask Mama as they were walking into the kitchen, "What was that all about?"

"I don't know. Sister has been going through some changes lately," I heard Mama say as she closed the door.

I know I had a stupid look on my face when I sat down. "I'm sorry you had to witness this. It's just that Sister hasn't been feeling very well lately."

"Rose, you don't have to explain," Jamal interrupted. "Alcohol will make you say things you don't mean. In the morning, she'll be embarrassed." I put my head down. Jamal lifted my head and kissed me.

"Look, baby. Maybe I should go. I mean, I think you need to be alone with your family right now. You know what I mean?" He said this in his steady, sincere voice. But even so, I wasn't sure what he was thinking.

"Sure, sure, baby. I understand. I'll call you later," I said.

"Come on. Walk me to my car."

"Okay."

When I went back inside, Daddy was just coming down the stairs.

"How is she?" I asked.

"She was sick for a little bit, but she's fine now. She's sleeping. Rose? Is Sister always like this?"

"No, I've never known Sister to drink like that."

"Where's your mother? I think I'm going to be leaving."

"No, Daddy," I whined. "Stay here. You can have my room."

"That's sweet of you, baby, but I think I'll just go back to the hotel. Tell your mother and Fannie I said bye. Come on, sweetie. Give me a hug. It'll be okay." I held Daddy tightly around his neck and whispered I love you in his ear. He returned my words and went out of the door. I flopped down on the couch, looked around, and put my face in my hands.

CHAPTER 27

Mama and Auntie sat up half the night talking. I went into Sister's room to check on her. She was sleeping soundly.

I walked over to her and gave her a kiss on the cheek. Just as I was turning to leave, I noticed her closet door was cracked. I opened the door to see what she had painted that day. I sat her paints out. The picture she'd painted had a sheet over it. I picked it up and quietly took it into my room to look at it. I was excited to see what she had painted. When we were younger, I always loved Sister's paintings. I lifted up the sheet and dropped it down again quickly. "Oh my god!" I slowly lifted the sheet again. Sister had drawn an abstract, black-and-white lines with several distorted faces. It was scary. There were also what looked to be huge rocks. It reminded me of the time I thought the devil had taken her over. I quickly covered it up and took it back into her room. The thought of that painting made my heart race. It was evil.

CHAPTER 28

It was noon. The summer breeze brushing across my face was refreshing. I stopped and inhaled. Hmmm! I started to skip down the street like a ten-year-old child. I was laughing. I was having so much fun. I started to run and run. I looked up. The blue skies were no longer blue. The more I ran, the grayer the sky became. I became frightened. There was someone after me. A dog? A person? I didn't know, but I could hear something chasing me. My heart was pounding, but I couldn't stop. I knew if I stopped, I would die. I tried to scream, but nothing came out. *I'm gonna die! I'm gonna die. Oh God! Please! Help me.* My legs were numb. I couldn't feel my feet under me, but I kept running. I wanted to look back, but I was afraid. But I had to see what was chasing me. I looked back. It was dark. I couldn't see what it was. My heart felt as if it was going to explode. I was slowing down. I couldn't do it. I couldn't keep running, "Help me, somebody!" I managed to scream out. I stopped and turned around. Just as I opened my mouth to scream, I felt someone touching my shoulders.

"Rose! Wake up! Wake up! Rose!" Mama shouted, shaking my bed. "Wake up!"

"What! What!"

"You're dreaming," she said.

I knew I was safe when I woke up and saw Mama and Auntie standing over me.

"You're soaked," Auntie added. "Are you okay, sugar?" My heart was still beating rapidly.

"Yes, I'm fine. Someone was chasing me, that's all. I'm fine, really. What time is it?"

"Four a.m.," Mama answered. "All right then. We're going back to bed."

"You go on. I'll be in in a minute. I want to make sure she's okay," Auntie said.

Auntie crawled into my bed with me. I was glad. I really didn't want to be alone.

"What was your dream about?"

"I'm really not sure. At first I was having so much fun. It was like I was a kid again. But all of a sudden, I became afraid. I mean really afraid. I felt like someone or something was after me, but I couldn't see who or what it was. I ran and ran. I tried to scream at first, but I couldn't," I explained. Auntie chuckled.

"You did a pretty good job of it. Scared the shit out of me! Me and your mama jumped up. We thought someone had broken in."

"I'm sorry."

"Oh! I'm just glad you're okay. You are okay, aren't you, Rose?" Auntie said as she rose and looked directly into my face.

"I'm not so sure, Auntie. I'm not so sure."

"Tell me about it, sweetie."

"Oh…Auntie, I don't know. Sometimes…I don't know…sometimes…I feel like packing up and moving into Grammy's house."

"Things can't possibly be that bad, sweetheart," she said, brushing my hair with her hands.

"Oh…Auntie, if you only knew."

"Knew what, sweetie?"

"Auntie? Do you know who my father is?"

"What? What kind of question is that? He was just here for dinner."

"No, not Daddy. That rapist son of a bitch."

"Rose!"

"I'm sorry, Auntie. I'm talking about David."

"You know about David?"

"Yes. Mama told me how he raped her and made her pregnant with me."

"What? I mean…she told you that?"

"Yes, but that's all she told me."

"Well, what else did you want to know?"

"I wanted to know if she knew where he was."

"Why?"

"Because I wanted to see what he looks like, how much I look like him."

"She wouldn't tell you?"

"She said she didn't know where he was. She didn't want to talk about it. Every time I'd try, she'd get angry with me. So finally, I just stopped talking about it." Suddenly, I sat up in the bed.

"Do you know where he is, Auntie?"

"No, baby. Your mother didn't press charges. So he went on about his business, I suppose. I'm sorry."

"Oh…that's okay."

"Rose, I know I haven't been here for you and your sister. I want that to change. It's just that your mother and I didn't always see things the same way. She had her life and I had mine, and at the time I thought it best we leave it that way. I know now that might have been a mistake."

"You and Mama didn't get along?"

"Well…we had our problems like siblings do. You and Sister don't always get along, do you?"

"No."

"I guess your Mama and I were both stubborn. We fought all the time. I promised myself when I was old enough, I would leave. And I did."

"How do you and Mama get along now?"

"I think we are both still stubborn women, but we're older. I love my sister, but sometimes I don't like her very much. You know what I mean?"

I smiled.

"I know exactly what you mean." I hesitated before speaking. "I…thought you didn't like me very much."

"What?"

"I did. I used to think you didn't like me."

"Why?" Auntie said. I could tell I hurt her feelings.

"I don't know."

"Oh, Rose, I love you and I always have. Your mother didn't like me telling her how to raise you girls, so I didn't say much. I know that's no excuse, but that's the way it was. But I'm here now, and I'll make sure you'll be able to get in touch with me no matter where I am."

"How long are you going to be here?"

"I'm leaving the day after tomorrow."

"Ah…that soon?"

"Yes, I have to. But I'll be back. I promise. Oh! Your friend is very handsome. What's his name?"

"Jamal. Oh, Auntie, he is so sweet. He shows me so much respect. I'm crazy about him."

"I can tell. You sparkle when you talk about him. Rose? Have you and he…danced the wild monkey dance?"

"Auntie!" I was embarrassed to admit it.

"Oh, girl! I'm your auntie. Did you use some kind of protection?"

"Yes, I'm on the pill, and I used a condom."

"My girl! I'm proud of you," Auntie said, smiling.

I hugged my aunt before she got out of my bed. "Do you think you can sleep now?"

"Yes, I think so. Good night, Auntie." She blew me a kiss before closing my door. But I didn't go back to sleep for a while. I kept seeing the picture Sister painted.

CHAPTER 29

Just as I had drifted off to sleep, I heard voices coming from the end of the hall. I sat up, hoping I could hear better. It was coming from Mama's room. When I heard David's name mentioned, I got out of bed and peeped out of my door. I saw Mama and Auntie standing in each other's faces. Just as I heard my name mentioned, Mama closed her door.

"Damn! I wonder what that was about." I started pacing the floor. I wanted to hear what they were saying. I grabbed my robe and pretended like I had to use the bathroom. I knew they wouldn't hear me because of the carpeting. I went in, but I still couldn't hear very well, just bits and pieces. I had the bathroom door ajar with my ear to it. Mama was talking.

"Who says they have a right! It's my choice, and if I don't want to tell them, I don't have to. Anyway, this is none of your business."

A right to what I wanted to know.

"You know it's not fair. Those girls are old enough to know. I just can't understand why you think you should keep this a secret from them!" Auntie yelled.

"Lower your voice. They'll hear you," Mama retorted.

Raising her voice even louder, Auntie said, "I hope they do! I hope they do hear me. Maybe Rose and Sister can get on with their lives."

"Their life's just fine! Thank you very much!"

"Fine! Yeah right! That's why Sister's drinking and Rose is having nightmares."

"You know what! I knew when you came up here, things would be like this. You never could mind your own business. That's why we didn't get along."

"No! We didn't get along because you are just as bullheaded now as you were then."

Auntie burst out of Mama's room and ran down the steps.

Mama's door was left open. When she went to the other side of her room, I ran down the steps. Auntie was in the kitchen making coffee, shaking the spoon and spilling the grounds.

"Oh! Hi, Auntie, I didn't know you were down here. What's the matter?" I asked.

"Nothing, sweetie," she said, gently touching my face. "I have to leave this afternoon."

"This afternoon? Why?"

"I got a call from my job. There's a problem that I need to go and take care of."

"You're lying!" I blurted out "Why are you lying to me?"

"I…I'm not lying, Rose," Auntie said calmly.

"I heard you and Mama arguing. She said something, didn't she? Tell me!" Auntie paused for a minute. She came over to me and said "Rose, Da…"

"Rose."

Auntie and I were both startled when we heard Mama's voice. We didn't notice she had come down. "What are you doing up so early?"

"I couldn't sleep. I came down to get a glass of milk." I kept my eyes on Auntie the whole time.

"What are you two talking about?" Mama asked as she sauntered over to the counter to pour a cup of coffee.

Auntie got up from the table. "Nothing." Auntie then looked at me and continued, "I'm going upstairs to pack." Mama kept her back to us as Auntie went upstairs.

"Well?"

"Well, what?" Mama replied.

"Aren't you going to stop her?"

"What for? Today! Tomorrow! What difference does it make?"

"Auntie's right. You are stubborn." Mama shrugged her shoulders and continued what she was doing. I knew I would never find out what they were talking about. "God! What is wrong with this family?" I stormed out of the kitchen and went back up to my room. Auntie left later that afternoon.

Since Thanksgiving turned out to be such a fiasco, Mama, Sister, and I decided to have a quiet Christmas at home. At twelve midnight on Christmas morning, we exchanged gifts and went to bed.

CHAPTER 30

Things continued to get worse at home. Sister became more and more distant. She spent a lot of time in her room, painting. Each painting revealed a side of Sister I didn't know existed. I wasn't sure how to reach out to her anymore. It used to be as simple as saying I love you. Now she looked at me like I was the crazy one. I would hear her talking to herself in her room at night.

I planned on going back to school this spring but decided against it. With Sister getting progressively worse, I didn't dare leave her. The flowers were beautiful in the front yard. I opened my bedroom window, hoping the smell of lilacs would lift my spirits. Mama called and said she wouldn't be home for dinner. I wasn't surprised.

I didn't feel much like cooking, so I made soup and sandwiches for dinner.

"Sister? What's the matter? Did you want bologna instead of ham?" I said, taking a bite of my sandwich.

"No, I'm just not hungry," she said while pushing her food away from her.

"Sister, are you sick? I haven't seen you eat anything in three days."

"No, Rose, I'm fine. I…I've been fasting."

"Fasting?" I repeated.

"Yes."

"Why?"

"What do you mean why? Why do people fast?" she said sarcastically.

"Don't get upset, Sister. Your clothes are beginning to fall off you. I just didn't think you would be fasting when you're so tiny already."

"People don't just fast to lose weight," Sister said with a certain hostility.

"I know, Sister. I'm sorry I didn't think about that."

"I'm sure you didn't!" Sister got up from the table, went upstairs, and slammed her door.

I lost my appetite. I grabbed a jacket from the hall closet and went for a walk. I needed to feel the wind on my face. I felt as if I was choking. *Am I my sister's keeper?* I thought.

I had been walking for hours. I noticed Sister's bedroom light was off as well as all the lights in the house. I went inside and turned on the lamp then went to the kitchen to get a soda. I could feel the presence of someone inside the house. I put my can down and slowly walked into the front room. I gasped.

"Sister!" I said, putting my hand to my chest. "Why were you sitting here in the dark? You scared me." Sister stared at me. She stared at me as if she hated me then got up from her chair, not taking her eyes off me, and went up the stairs to her room. My heart was pounding. I was afraid. I turned all the lights on and waited downstairs for Mama to get home.

I hadn't realized I dozed off until I heard Sister's door open. I wasn't sure if I wanted to sit up or pretend I was sleeping. The choice was easy because I couldn't move. I felt as if my senses were magnified. I could actually hear Sister coming down carpeted steps. My heart was beating faster. Why was I afraid of my sister? I opened my eyes and sat up. Sister was standing over me with a butcher knife in her hand. I screamed. Tears streamed down my face. I looked up into Sister's eyes. I froze.

"Where were you tonight?" Sister's voice was deep. She was stroking her face with the knife. I had both hands touching the seat of the sofa to get up quickly if I had to.

"Walking…just walking!" I replied, looking at the knife in Sister's hand.

Sister snarled. "I…saw…you…talking to her! Conniving—"

"Sister!" I jumped as she made a short and sudden move toward me. "What's the matter? What are you talking about?" Sister slowly backed up, her back straight. She didn't take her eyes off me. She had the knife pointing straight out in front of her. She stood there, looking at me. Sweat was pouring down both our faces. I was afraid to move. I heard someone coming up the walk. I looked out of the window and saw Mama. I gasped! Sister thought I was out talking with Mama? Sister lunged at me with the knife. "Oh my god! I'm bleeding…I'm going to die…"

"Rose! Wake up!" Mama said, shaking my shoulders. "Rose, you've spilled that pop all over you. Where's Sister?"

"What?" I said groggily. "Are you sure she's not here?"

"Yes, I'm sure! Well…I'm going to bed."

"Mama?"

"What!"

"Gee! Why are you snapping at me? I think Sister should have some more psychological evaluations done."

"Come on, Rose! Not tonight. I'm tired."

"You're not tired," I growled as Mama turned to look at me. "You're high. I can tell by your eyes. They look like saucers. I…I give up! Mama, I can't do this by myself. Something is wrong! Sister needs our help. I…I can't believe you. I thought you quit doing that." Mama started to speak, only she sounded like she had a mouthful of peanut butter.

I raised my hand up to her face. "Shh! Mama, I don't want to hear it. Just go to bed. Shit!" I looked out of the window for Sister.

CHAPTER 31

"Sister! Hi…come on in," Tweety said, smiling. "What are you doing out so late?" he added, looking for the car she might have arrived in. "How did you get here?"

"I walked," Sister said, pulling a cigarette out of a half-smoked pack.

"Walked! Sister, I live a good thirty blocks from you. Why didn't you call me to come get you? And when did you start smoking? Girl, get in here."

"I didn't know if you felt like coming out and…I really felt like walking. Oh!" she said, raising her cigarette. "Someone left these on a bench at a bus stop. I thought, why not?" Sister said, trying to keep from coughing. "Actually, it doesn't taste so bad," she said, coughing harder.

"Give me that. These will kill you. Besides, you know I have a no smoking policy." Tweety took Sister's cigarette and tossed it far into the street.

"Oh, you got some new stuff since I was last here," she said while examining his small crystal collection.

"Yeah, a few things."

"This is neat. So what do you have to drink?" Sister asked, plopping lazily on his sofa bed. Tweety lived in a small one-bedroom apartment, just right for him. He kept it immaculate.

"Well…I have pop, beer, coffee, tea…uhh…"

"Pop, any kind. Thanks. Hey…you have any new CDs?"

"Of course. They're in the case over there. Take a look," he said, pointing to his collection. "So you still haven't answered my question."

"What question?" she asked, looking through his CDs.

"What brings you out so late? Walking, no less."

"Tweety? Have you ever felt as if you were falling apart? I mean… have you ever felt like you weren't yourself?" she asked, continuing to look through the CDs.

"I…I guess so," Tweety responded, walking over to her. "What's the matter, girlfriend?"

"I think my family wants to put me in some institution."

"For what?" Sister put in a CD and sat down on the couch, Tweety following close behind.

"I'm not sure. I can just feel it. Something is telling me they want to commit me. I'm afraid."

"Move."

"What?" Sister asked, looking at him.

"Move. If you move, no one can tell you diddly squat."

"Oh… Tweety, I can't afford to move. I'm not working."

"Get a job! The telemarketing department where I work is hiring. They'd hire you."

"How do you know?"

"Girl, that company hires everybody that comes through that door. I have an extra application if you want one. You probably can start in a few days. They pay weekly. There's overtime. You could be up outta there in less than a month. Not only that, there's an apartment available on the second floor right above me. We could be neighbors."

"Oh… Tweety, that would be so great. Give me the application. I'll fill it out now and you can take it in when you go," Sister said, smiling.

"Look, girlfriend, you can crash here on the sofa bed or I can take you home. What's it going to be? I have to be at work an hour earlier in the morning."

"I'll crash here. That way, I can listen to your CDs."

"Good! There's the phone just in case you need to call home. The earphones are on the bottom shelf. See you in the morning," Tweety said as he retired to his bedroom.

* * * * *

"Hello? Sister, where are you? I've been worried sick. Why didn't you wake me and let me know you were going out?"

"I'm sorry, Rose, but I'm fine. I'm staying here at Tweety's tonight. I'll be home tomorrow. Is Mama home yet?"

"Yes, she got in a couple hours ago. She went to bed."

"Nice to know she wasn't worried."

"Well, you know Mama!" I added.

"Yeah, I do. Good night, Rose."

"Good night, Sister." Damn! I could have been asleep hours ago. All this worrying.

CHAPTER 32

Mama and I both slept until late afternoon. I knew she was up when the aroma of coffee tickled my nose. I thought this would be a good time to talk to her. Mama had a cup of coffee sitting there waiting for me.

"How did you know I was up, Mama?" I said as I sat down and reached for the cream and sugar.

"Rose, I apologize for last night. I knew when you smelled the coffee you would come down, especially when there is something on your mind," Mama said while pouring her second cup.

"Yes, there is something on my mind, but first…Mama? How long have you been smoking that stuff again?"

"I…don't know, Rose. For a while." Nervously, Mama reached for her cigarettes. "I've tried to stop. I just can't."

"Mama, it's going to kill you! If you don't stop smoking that stuff, it's going to kill you! Anyway…I need your help. It's like you never see anything that's happening around here. Do you purposely ignore the things that go on? Do you just not care? Mama, what is it? Sister is getting worse! She's talking to herself. She has all these weird paintings. Did you know Sister was painting again? Sister looks at me like she hates me sometimes. And then there are times when she's perfectly okay again. I don't know what to do. Something's wrong. Have you noticed all the weight she's lost? Mama, Sister is still sick. Come with me. I want to show you something in Sister's room."

"What?" Mama said, rising from her chair. "Rose! What are you doing?" Mama asked as she watched me pull some paintings from Sister's closet.

"Look at these."

"Oh my god. What is it supposed to be?"

"I don't know, Mama. But all of her paintings are weird like this."

"Well…I mean…maybe it doesn't mean anything. Maybe she just likes painting stuff like this."

"Mama, this stuff is evil. It's devilish. Why would she paint stuff like this?"

Mama and I were so involved in looking at Sister's painting, we didn't hear her come in. She startled us standing, in the doorway.

"Oh! Sister…I…I just wanted to show Mama your paintings."

"Yeah…they're lovely." I couldn't do anything but look at Mama stupidly when she said that. I got up off my knees.

"Get out!" Sister scolded. "Get out of my room right now! You have no right to come into my room and touching my things. I hate you!" Sister screamed. "Now!" Mama and I hurried out of Sister's room as fast as we could. She slammed the door behind us. Loudly. We went into Mama's room and closed the door.

"See, Mama, I told you. Those paintings are weird. Why did you tell her they were nice?"

"I don't know," Mama said, whispering back to me. "She scared me standing there. I didn't know what to say. Maybe you should ask her about the paintings. What she might be thinking when she paints them."

"Me? Why can't you ask her? Mama, I do everything else. You ask her!" I left Mama's room and went into mine. A half hour later, I heard shuffling in Sister's room. I peeped out of my door and noticed her throwing away some of her things. All the things she thought we touched were thrown away.

Mama said she was going to observe Sister for a while. Sister stayed in her room for the rest of the day until Mama called her down to dinner. Mama made a very nice dinner, which included several of Sister's favorites. Sister came down, sat at the table, looked down at her plate, and pushed it away.

"Sister? Why aren't you eating?" Sister looked at Mama but refused to answer. I looked at them both and decided to let Mama handle this one. "Sister, would you rather have something else? A sandwich or something?" Sister continued to ignore Mama. Sister got up from the table, put on her jacket, and left. She was only gone for a short while. When she returned, she had a grocery bag that she took to her room. This continued for several weeks. Sister wouldn't eat anything either one of us prepared. Everything she ate, she bought.

CHAPTER 33

Sister was going through what I called a normal spell, when everything was fine. It was during these times that her paintings were full of cheer, butterflies, and pretty flowers. She had started her new job where her friend Tweety worked. She told me one of her coworkers had asked her out. Sister had not dated since her and Brenda broke up. I was real happy about it. We went on a shopping spree with her first check to find her the perfect outfit for her date.

"Rose, I'm thinking about getting my hair cut. What do you think?"

"Oh…Sister…I don't know. You have such beautiful hair. Are you sure?"

"Yes, I am. I need a new look. I mean…my hair just hangs. I need a style."

"I know…but it hangs so pretty. But all right. What kind of style do you want?"

"I don't know. That's why I'm asking you. I don't want a lot cut off. Just some shaping here and there."

"Okay, why don't we go into the salon and look through their hairdo books and see if you see anything you like?"

"Okay," Sister said, smiling.

"So…what's this guy's name again?"

"Henry. And he's so fine. He looks sort of like that guy that plays in…oh, what's that movie. Ah…*Jason's Lyric*. The one who was in love with Jada Pinkett…oh shoot!"

"Oh, I know who you're talking about. I don't remember his name...but he is fine. Where is he taking you?"

"Well. he asked me out to a movie and maybe dinner."

"That's nice," I responded as we shuffled a few dresses around on the rack. "How about this skirt outfit?" I said, holding up a short white skirt with a vest to match.

"That's cute. I like it. What size is it?" Sister asked.

"Um...it's a five."

"Okay, what about these I have?"

"Those are cute too. The dressing rooms are over here. I'll wait right here so I can see what you look like when you have them on." Sister was as happy as a lark. When she went into the dressing room. her smile could've lit up the sky. She came out of the dressing room wearing the white outfit I picked out, looking like an angel. "Oh... Sister...you look gorgeous. You have got to pick this one."

"I know. Rose. I love it. When we first came into the mall, I saw these real cute white sandals that would go perfect with it. Oh... Rose, I'm so excited." She was so bubbly, it was great.

"Okay, let's get it, and then we can check out that salon." I put my arms around Sister's shoulders. It was like old times. I didn't want it to end. As we thumbed through a few of the salon books, Sister found the perfect style for her. It was one of those short on one side, long on the other with just a little cut off the back. It really was quite attractive. When we left the salon, every male walking took a double take at the way my sisters hair flirted with the wind.

It was the night of Sister's date. She was getting ready for her shower. I could tell she was nervous, so I decided to set up the bathroom for a candlelight bath. I wanted her to be totally relaxed, and it always worked for me. I went to my room and retrieved some of my precious scented candles. I ran a warm scented bubble bath, lit the candles, and turned off the light.

"Sister, are you nervous?" She nodded yes. "Come with me. I have a surprise for you."

"What?" Sister asked, looking at me strangely. I took her hand and led her into the bathroom. Sister gasped.

"Oh, Rose, it's lovely, and it smells so good in here." We both stood in front of the mirror over the face bowl. I put one hand on her shoulder.

"Remember when I told you about the first date I had with Jamal?"

"Um hm."

"Well...I was so excited and nervous. This was what I did. I took a romantic candlelight bath to relax me. I treated myself like a queen. That's what I want you to do. I'll lay everything out for you, so take your time." Sister turned to me and put both her arms around me and whispered thank you into my ear.

I told Mama to come into the living room with me for a minute.

"What is it, Rose?"

"Just wait a minute. She'll be down in a second."

"Who...who'll be down in a second?" Mama looked up at the top of the stairs and saw Sister.

"Oh my god! Is that Sister?"

Smiling I, said, "Yep!"

"Oh my goodness, Sister, you look so beautiful."

"I know," I said, taking a bow.

"And your hair. I didn't like it at first, but you've added more curl. It's gorgeous, baby."

"Thank you, Mama." Just then, someone knocked on the door.

"Oh, Rose!"

"Don't worry. You're fine...you're okay. Answer the door." Sister slowly walked over to the door. I could hear her take a deep breath. She paused before opening the door. Mama and I both walked quickly to the kitchen, peeping out through the door. Henry was very attractive. He had naturally curly hair, was not very tall, but muscular. He handed Sister something. I couldn't quite tell what it was.

"Thank you, Henry," Sister said, smiling.

"Sister, you look...you look." Mama and I started to chuckle. Henry was at a loss for words.

"You look b...beautiful," he said, staring.

"Thank you, Henry. I want you to meet my mother and sister. Here, have a seat on the couch." Sister came walking our way into the kitchen. When she got inside the doors, she took another breath. We all screamed. I know he heard us.

"Sister, he is cute," I said.

"Girl, he didn't know what to say," Mama replied.

"I know," Sister said, giggling. "Come on. I want you to meet him."

"Oh, Sister," Mama said. "I look a mess."

"That's okay. Mothers always look a mess. It's expected," Sister said.

"Come on, Mama," I said, pulling her hand and letting it go when we got outside the door.

"Henry?" He stood. "This is my mother. And this is my sister, Rose" Henry stretched out his hands to both of us.

"Nice to meet you both."

Mama put on her fake voice and said, "Likewise."

"It's nice to meet you, Henry," I responded. Mama and I went back into the kitchen.

When Sister and Henry left, we looked out of the window to see if he would open the door for her. He did.

"See! There's nothing wrong with Sister. She just wanted some attention," Mama said.

I didn't say a word. "Rose, did you need to get in the bathroom before I take my shower?"

"Where are you going?"

"To a friend's house…to play cards."

"Yeah right!" I whispered under my breath. "Sisters been dating Henry for a few months now." "Oh, Mama, I was thinking about going to visit Jamal. Sister seems to be doing okay right now, and I haven't seen him for a while. I'll only be gone for a few days."

"That's fine, baby. When are you leaving?" Mama asked while gathering up some dirty dishes.

"Tomorrow afternoon."

"All right. I hope you have fun," Mama said as she went up the steps to take her shower.

"Hm…That was easy."

CHAPTER 34

"Jamal?"

"Hey, baby. I was just thinking about you."

"You were?" I said, smiling.

"Yes, I miss you."

"Would you like to see me?"

"Yes! When?"

"How about…tomorrow?"

"Sure, that's great. Will you be arriving at the same time you did before?"

"Yes."

"I'll be there…Oh, and, Rose, I want to ask you something."

"What?"

"I'll ask you tomorrow, okay?"

"Okay."

"Bye, baby."

"Bye." Oh…my…god. He was going to propose. I had to call Nina. What's that number? I couldn't remember the number. My heart was racing. "Nina? Wake up, girl. I have to tell you something."

"Hi, Rose. What time is it?"

"I don't know. Guess what?"

"What?"

"I think Jamal is going to propose to me."

"Wait…wait a minute…what?"

"I told him I was coming to see him tomorrow, and he said he had something he wanted to ask me, so…I told him to ask me now. But he said he wanted to wait until I arrived. I think he's going to propose."

"Well, have you all discussed marriage at all?"

"No."

"I don't know, Rose."

"But what else could it be? We've been dating for a long time now."

"Would you marry him, Rose?"

"In a heartbeat, girl. Jamal is great. I'll never find another man like him."

"Oh, Rose, I wish you all the best."

"I'm scared, Nina. My hands are shaking."

"Calm down, girlfriend. Let's talk about something else. How is your sister? Has she been doing any more weird things?"

"Girl…Sister went out on a date tonight…with a man."

"You're lying."

"No, I'm not. He's cute too."

"So…she's okay then?" Nina asked.

"I…really don't know. Mama thinks she just wanted some attention, but I don't think so. I think she's at some kind of resting stage, if that makes any sense."

"What do you mean?"

"It's hard to explain. I just don't think it's over. I think there is really something wrong with her. Man, you haven't seen what I've seen. Remember, I told you about her sitting in the dark and throwing all her things away. You don't do that sort of thing just for attention, Nina."

"Yeah, I see your point," Nina responded.

"What do you think is wrong with her? I think her paranoia is back. You know, Nina, sometimes, I'm really afraid of her."

"Oh…Rose."

"I am."

"I just hope she stays okay until I get back."

"So…I know you're going to stop in to see me."

"Of course, I mean…not the first day I get there."

"I know. You have to take care of business."

"And you know this!" We laughed. "All right, girl. I'll see you in a couple of days."

I could not get the thought of Jamal proposing to me out of my mind. I wondered how he was going to do it. I needed a new negligee, a trip to the mall.

"Mama! On your way out, will you drop me at the mall?"

"I'll be ready in five minutes, so you'd better hurry up!" she yelled from upstairs.

"I'm ready. You're the one that wasn't dressed!" I yelled back.

"All right, smart ass," Mama said as she came down the stairs. "Where did you get the money to do all this anyway?"

"Daddy sent me and Sister some money."

"Um!" she said sarcastically. "Let's go."

CHAPTER 35

When I arrived, I saw Jamal coming toward me. He was so fine. When he noticed me, I saw him smile. His pace quickened, and so did mine. He picked me up and swung me around, followed by a passionate kiss. "Hey, baby! How was your trip?" he asked.

"Fine, now that I'm here. I'm so glad to see you!" I put my hands around his neck and kissed him again.

"Come on. Let's get out of here," he said. "Are you tired?"

"No, not at all." He looked at me and said, "Good." We laughed.

"Um…what's that smell?" I asked, lifting my head to get a good whiff.

"I cooked some shrimp for us. Are you hungry?"

"Famished," I said, rubbing my stomach.

"Well, while you're freshening up, I'll get it ready. How about some wine?"

"Sure."

After we ate, we went into the living room. Jamal put on music and lit a fire. By this time, I was dying to know what he wanted to ask me. I couldn't wait any longer.

"Jamal, what did you want to ask me?" He started laughing.

"I'm sorry, baby. I know you've been waiting. Rose?" he said softly. *Oh my god, here it comes.* "I want you to come and live with me." I looked at him with a blankness. He continued, "We don't get to see each other much. Talking on the phone is just not enough.

You don't have to answer now. Think about it." My heart fell. Live together...what! "Will you think about it?" I didn't answer. "Rose, what's the matter?" I was stunned.

"Jamal...I don't know what to say."

"Say yes."

"I can't...not now. I mean...I can't. Will you excuse me? I need to go to the bathroom." I quickly got up and went into the bathroom and stared into the mirror. I couldn't live with him. Why was it that men always wanted women to live with them? Why! So if the going got rough, he could put me out. I felt so stupid. What made me think he would want to marry me?

"Rose, honey, are you okay?"

"Yes, I'm fine. I'll be out in a minute." I didn't want to go back out. What was I going to say?

"Are you okay, baby?" he asked me again when I returned.

"Sure, baby. I'm fine. I was just a little surprised, that's all."

"Let's not talk about it anymore. You think about it, okay?" I nodded. "May I have this dance?" he asked me.

I smiled. "Yes, you may." As we danced, we kissed and forgot the bedroom even existed.

The next morning, Jamal had to work, so I had him drop me off at Nina's.

* * * * *

"How was your evening?" Nina asked me. "Never mind. I can see it in your face."

We hugged and went inside. "I can't believe you're here."

"I know. Oh, you've got some new furniture since I was here last."

"Yeah. It was a birthday present from my dad," she said while rubbing the top of the sofa. Nina was looking at me strangely.

"What?" I asked her.

"Well, aren't you going to tell me what he had to ask you?"

"He asked me to move in with him," I said, more flatly than I'd intended.

"Well!"

"Nina? I don't want to just move in with him."

"Why not!"

"Because!"

Nina motioned for me to continue.

"Because…"

"Nina…there is no security in moving in with someone."

"What do you mean?" Nina asked me as she pulled a chair out for me to sit down.

"I mean…what if things just happen not to work out for us? Then what?"

"You move on."

"Right! I have to move on. No, I don't think so. Besides, right now is a bad time, with Sister acting goofy all the time and Mama's addiction."

"Your mother is still smoking cocaine?" Nina asked me, putting her hands to her face.

"She says she's not. I don't believe her."

"Oh, Rose."

"If he had proposed, it could have been a long engagement, which would have given me time to see what's up with Sister, you know?"

"Yes, I guess I can understand what you're saying. Well, did you tell him all that?"

"No. I just told him I would think about it. So what's on the agenda for today?"

"Anything goes. I took off today, so whatever you want to do is fine with me," Nina said.

"Let watch soaps all day and find out what's happening in the real world."

"Yeah right!" We laughed as we went into her living room.

"But you know, Nina, Sister was doing real well. She's been seeing Henry about three months now and seemed to like him a lot. I was thinking maybe that's what she needed—a man in her life. At least that's what I thought until she came in late one night and started in on me."

"What did she do?"

"I was just hanging up the phone when I heard Sister come into the living room. 'Who were you talking to?' she asked me with a piercing look in her eyes. I looked at her. 'Jamal…why?' 'You lying bitch! That was Henry, wasn't it?'" Nina put her hand to her mouth in awe.

"Sister called you a bitch?"

"Girl, yes! So anyway, she said, 'I see the way you look at him.' All I could do was stare at her."

"What!"

"I said I looked at her like she was crazy, and she was. So then she said, 'You think I don't know the way you look at him whenever he comes over?' 'Sister? What are you talking about? I don't look at him in any way. And I was talking to Jamal. I picked up the phone and held it in her direction. Call him! Sister, I was talking to Jamal. Here, call him,' I said to her again. Sister turned and ran up the steps. I didn't know what was wrong with her.

"A few hours later, she was fine again. Mama had come home and asked if we wanted to go to the grocery store with her. So we did. We were having a pretty good time. It's been a long time since we all went grocery shopping together. So Mama told us to go and pick out some kind of beef for dinner. I said, 'Okay, come on, Sister. It's over here. I feel like steak…they look good too.' 'I wonder if Mama will care.' 'You think she will?' I said. I didn't get an answer. I turned to see where Sister was. Girl, she was standing there, staring at the meat."

"What?"

"I said, 'Sister? What's wrong?' She then started to mumble. 'Sister?' When I touched her arm, she quickly pulled away from me and started walking fast. Oh my god! I was thinking. I followed Sister, but I had a hard time keeping up with her. I spotted Mama in the vegetable section. I called her and pointed at Sister ahead of me. Mama dropped the tomato and came running over to me."

"Was she still mumbling, Rose?"

"Like she was on speed or something. I didn't know what to do. 'Sister?' Mama was calling her. 'Rose, what's wrong with her?' Mama asked me. I was losing my breath, mostly because I was afraid.

"'I don't know, I told her. We were looking at the beef and all of a sudden, she was just standing there.

"'What is she saying?' Mama looked at me.

"'I don't know, Mama. Look, she's going out of the store. I'll get the car. You keep up with her.' So Mama ran to get the car.

"'Sister! I called her. She was a few feet away from me, Nina. Then I asked her, 'Sister, where are you going? Sister?' Girl, she didn't say anything. Mama pulled up beside us and started driving to our pace, yelling loud from the car.

"'Sister? Get in, Sister. Get in.' I hunched my shoulders at Mama and continued to follow her. After a while, I was tired. I didn't want to walk anymore. My feet were killing me, and I was having a hard time keeping up. I flagged for Mama to stop. We followed her. I managed to hear a few curse words. Sister had speed walked all the way home. Nina, it was a good twenty blocks away. Sister opened the door and went upstairs. Mama and I didn't know what to do or think. Me and Mama sat down on the couch in amazement."

"So did you ever find out what happened?"

"Nope, it was strange. I wanted to see what kind of painting Sister was doing, so I sneaked into her room one day when her and Mama left. Just as I was going into her closet, I picked up a sheet of paper lying on her floor in the corner of her closet. I read it. Girl… Sister is a paranoid schizophrenic." Nina had to sit down.

"Girl, I went into my room and lay across my bed and put on my favorite gospel CD. I didn't want to be a part of the family anymore. Because I knew Mama wasn't going to do anything, I didn't even tell her. I wanted to be Mrs. Jamal David. I wanted to move in with him like he asked me to. I wanted to work and not have to worry about my mother or sister. I wanted to go back to college and become a writer. Nina, I got angry. I said, 'Are you listening, God! I'm tired of it all. Every night I pray to you and nothing! I thought you were supposed to be all-powerful. So why is this happening? Huh! I've gotten down on my knees. If you're so omnipotent, why is my sister suffering so? I don't understand. Please help me to under-stand.' I mean, Nina, I was screaming and pacing the floor back and forth. 'Am I not praying hard enough?' I screamed. 'Can't you hear me! I need your help. I love my sister, and believe it or not, I love my mother.' I knelt down beside my bed and put my hands together. I whispered, 'I'm sorry, God. I love my family. They're all I got. I don't know what I would do if anything was to happen to them.' Girl, I was scared. I thought God was going to strike me down and I said, 'Don't take them away from me. Please forgive me for speaking to you in that tone. I love you, I love you, I love you. I know that you are a forgiving God. I am thankful, Jesus. Thank you, Jesus. Thank you, Jesus. Thank you. Thank you. I said it over and over and over until my body felt hot. All of sudden my body just seemed to jump up on its own to my feet. The words *thank you* became louder and louder and my eyes filled with tears as I shouted the words 'I love you' and 'Thank you, Jesus! Thank you, Jesus!' I'd forgotten where I was because, Nina, the next thing I knew, I was downstairs sitting on the edge of a dining room chair, my arms crossed and rocking. I knew what had just happened. I closed my eyes again and said, 'Thank you, Jesus.' That was the first time I ever got the spirit. Nina, it felt so good."

"That's what I heard."

"But the last couple of months she has been doing well. She hasn't tripped about anything, and she's been really sweet."

"I hope it lasts," Nina said.

"I know, girl. So do I. So do I."

"So, Rose, when will you be back?"

"I don't know, but I'm sure it'll be soon."

CHAPTER 36

I always hated when it was time to leave Jamal. He took my answer about moving in with him very well. He told me he would keep trying. I had no problem with that at all.

I was hoping Sister would tell me about the paper I read in her closet. Weeks went by, and she didn't utter a word. I didn't want to tell Mama. She probably wouldn't have believed me anyway. I went into Mama's bedroom and took her phone book from her vanity.

"T?"

"Rose…hi…how are you?"

"I'm…fine."

"How's your Mama? And Sister, how is she doing? I heard she had a boyfriend." Auntie chuckled.

"T…I was wondering if I could come up to see you?"

"Sure…Rose. You know you don't have to ask."

"Well…I'm asking because I don't have any money…and I was hoping you would pay for me to come up for a week…maybe."

"Oh, sweetie, of course. When do you want to come?"

"Well…how about Saturday? Can you wire me the money tomorrow?"

"Sure, baby. Rose…what's wrong?"

"I just need to talk to you. That's all…okay?"

"Okay, sugar. The money will be there by noon. Are you bringing your sister with you?"

"No, I haven't told anyone yet. Thanks, Auntie. I'll call you to let you know what time to pick me up, okay? I really need to be going now. I need to do laundry and get ready. And thanks again."

"No problem. I'll see you Saturday…bye."

The next morning, the doorbell rang. Mama answered.

"Yes," Mama said, trying to sound sexy when she noticed it was a handsome man at the door.

"I have a telegram for Rose Sinclair."

"That's my daughter. I'll sign for it. Thanks."

"Rose! You have a telegram!"

"Really," I said, coming quickly out of the kitchen.

"Who's it from?" Mama asked.

"Well, gee, give me a chance to open it."

"Fannie! Why is she sending you a telegram?"

"I'm going to visit her this weekend."

"What? Why didn't you tell me…again? You are always going somewhere. You just got back from seeing what's his face."

"I'm telling you now. Besides, I only decided yesterday."

"Why?" Mama snapped.

"Because she's my aunt, and I want to see her."

"Uh uh, you got something up your sleeve. You've never wanted to visit her before."

"There you have it," I said, taking it from her hand. "I never visit, so I decided I would."

"Well…what is she saying?"

"She made my plane reservations, and she's sending me a few dollars in spending money. Oh! And she's sending Sister some money too."

"Oh, isn't that sweet?" Mama snarled.

"You're just jealous, Mama."

"Jealous of what?" Mama then turned and walked back into the kitchen. I could hear her mumbling as I went up the steps to pack.

Mama took me to the airport. I handed her a note to give to Sister, telling her bye. I would have told her myself, but she had been spending a lot of time at Tweety's.

CHAPTER 37

I saw T in the distance. She was wearing jeans and a white T-shirt. She saw me and raised her hands so I wouldn't lose track of her. She smiled widely and gave me a big hug.

"How was your flight, baby?"

"Fine. Man! I didn't realize how big this airport is. You can get lost."

"I know. I've gotten turned around myself a couple of times." We laughed. "Come on. Let's get your bags and go home."

"Do you live far from here?"

"About an hour away."

"Ooooh, is this your car?"

"Uh hum."

"It's bad!"

"Girl…this car is a couple of years old. It's time for a new one."

"A new one!" I said, opening the door and sliding onto her plush velvet seats. "This feels good. I love this royal blue. What color is the car? I know I've seen it, but I never really knew the color."

"Champagne."

"It's gorgeous."

"I'm glad you like it."

The sun was just starting to go down. "T, I ain't seen so many black folks in one place in all my life. What side of town is this?"

"That's because your mama had a thing about being around so many black people. I never understood that. This is the west side."

"Do you live over here?"

"No, baby, I come over in this section just to work. I need to pick up some forms I forgot to finish earlier today. Would you like to come in and wait?"

"No, I'll wait out here in the car."

"Okay, lock the doors. I'll be right back."

Just as T went inside, an ambulance and two cars pulled up. I saw doctors come running out. Two women and three men got out of one car, and three women got out of the other. They were all screaming and hollering, telling the doctors to hurry up. Someone was bleeding to death. They all looked like they hadn't bathed in weeks. I was then startled by a man knocking on the window of the driver's side, asking me if I had a quarter. I quickly shook my head no. "Just one quarter," he asked.

I shook my head no, but harder that time. He walked away, calling me a stingy bitch. I was just getting ready to scoot down in my seat when I saw T coming. I was glad.

"What's the matter? You look scared," Auntie said, smiling.

"Some man came and knocked on the window, asking me for a quarter."

"Did you give it to him?"

"I wasn't opening that door. He looked crazy"

"I'm sure he did. He was probably a crackhead." I immediately thought of Mama.

"They had just brought in some little boy caught in a drive-by," T explained.

"Is he going to die?"

"No, he was shot in the leg. He'll be fine."

"T, there's people on every corner."

"Did you notice why?"

"No."

"Just pay attention to when you see a group of men or young boys or whatever standing on the corner that is nearby. Just pay attention."

After about five minutes, I said, "T, there is a store with a liquor sign almost on every corner."

"And did you notice cars pulling up and stopping for a few seconds and pulling off?"

"Yeah."

"Drugs. These young boys are selling drugs."

"The police don't do anything?"

"They do, but it doesn't matter. They're right back out here the next day, or a different group will be out here. Girl…the police can't do anything about it, as big as this city is. Please! Some of the police are crooked. They'll take marijuana off these young boys and take the shit home and smoke it themselves."

"Really?"

"Girl, yes."

"What side of town do you live on?"

"The north side. It's a little more quiet, I think."

We drove for a while, then I saw sails from boats.

"Where are we now?"

"Lake Shore Drive. Beautiful, isn't it?"

"Yes, it is," I said, looking out at the water.

There was a moment of silence. I thought about Jamal. I could see us on a boat, docked somewhere. Before I knew it, T was pulling up to this huge white brick apartment building. I was surprised.

"Is this where you live?"

"Yep!"

"I thought you lived in a house."

"Oh, I used to, but I got tired of the yard work. I'd work so many hours at the hospital. I just didn't have time for it. Not only that, it's just me. What do I need with a big house? I like it much better here. It's a condo, and to me that's just as good."

"It's huge. What floor do you live on?"

"I live on the twenty-third floor. I could have lived on the second floor, but I like sitting on my balcony, staring out at the water. It's so quiet and peaceful, and I get a lot of reading done. You grab that bag and I'll carry this one," she said as she led me into the foyer. It was beautiful. The floors were marble with specks of black in them. There were huge plants sitting everywhere. Two huge chandeliers hung from the ceiling, accompanied by smaller ones. When we reached the twenty-third floor, the red carpet delighted my eyes. Plants lined the hallway. Each door had numbers in thick gold letters.

"Which one is yours?"

"I live in 2304. It's toward the end of the hall. Here we are." T opened the door.

"Umm, what's that smell?" I said, looking around her apartment. Something brushed my leg and startled me. T noticed me jump.

"Hi, Purina. How Mama's pretty kitty? Did you miss me? Yes," she said, picking up the most beautiful all white cat I had ever seen.

"Oh, T. She's gorgeous. Look at her fur. It's so long," I said, stroking her.

"I know. Isn't she beautiful?"

"Yes. How long have you had her?"

"Two years. I fell in love with her eyes," T said.

"Oh my goodness, they're purple."

"I know. Isn't that precious? My girlfriend moved to Italy. She's a photographer. She couldn't take her, so she gave her to me. I just love her." T looked into Purina's eyes. "Yes, I do…yes. Oh, I have a roast and some potatoes simmering in a crock pot. Are you hungry?" she said, gently putting Purina to the floor.

"A little bit, I guess."

"Come on. Let me show you around."

"T, it's beautiful in here. Oh, look at your chandelier. It's beautiful."

"Yes, it's hell keeping it clean too."

"I'll bet. This apartment is almost as big as a house."

"I know. This is my room."

"Do you have white carpet in all the rooms?"

"Um huh."

"How do you keep it clean?"

"It's only me, and I don't wear shoes in here," she said, looking down at my feet.

"OOPS." I took them off and carried them.

"This will be your room."

I gasped. "Oh, T, it's lovely."

"Your bathroom is through that door."

"I have my own bathroom?"

T nodded.

"This is the living room."

"Man! it's humongous." I noticed her north wall was full of black-and-white pictures. I walked over to them.

"Is this you and Mama?"

"Yes."

"How old is Mama here?"

"Ten."

"She's pretty."

"Yes, she is."

"Who is this? Why do you have this old-fashioned picture of this lady here?"

T laughed.

"What's so funny?"

"Girl...that's your grandmother."

"Grammy! Oh my goodness. She was so skinny. And look at that dress. It's down to her knees." We laughed. "Who are these people looking like they're getting ready to go to a party?"

"That's your grandmother too. And your grandfather."

"I've never seen him. That's what he looked like?"

"Umm, hm. Your grandmother knew she loved that man. I knew she would never marry again."

"He looks white almost."

"He did have some white in him, but nobody talked about it very much. That's how your mama turned out to be such a beautiful caramel color."

"Don't you and Mama have the same daddy?"

"No, my daddy was someone your grandmother knew for a short while. He was married, but your grandmother didn't find that out until she was already pregnant."

"Oh," I said softly. "Why are you looking at me that way?"

"What way?" T asked me.

"I don't know...like you're deep in thought."

"Oh…well I'm just glad you're here. I can't believe it. You've never visited before. I'm wondering why now…not that I don't want you to. I'm glad you're here, but I can't help but think there's more to it."

"Maybe, but can we talk about it later? I just want to unpack and chill out for a while, okay?"

"Sure, honey. You go on and unpack. I'll get the salad ready and we can have a nice dinner and talk, okay?"

"All right. I think I'll take a shower and put on my nightgown. T, do you have any movies?"

"I have a couple I rented yesterday that have to be back by midnight. I haven't seen them yet. Maybe we can watch those."

"Okay."

When I came into the living room, T had dinner set up on her glass cocktail table protected by a blue bath towel.

"T, we could have eaten in the dining room."

"I know, but it's getting late, and I thought we could watch movies while we eat."

"Sure, what are we watching?"

"Well, I have *Rosewood* and *Face Off*."

"Let's watch *Rosewood* first. I've heard a lot about that movie."

"Rose? How are things at home?" I hesitated for a second.

"Strange."

"Strange how?"

"Do you and Mama ever talk?"

"No, not really."

"That's awful," I said, putting some roast in my mouth. "Um, this is good."

"Thank you, my dear. What do you mean strange?" T asked me again.

"I don't know how to begin."

"Anywhere."

"Sister's sick."

"Oh no! What's wrong with her?"

"We don't know." While we ate, I told T everything there was to tell about Sister. When I was done, I noticed T hadn't touched a thing on her plate.

"What is your Mama doing about all of this?"

"Nothing. You know Mama. She gets so wrapped up in what's she doing that she doesn't have time for anything else."

"Yes, that sounds like your mother all right."

"T, if I tell you something, will you keep it just between us?"

"Of course, baby. What is it?"

"Mama's…Mama's smoking dope."

"I know that. She's been smoking marijuana for years." I held my head down as I shook my head no.

"Mama's smoking crack." I looked up at T. She was stunned.

"I think that's why she can't seem to help Sister like she should."

"That stupid bitch. How could she have gotten herself caught up in some shit like that?" T got up and paced around the floor. "Are you sure, Rose?"

"Yes. She says she doesn't smoke it anymore, but I know she still does. I can smell it on her sometimes, after she's come back from being gone for a long time."

"Oh my god! I knew there was something up with her. I think she wanted me to leave when I was there so she could get back to that pipe."

"That's why I haven't gone back to college. Between Sister being sick and Mama's addiction, there was no way I could go back and concentrate on my studies."

"Well…I know," T responded.

"T, there's something I want to ask you." T looked at me.

"Mama said she was raped when she was younger and became pregnant with me." As I was telling T this, I saw her expression change. "She said she was raped by a friend when she and a group of friends went up to Myers Lake one summer. She said that's why Sister and I looked so different." My eyes started to fill up. "But anytime I try to find out more information, she gets angry and says she don't want to talk about it. She said his name was David. But she don't know where he is now."

T sat down on the couch and put both her hands to her face.

"I never understood why she treated me and Sister so differently until I found out we had different fathers. I always thought it was because Sister was so much prettier than I was." T sat in silence. "I asked Daddy about it, but he acted as if he didn't know anything. So now I'm asking you. Do you know anything about this?"

T just sat there, rubbing her face. She then got up and walked over to the window and stared out into the water.

"T?"

She waved her hand at me without looking in my direction and said, "Just let me think for a minute. She said David raped her?"

"Yes."

T started to laugh, like she didn't believe what I had just told her. I then heard her mumble under her breath.

"That sick, twisted…I don't believe this."

"Believe what! T? Believe what?" I asked again.

"Your Mama has went stone crazy." T continued to stare out of the window, mumbling. "Why would she tell you something like that?"

"Like what?" I said. I stood and walked over to where T was standing. "T, is David my father?" I asked. My heart was beating rapidly.

"Yes, David is your father." I stepped back and started to sob. T walked up to me and removed my hands from my face.

"But David didn't rape your mother."

I didn't have words.

"David didn't rape your mother. He and her were dating. She willingly had sex with him."

"Mama lied to me?" I started to sob again, only this time I was angry. "Mama hates me that much that she would lie to me about something like that."

"I don't know why she lied, Rose. All I know is David did not rape her."

"I don't understand, T."

"The only person that really knows what happened and why she might of lied is your grandmother."

"How do you know?"

"Mama wrote everything down. She kept a diary that she would write everything in about your mama and I from the time we were babies. She burned them all except one."

"How do you know she burned them all except one?"

"Because one night, she was looking at them. It had to have been about ten of them. She was crying. She asked me to take them out to the trash can where she had been burning leaves and toss them in. I asked her why she was saving this one particular diary. She held it tight and said, 'God told me to.' As far as I know, that diary still exists. I know Mama wrote everything you need to know in that diary."

"Does Mama know about that diary?" I asked T.

"Yes, she knew about the diaries. But even back then your Mama didn't pay attention to a lot. She was self-centered even then. At least that's what we thought. But one night, when Mama was out, I heard some noise in Mama's room. I went in to see what the noise was. It was your Mama. I don't know what she was doing, but I saw the diary on the floor by Mama's bed. Before I could ask her what she was doing in Mama's room, we heard your grandma coming through the door and ran out. A couple of days later, Mama asked us if we had been messing around in her room. Of course we said no. The key was missing to her diary. Your grandma had us tear the house apart, looking for that key. It was as if her life depended on it. We never did find it. Oh, baby, don't cry."

"I'm tired, T. I'm just so tired. I don't know what to do."

"You know what…stop crying. You know what, it may not seem like it now, but it's going to get better. It is."

"How, T? I have to go back there. I have to go back there and face her. I don't want to talk to her because I know she is not going to tell me the truth. I hate her! I hate her! How could she do something like that, T?" I sobbed.

"I don't know."

"Where is David at now?"

"I have no idea. I really don't. All I know is that he moved out of town. At least that's what I heard. I'm sorry, sweetie," she said as she hugged me. T laid my head down in her lap. We were silent the rest of the evening. Neither one of us was paying attention to the movie.

It was really hard trying to enjoy the rest of my visit. T didn't have a lot to say to me after that night. I would catch her looking at me, like she pitied me. As much as I hated going home, I cut my visit short. T understood and took me to the airport two days early.

CHAPTER 38

I didn't tell anyone I was coming in early. I could not take a ride in the car with Mama. I needed time to sort things out. T gave me enough money to catch a cab from the airport.

When I arrived in front of the house, my hands were trembling. It was 3:00 a.m. I knew Mama and Sister should be asleep. As I approached the house, it was dark, except I saw a light coming from the basement. I thought nothing of it. We often forgot to turn the light out after laundry. I turned the lock and very quietly closed the door behind me. I did not want a confrontation with Mama, not tonight. I noticed a very weird smell as I entered the living room. I put my bags down and turned on the small lamp sitting near the basement door. The door was cracked, so I slowly opened and took in a breath to see if the smell was coming from down there. It was. I slowly descended the steps. The basement had three rooms—a room with a washer, dryer, and table; a room with a television couch and love seat; and a room we use for storage, which hardly had anything in it. The light coming from the window was the storage room that also had a small closet. I went into the storage room where the odor was the strongest. I noticed pieces of white paper on the floor and little burnt pieces of cotton balls wrapped around a broken off wire hanger. The closet door was cracked, so I walked over to it and opened the door. I screamed!

"It's me!" Mama yelled.

She was hugging a plate with a small pile of white powder, a glass pipe, a razor blade, and a spoon. I looked at Mama. She looked at me. I turned abruptly to walk out of the room. She came after me, trying to call my name. "Wose." Her mouth sounded very full even though it was empty. I stopped and turned to her. I could not believe what I was seeing. Mama's face was sweating, her eyes were bulging, her jaws were tight, and it looked as if her tongue was moving around in her mouth. "Wose...I—"

"I hate you!" I turned and ran up the steps. Just as I expected, she didn't follow me.

Before entering my room, I peeped into Sister's room to see if she was there. She wasn't. I tossed and turned all night.

I was awakened by the garbage trucks. My head was pounding, so I went into the bathroom to get a couple of Ibuprofen out of the medicine cabinet. There was a note on the mirror.

> Rose, I am sorry about this morning. I'm sick. I've tried to stop, but I can't. I've checked myself into Taylor House. I will never forget the look on your face. After you went to bed, I went and took a long look at myself in the mirror. I didn't like what I saw. I've never tried a drug treatment program before. I've heard Taylor House is the best around. I'm sorry.
>
> Mama

I balled up the note and threw it in the wastebasket. I took the medicine, got back in the bed, and balled myself up like that note. If that piece of paper could speak, we would have a lot to talk about. I lay there, feeling my body sink into the mattress, my arms, my legs, the warmth, yet wondering if I was real.

I wanted my sister back. I wanted to talk to her like we used to when there was a problem. I wanted to feel the warmth of her hand in mine, the love that generated when she held it, protecting me from my fears.

I heard loud banging on the front door. I wasn't going to answer until I heard Sister's voice. "Rose! Rose? Open the door! Rose!" I got up, put on my robe, and ran down the steps to open the door.

"Sister! Where is your key?"

"I forgot it. Hi."

"Hi." I wrapped my arms around my sister and hugged her tightly.

"What was that?" she asked, looking at me strangely.

"Oh, I've missed you. I miss talking the way we used to, you know?"

"I know. That's why I'm here. I need to talk to you." she said, taking my hand and leading me to the dining room table. "Where's Mama?"

"She's not here."

"Where is she?" Sister asked.

"I'll tell you that later. What did you want to talk about?"

"Well, I'm not quite sure how to start."

"How about the beginning."

"That's just it. I'm not really sure when it all began."

"Sister!"

"Okay, okay. I've been seeing a new psychiatrist."

"Wh—"

"Wait! Wait! Don't say anything. Let me finish."

"Okay."

"I've been seeing a psychiatrist. I know I have been doing some really weird things lately. I couldn't understand why, and I didn't seem to have any control over it. I didn't really think I was doing anything weird until one day, I was at Tweety's house painting while he was at work. He said he came in and was talking to me, but I didn't respond. He called out to me and I still didn't answer. I didn't notice he was there until he put his hand on my shoulder and called my name. I looked up at him and then at the picture I had painted. Rose, I didn't remember painting that picture. I don't even know what it was a picture of. It was all kinds of weird lines and faces. Tweety said I didn't look like myself. He said he was afraid at first. He sat down, and we had a long talk. I told him about some things I was experiencing that I hadn't been able to speak of before."

"Like what, Sister?" I asked intensively.

"Like feeling I wasn't me sometimes. There was a lot of times I wanted to talk to you, but I was afraid you were going to think I was crazy."

I smiled inside myself when Sister said that.

"Anyway, I would hear these voices, lots of voices. I can't really explain it, but...I know that after I heard the voices, I would have painted a picture or said or done something I know wasn't right. Anyway, Tweety took me to see this doctor and to explain to him everything we had talked about. The doctor ran some tests. Now, Rose, before I tell you, I don't want you to worry. The doctor said it can now be controlled with medication."

"I know, Sister."

"What...what do you know?" she asked me.

"I found the doctor's report on the floor of your closet."

"Why didn't you tell me?" she retorted.

"I didn't know how. I wanted to do some research first. I was afraid. I saw some of your paintings. I was scared."

"Does Mama know?"

"No, I haven't told anyone. I've heard of paranoia schizophrenia before, but I never knew anyone who actually had it," I said.

"I'm sorry for the things I've put you through, accusing you of seeing Henry and pulling that knife on you. I had no control. I felt so much hatred and confusion. I've been on the medicine for a couple of days, and I feel like a different person. Rose, don't cry. I'm fine."

"I can't help it. I was just thinking, I wish I had my sister back. I need you so much."

"What's the matter, Rose?"

I hadn't heard those words in a long time. Hearing them, I couldn't help but cry. I held on to Sister tightly as I cried and cried and cried. "Come on, Rose. Tell me...please!"

"T told me that Mama lied to me again." Between sobs I explained, "Mama was never raped by my father." Sister held my shoulders up.

"What!" Sister looked horrified "Oh my god! Why would she say that? How could she say that if it wasn't true? What else did T say?"

"She said she doesn't know why Mama lied to me. She said Grammy kept diaries when her and Mama was smaller. She said she knew Mama kept one diary that probably talks about it. But she doesn't know what happened to it. She thinks Mama took it."

"Did she say that?" Sister asked.

"She said one day Mama was in Grammy's room, and later on Grammy noticed the key was missing."

"You mean the diary?"

"No, the key."

"But you said you think Mama has the diary."

"I meant to say the key. T don't know where the diary is either."

"That diary is probably long gone by now," Sister said.

"T said she thinks the diary still exists."

"Really!" Sister said. "When you went to see Grammy that time, did she say anything at all about the diaries?"

"No, she said she had...oh my god! Oh my god! Sister, there was a diary in Grammy's trunk in the attic...oh my god!...I remember trying to open it but I couldn't." I wiped my eyes.

"Where is it now?" Sister asked.

"I put it back in her trunk. I brought it home but took it back, just in case she missed it."

"Rose, you have to go down there," Sister suggested.

"To Mississippi?"

"Yes!"

"How am I supposed to get there? I don't have any money." Sister said, "Oh" and held her head down, and then abruptly raised it again.

"I know. I'll bet T would give you the money to go."

"You think?"

"Sure, she would."

"Okay, but I'm not going alone. I'll go if you go with me."

"Yes, you would. You've been trying to find out about your father for a long time."

"Yeah, I would, but please come with me. I don't want to do this alone."

"If T lend us the money, then yes, I'll come with you." We hugged. It felt like old times. Regardless of everything that had happened, I felt a certain joy.

"I'll call her."

"All right. When you're done, I'll need to call Henry and Tweety to let them know I'm going to be gone for a while."

"What about your job, Sister?"

"Girl, I lost that job. I was acting crazy, so they fired me."

"Oh," I responded quietly.

* * * * *

"T?"

"Rose! Are you okay? You didn't call me when you arrived," T said.

"I'm sorry. I forgot."

"What's the matter?" T asked me.

"First, I want to tell you that Mama checked herself into a drug rehab."

"You're kidding me."

"Nope. When I got home at three a.m., she was hiding in the basement with a plate of cocaine. I got angry. When I got up the next morning, she had checked herself into a drug rehab."

"Well, good for her," T said with a sigh of relief.

"But that's not what I called for. Remember the diary you were talking about?"

"Yes."

"Grammy has a diary and some other books in her trunk in the attic. That might be the one."

"It could be. Are you going up there?"

"Well, that's why I'm calling. Sister and I were wondering…"

"You don't have to say another word. Of course I'll send you the money."

"It'll only be a loan."

"I won't hear of it. You deserve to know. How did you want to go?"

"Bus is fine."

"I'll call the bus station here, find out the cost, and wire the money out right away."

"Thanks, Auntie."

"You're welcome, sweetie. How's Sister?"

"She's going to be okay. Really, she is. I'll fill you in later."

"All right, sweetie. Have a safe trip."

"We will. And thanks again."

Before I could hang up the phone, she asked, "Call me when you find out something, okay?"

"I will. Thanks, bye." I heard Sister come running down the steps, slightly out of breath.

"What did T say?"

"She's sending it out today."

"Great!" Sister responded.

"What about Mama?" Sister asked.

"I forgot to tell you. Mama checked herself in at Taylor House."

"That drug rehabilitation center?"

"Yep."

"I knew she was still smoking that shit. I'm not surprised," Sister commented.

"How did you know?" I was curious.

"She stanked. And sometimes she looked crazier than I did." We laughed. "So when are we leaving?"

"First thing tomorrow. Sister, when you get off the phone, call the bus station and get the schedule and see if your friend Tweety can take us to the Greyhound bus station."

"I'm going to take a shower before I call and pack," Sister said.

Sister did an about-face and ran up the steps. I went to my room to pack again. The traveling was beginning to tire me out. Most of my clothes were dirty. I thought I would borrow some things of Mama's. I went in Mama's closet to borrow some of her shoes. And like a bolt of lightning, it hit me. This was where Mama would hide the key. I rummaged and tossed everything around, thinking how lucky it was Sister took such long showers. Finally, taped to the bottom of a shoebox that I had already looked inside of twice, the key.

When I heard Sister coming out of the shower, I ran to her.

"Sister! Yo…you cut your hair again."

"It was cut before the shower. Are you just seeing it?"

"Sister," I whined. "Your beautiful hair."

Looking into the mirror, she asked, "You don't like it?"

"Oh…no…no, it's not that. It…surprised me. I think it's cute. Yeah! I think it's really cute. You have just the face for a haircut."

"You don't think it's too short?"

"No, not at all."

"I needed a new look. My long hair just made me…I don't know. I looked wild sometimes when I was going through one of those spells. Now when I look in the mirror, I see a different person."

"I like it. But, Sister, listen…" I reached out my hand and showed her the key.

"What's that?"

"This key was taped under a shoebox with pictures Mama kept on her closet shelf."

"Rose, that's probably the key to the diary T was talking about."

"I know. It's all coming together."

"Are you afraid?" Sister asked me.

"Yes."

CHAPTER 39

The ride was long and tiring. Sister and I went directly to the attic. The trunk was still there. Sister and I approached it. We stood there, looking at it. Sister looked at me. I looked at her. We both looked at the trunk. She nudged me. I knelt down, my hands trembling. I slowly lifted the lid. It was empty. I screamed.

"It's not here!" I shouted. "It's not here!"

"It's got to be here. Are you sure this is the trunk?"

"Yes, I'm sure. What? You think I'm stupid or something? It was here!" I cried.

"Calm down. There's a lot of stuff up here, Rose. Let's just keep looking." It was creepy. The dust was so thick, we could have worn skis. "Look over there. What's that?"

"Sister, that's it." We walked quickly over to the shelf the diary was sitting on.

"Where's the key, Rose?"

"It's down in these tight jeans somewhere...here." I put the key into the lock and tried to turn it.

"It won't open?" Sister asked.

"No!" I jiggled and jiggled. It was no use. The key just wouldn't open the lock. "Come on. I know what I'll do."

"What, Rose? What are you going to do?" We went down to the kitchen. I pulled out a sharp knife.

"Rose? You're going to cut it?"

"Why not? Grammy isn't here, so what should it matter? This house was left to us. This stuff is ours anyway," I said, taking a knife from the kitchen drawer. "There!"

"Let me see."

> *Mama told me to stay away from him, but I couldn't. He was so handsome.*
>
> *I know his family has a lot of money. You can tell by his house. It's big and white sitting up there on that hill. I remember walking past it and smelling the flowers along the fence. I'd see him looking out of the window at me. I'd purposely walk past there, going a mile out of my way just to go to the grocery store. Fannie thinks he likes her, but I know he likes me. I can tell by the way he's always looking at me. I'm so glad Mama came up here to visit. I hope we move here. I hope we never go back to Mississippi. I hate it there.*

"Didn't T say Grammy wrote the diaries?"

"Yes, but that's been so long ago. She could have made a mistake."

"Yeah, I guess. Read some more."

> *Mama said we would be leaving as soon as her friend got better. She had cancer or something. I went to my room and cried. I didn't want to go back to Mississippi. I like it here. He was just beginning to talk to me. He said I was pretty and had beautiful skin. I know he wanted to kiss me. I wanted to kiss him too. If Fannie hadn't been so close, I would have. I would have leaned right over and kissed him. He said his parents were going to a party tonight. He asked me to come over when everyone goes to sleep. I told him I would try.*

"I wish I knew who she was talking about. I wonder if it is David," I said.

"Maybe it's Daddy," Sister added. "You think she went?"

"Went? Oh! To his house?" I looked at her. Together we said, "She went."

I didn't think they would ever go to bed. I pretended to go to bed early so that I could make myself look really pretty. I was going to that big white house on the hill. I've wanted to see what the inside looks like. I brushed my teeth three times. My teeth looked dull, and I knew I would smile a lot. I always smile when I'm nervous. I was very nervous. Okay, diary, here I go. See you when I get back.

Sister and I looked at each other, each wanting to say something and neither of us having words.

The house was everything I imagined it to be. The rooms were huge. Everything was so white. The sofa, carpets, kitchen appliances, beds, everything was white. I asked him about it. He said he didn't like it like that. But he didn't have a choice. He has to go with whatever his parents liked. His music collection was awesome. He DJd for me. I loved it. I couldn't keep my eyes off him. Of course I would never let him see me looking at him. He sat next to me and tried to kiss me. I turned away at first. But slowly turned my face back in his direction and let him kiss me. He tried to put his hands inside my blouse. I jumped and scooted away from him. He said, "You know, I really like you a lot. The way your skin glows in the sunlight, your full lips, and that cute little way you swing your hips." He didn't know I didn't really walk like that, only when I knew he was looking. I became nervous and made an excuse to go home. At first he grabbed me and said I couldn't go, but he then let go, saying he was only kidding. I kissed him really quick and ran out the house. Oh, diary, I don't want to leave here.

"I'm surprised. I thought she would do it for sure."

"Me too," said Sister.

"I hope we didn't come way down here for nothing." I wanted to slam the book hard on the table, but I just handed it to Sister.

"You read."

Sister turned to the middle of the diary.

"Rose! Look! Read this."

I cried all the way. I knew I would never see him again. I hate my life.

"So?"

"No, Rose! Not that! Down here."

Dear Diary

We've been home for months now. I still can't get him out of my mind. I've written him eight letters. He hasn't wrote me once. I am mad at him. I thought he really liked me. That's the only reason I slept with David. I didn't even know him that well. He wanted to, so I did. I know I'm pregnant. What am I going to do? What am I going to do with a little nappy head baby? David works in a grocery store as a stock clerk. I can't believe I let his black hands touch me. What am I going to do? I'm not going to tell him. I am not going to tell anyone. I want an abortion.

I turned the page quickly.

Dear Diary

I caught Fannie reading my diary. I asked her what she read. She said nothing. I know she's lying. I know she knows I'm pregnant. I can tell the way she keeps looking at my stomach. I wish I was dead.

Yep, dear diary

Fannie knew all right. She told David I was pregnant but promised me she hadn't told anyone else. David came over one night when no one was home except me. He begged me to keep the baby. He said we could get married and raise it together. He told me that he has always been in love with me and that he would get a better job. I told him it was too late. I'd already had the abortion. I lied to get him away from me. I hate him.

The more I read, the more my hands trembled. A tear from my eyes hit the page we were reading. Sister took the diary from me and closed it. We said nothing. I cried. But I couldn't stop there. I had to continue. There was only one page left.

Dear Diary,

Mama could see I was pregnant. I told her he raped me. I purposely stayed out late as part of my plan. I purposely would not eat and kept myself distant. I knew Mama would come into my room soon and ask me what the problem was. She did. I started to cry. She kept asking me what was wrong. I pretended I didn't want to tell her. Finally, I told her the story I'd made up. She was furious at first, then calmed down when I pretended to look afraid. She wanted to know why I didn't tell her before. I told

229

her I was afraid to. She asked me if I had went to a doctor the night it happened. I told her no again because I was afraid. She tried to comfort me. She told me how much she loved me and that it wasn't my fault. When I looked into her eyes and saw I had won her over, I told her I was pregnant. She said she knew it all the time and was waiting on me to tell her. I asked her to help me get an abortion. She said no. She said that it would be okay, that she would help me as best she knew how. I cried in her lap and said, "Okay, Mama." She stayed with me until I pretended to fall asleep.

My eyes were swollen when I looked in the mirror the next morning. Sister looked at me and knew I didn't sleep a wink. We decided not to stay long after that. I tied up some loose ends about the house and we left.

When I checked the mailbox after returning home, there was a certified package for me to pick up at the post office from T. I took a shower and walked to the post office. When I opened the package, there was a floral diary with T's name marked on the front of it in black marker. There was also an envelope with my name on it.

"Rose, I thought this might be of help to you. This is my diary from many years ago. No one ever knew I kept one. I love you, T." I noticed on the letter from T she had certain pages circled.

I stopped at a neighborhood grocery store for a pop then walked to the park near our house and sat on a bench overlooking a small creek. I sat there for a moment, staring at T's diary. Before I knew it, I had it open, reading the first circled entry.

Dear Diary

Entry 12

Maxi thinks she's all that just because some white boy likes her. Now she's up at that big white house, probably doing the nasty. I should tell Mama. My sister is so stuck on herself. David is so cute, and the only reason she doesn't like him is because he's dark skinned. He would do anything for her. Yes, diary, I guess I am a little jealous. Okay, a lot jealous.

Dear Diary

Entry 24

I'm so glad to be back home. I like it here. I like all the grass and fields, the beautiful flowers. Maxi is crazy. She only likes it there because Mama's friends live around a lot of white people. Although Steven is cute.

I sat straight up when I read that. "Daddy."

She cried like a baby on the way home. Hmph! Steven didn't write her once. He only wanted to get in her panties. I told her he had a reputation for only wanting one thing from a girl. Of course, she didn't believe me.

Dear Diary

Entry 30

David was so glad to see Maxi when we got home. He hardly even noticed I was back. Maxi barely spoke to him. He's a fool. If he'd pay attention, he'd know who really loves him. Yes, dear diary. Me.

My back started to hurt, so I got up and walked over to a huge oak tree and sat under it.

Dear Diary

Entry 42

I knew it. Maxi's pregnant, and by David, no less. I hate them both. I can't believe she told Mama she was raped just to save her skin. I don't care that my sister is pregnant by him. I still love him. That's crazy, I know. I can't help it.

I closed the diary and took a deep breath. I sat there.

CHAPTER 40

Mama was coming home in a few days, but I was antsy. I needed to talk to her. I refused to wait any longer. I called Taylor House to find out about their visiting policy. When I arrived, Mama had just come back into her room from watching a movie on drug addiction.

"Rose! Hi."

"Hi, Mama."

"I'm glad you came. I didn't think you would. It's been over a week and I—"

I held my hand up to her face to cut her short. She widened her eyes.

"Rose, I thought you'd be happy."

"Mama, shut up! You just shut up for once." I felt a lump in my throat. I looked at her. My eyes filled up. She didn't say a word. "Mama." I was trying hard to compose myself. I didn't want to be crying. So I stood there for a few seconds. Mama didn't take her eyes off me. She let me take the time that I needed.

"Mama, why did you lie to me about David?" I said, wiping my eyes while I looked directly at her.

"Lie? What are you talking about, Rose?"

"You told me you were raped! And that's how I was conceived."

"That's true. I was r—" Before Mama could finish, I took the diaries out of my shoulder bag and slammed them down on a table in her room.

Surprised, Mama asked, "Where did you get those?"

"I went to Grammy's house. I found them in the attic."

"You went all the way to Mississippi? When?"

"Never mind. Why did you lie to me?" I became very calm at that point.

Mama picked one of the diaries.

"I...I..."

Keeping my calm and speaking in a low tone, I continued, "You first made me think my father was dead." I started to slowly walk around her room, her eyes following me. "You then told me my real daddy was a rapist." I chuckled and shook my head. I could feel my body tightening. "Now, what I don't understand, Mama, is you say you love me."

"I do love you."

I wanted to lunge at her with my hands around her throat. I could imagine things falling around us, not hearing them fall, Mama gasping for dear life.

But I just turned and walked out of the room.

Sister was waiting for me in front. "Rose, what happened?"

"I could've killed her right there. She stood there and tried to tell me she loves me. 'I love you, Rose.' I couldn't take it, Sister. She makes me sick."

"I know, Rose. Here, sit with me for a moment. I just poured this glass of pop. Drink some. What else did Mama say? What did she say about David?" I looked up at Sister.

"Nothing! What was she going to say? She couldn't say anything. She lied."

"T called."

"What did she want?"

"She wanted to know if you received her package."

"Oh yeah."

"What was it?" Sister asked.

"What was what?"

"What was it that T sent you?"

"Oh, I'm sorry. A diary she had."

"Did it tell you anything different?"

"No…not much," I answered.

We went back home. I didn't say anything on the way there. When I got through the door, I went over to where Mama kept the alcohol and picked up a bottle of rum to mix in with the Coke Sister had in her glass.

"Rose! What are you doing?"

"Shut up, Sister!" She didn't say another word. She went into the kitchen, got another glass, poured the rest of the Coke for herself, and also mixed in some rum. I looked at her. Her response was "If you can do it, so can I." I said nothing and proceeded to empty my glass. I poured another. After an hour, we were smashed, talking and laughing until I glanced at a picture of Sister hanging on the wall when she was very young.

"What's the matter, Rose?"

"You were so pretty in that picture." We both looked at that picture and remembered how Mama was back then.

"Mama, can I help you get ready for the party?"

"Of course you can, Sister. But first go and put on that pretty pink dress I laid out for you on the bed."

"Can I help too, Mama?"

"Did you forget? You were going across the street to spend the night with your friend Amanda?"

"I don't want to spend the night over there," I answered. *"It stinks, and she always makes me clean out that nasty cat box. Why can't I stay here and help, Mama?"*

"Because we promised Ms. Jones you would stay over there. You wouldn't want to upset little Amanda, would you, Rose?"

"She doesn't even like me. She never plays with me. She just sits and looks at me. I don't like it over there. I got a pretty dress. I got a pretty dress too, Mama."

"All your dresses are dirty. You wouldn't want to wear a dirty dress now, would you, Rose?" I held my head down.

"Go on, honey, run along. I promised her you'd be there in a little while. Oh, and don't forget your bag over there in the corner, okay, honey?" I picked up my bag and dragged it. I could see Sister out of the

corner of my eyes, spinning around in her new pink dress. I could see the lace petticoat underneath and her shiny black patent leather shoes.

I remember knocking on Ms. Jones's door. She came to the door with a glass of something light brown. I saw Amanda sitting on the couch behind her. She jumped up and said, "Is she here again?" She then ran up the steps and shut her door. I didn't like her at all. She would always swing her long blond hair in my face. She would come and sit right in front of me and brush it. She would always say, "Isn't my hair a pretty yellow? Everyone says it's so pretty in the sun. Do you think it's pretty, Rose? Sister's hair is pretty like mine too, except it's black. Why isn't your hair pretty, Rose?" I walked away from her and went and stared out the window. I saw the people coming to Mama's house for the party. They had on long pretty dresses. Even the little girls like me had on pretty dresses. I saw Sister standing there with Mama, laughing and talking. Everyone that came up would touch Sister's hair or her dress. I cried. I watched as Mama and Sister had the time of their lives. I sat there so long, I fell asleep until Ms. Jones came over to me and told me to get in bed. Amanda was already asleep. Just as I climbed into bed, I noticed a pair of scissors on her dresser. I took the scissors and started cutting Amanda's hair. I cut and cut and cut and cut. I quickly dropped the scissors. I ran down the steps. Ms. Jones was busy keeping company in her room as she always did. I ran out of the house, went to the back door, and sneaked up the steps. I hid in the closet. I heard Sister's voice, so I cracked open the closet door. I saw her coming toward it, so I closed it quickly. She heard the door close. She must have noticed part of my gown hanging outside the door because she opened it without being afraid.

"Go away. Leave me alone!" I whined. We had a walk-in closet big enough for us to share. She came in. Her dress had a matching purse attached to it. She opened it, pulled out a tissue, and gave it to me to dry my eyes then left. But when she came back, she had some chips and candy. She started to leave again. I didn't want her to this time. "Where are you going?" I asked.

"I'll be back." Sister went downstairs. Mama was busy laughing with some friends.

I heard Sister tell her, "Mama, I'm tired. I think I'll go to bed now, okay?"

"What's the matter, baby? Are you feeling okay?" I heard one of Mama's friends say. "She's a doll. I know your husband's crazy about her." Mama smiled. "All right, sweetie. You go on the bed."

"Mama?"

"Yes, honey?"

"When will Daddy be back?"

"He'll be back in a couple of days." Mama would always have parties when Daddy would go out of town. She was like that. Sister gave Mama a kiss and came running up the stairs. But she didn't come into the closet right away. I wondered what she was doing. When Sister came into the closet, she had on her nightgown. She also had a can of pop for us to share and a flashlight. It was the best party ever.

"Do you remember that, Sister?" I asked her.

"Of course I do. I wonder whatever happened to Amanda."

"You don't know?" I said.

"Know what?"

"Her mama put her out because she got pregnant by a black boy." We laughed.

"But there were times, Sister, you was a brat."

"What!"

"Yes, a brat, and you know you were. When we were in grade school, your friends would always make fun of me. You never stuck up for me. Remember that girl...what was her name...oh, what was her name... Jenny. Jenny Millhouser. You remember? She was tall, skinny, blond, and always wore a headband to match everything she wore...you remember. She was popular."

"Oh yeah, I remember her. She used to wear three pairs of socks at a time to make her legs look big."

"Yeah...that's the one," I said. "She didn't like me, and she would always try to get you to do things without me, and she would talk about me and you would never say anything. Mama said we were to always walk home together after school. One day, Jenny wanted you to go with her to get a slice of pizza with some other girls. So you came to me between classes and told me, and I reminded you what Mama had said. I asked you if I could come too. You said no. But I knew if I came home without you, Mama was going to whoop me. So I tried to come with you all anyway…remember?" I could tell Sister didn't want to remember, but she admitted it. "Do you remember what happened? You, Jenny, and a couple of other girls were standing out front, waiting on Mindy. I was standing out there too, a few feet away.

"Jenny said, 'Why is she standing there? She's not coming with us, I hope. Is she, Sister?'

"'I don't know,' you said.

"'Well, here comes Mindy. Let's go,' Jenny said. Then she turned around.

"'Where are you going?'

"'I'm going with my sister, if that's any business of yours.' Everybody stopped walking.

"'Sister, you'd better talk to your sister.'

You came over there and whispered to me to please go home and tell Mama you had to stay after to finish an assignment. I told you no, because Mama said no matter what, we were to come home together.

"'Well…' Jenny said.

"'Jenny, she won't go home,' you said. Then they started to make fun of me.

"'You need to go home and change clothes. You get that at the secondhand store? Don't her skirt look like her mama got it off the dollar rack?' Everybody laughed. Even you. Then they started talking about my hair. You knew how sensitive I was about my hair because of yours. Even that black girl that was with you all, she was the one talking about it.

"'You need to go home and get out the straightening comb and press out them naps.'"

You didn't say anything. I looked at you, hoping you would say something, but no. So I turned around and went home. That happened a lot."

"I know, Rose, and I'm sorry. I didn't know any better back then. You know Mama. She only…"

"You can't blame this one on Mama. I mean, I spoke up. Why didn't you help me?"

"I don't know, Rose. Stupid, I guess." Sister got angry all of a sudden. "How many times am I going to have to apologize for all that stuff I did way back when?"

"You don't have to keep apologizing, Sister. We were talking, and it just came up. I know you would never do anything like that now. Anyway, if you did, I'd beat your ass," I said, laughing. Sister laughed too.

"Yeah, you and what army?" I looked around at a cookie left on the floor in the kitchen.

"Me and that army of ants over there eating that cookie." Sister jumped up.

"Yuck!" she said.

"Oh, Sister!"

"What? What is it?"

"I don't feel well." I struggled to get up. Sister moved quickly out of my way.

"Look at you, talking about beating somebody up. You can't even get up fast enough to go…oh, Rose, gross!"

Mama was due home in a couple of days. I'd thought long and hard about leaving. Sister was doing better. There really wasn't any reason to stay. I knew Jamal would be glad to have me. But I still wasn't sure living with him was a good move. Auntie said I could live with her.

Finally, I'd made my decision. The hard part was telling Sister. I had a few dollars left of the money T sent, so I decided to take Sister out to dinner and tell her then. I was waiting for Sister to get in from her date with Henry when the phone rang.

"Rose?"

"Hi, T. I was just getting ready to call you."

"How are you, honey? I hope my diary was of some help to you."

"Yes, T, it was. I wanted to know if the offer to come and live with you is still good."

"Sure, baby. I meant it. You can come anytime you like. Are you sure this is what you want to do?"

"Yes, T, it is. I know that if I stay, I'll end up killing your sister."

"Well…we don't want that. When are you coming?"

"Mama's due home in a few days. I thought maybe you could wire me the money and I could leave maybe the day after tomorrow. I need to talk to Sister and, of course, Jamal."

"You are willing to move that far away from him?"

"I know…but I don't have a choice, T. I can't stay here. I just can't. Jamal won't give me a problem. At least he never has before."

"All right, baby. I'll send the money today."

"T, I hear Sister coming. I think I'll tell her now. Can I call you later and give you the flight information?"

"Sure, honey. Tell Sister I said hello here."

"I will, T. T? I wish you had been my mother." There was just silence. Then she said bye and hung up.

As I heard Sister turn the lock, I took a deep breath.

"Hi, Rose."

"Hi, Sister. How was your date with Henry?"

"Fine."

"Have you eaten? I want to take you out to dinner. There is something I want to talk to you about."

"You're leaving, aren't you?" I was surprised.

"Sister, I have to. There's no way I can live here knowing what Mama has done. I've thought about it a lot. I can't deal with it. I can't eat. I can't sleep. I'm tired, Sister. You're better now. You can handle Mama."

"I'm not afraid of Mama, Rose. It's just that…you can't leave!"

"Sister, I have—"

"You can't. You just can't. I'm pregnant."

I stared at her. I couldn't say a word. I had to sit down. I rubbed my face. I couldn't believe what Sister had just told me. She came over to me and took my hand.

"So you see, you can't leave. What would I do without you? Rose?"

"Does Henry know?"

"I just told him."

"What did he say?"

"He asked me to marry him, but I don't want to marry him, Rose."

I became angry.

"I can't do it, Sister! I can't do it anymore. I need a life too. Sister, I have to do this. Do you understand? I have to." I went upstairs to pack…again.

Although I felt bad leaving Sister, she understood. I explained that I would come back to see her once the baby was born. I didn't tell Mama I was leaving. I no longer wanted her to be a part of my life.

Jamal wasn't as understanding as I'd hoped. He couldn't understand how I could move with my aunt and not with him. He had a problem with me being so far away. I said we would discuss it later once I arrived in Chicago.

After I arrived, T wrote Mama a letter. I don't know what she said to her, except that I was welcome there for as long as I liked.

I never called Mama's house in fear she might answer the phone. Sister wrote me a long letter, telling about how Mama accepted her pregnancy, not without first asking her to have an abortion. Mama finally left her alone when Sister said no way. Sister would call me often when Mama left the house.

I wanted more than ever to find David, especially since I know he wanted me all along. I stared out of the window in a daze, wondering what he looked like. I was startled by the phone ringing. I really didn't feel like talking to anyone. I sauntered slowly over to the phone, hoping whoever was there would have hung up.

"Hello?"

"Rose…baby, is that you?"

"Oh…Jamal. Hi!"

"Were you busy? I can call back la—"

"No, no, no. I'm not busy. Just standing here, looking out of the window. As a matter of fact, I'm glad you called. It'll take my mind off of…" I realized what I was saying and quickly stopped.

"Take your mind off what?" Hearing the curiosity in his voice, I knew there was no way out.

"I've been going through a lot, Jamal, and I'm not sure I want to discuss it now."

"You know, Rose, I've been very patient with you. I see you when it's convenient for you. I've tried to be as supportive as I can. I just don't understand. Why is it I have to pry things out of you? You can't come up as much because your sister is sick. I can't come up there because of one problem or another. Rose, I am trying to be your man. When are you going to be my woman?" I didn't know what to say behind that.

Except something stupid like "Jamal, I am your woman."

"And now you've put all this distance between us as if it wasn't hard enough to see you before. What's the problem, baby?" We were both quiet for a minute as he waited patiently for an answer. "Rose?"

"Jamal, no man wants a woman who is always complaining about this or that. I'm sure you have problems of your own. You never call me crying. Maybe if you shared some of your problems with me, I would be a little more open with you about mine."

"Do you really want to hear about what problems I'm having? Do you?" He sounded angry.

I answered, "Yes."

"I have this woman in my life that I am crazy about. I just can't seem to reach her. I've told her how much I love her. I told her I would be there for her. I told her I would give her the world...as much of it as I could. I told her I would support her in all her endeavors. I want to share my entire life with her."

I could not stop the tears from falling. I didn't want him to hear me crying. I'd raise the phone to keep him from hearing me sniffle.

"I don't know what to do," he continued. "Maybe you can help me. Can you help me, Rose?"

I couldn't answer. I was fighting the sobs.

"I'm sorry, baby. I didn't mean to make you cry. It's just that I can't go on like this forever. We can't go on like this forever." I put the phone on mute, coughed, and blew my nose.

"Jamal?" I couldn't keep my voice from shaking. "It's a long story."

"Start at the beginning," he answered.

After talking to Jamal, I felt as if I had gone through six months of therapy. I slept.

CHAPTER 41

It was nice staying with T. She took me shopping and showed me some of the better sites in the city. Sometimes when I was in bed, I could swear she was there watching me sleep.

I was in a better mood the morning after I talked to Jamal. When T came into the kitchen and saw me, she smiled.

"You seem to be feeling better this morning," she said, returning a smile I had given her.

"I do. I feel much better. T, how come you never had any children? You didn't want any children?"

"I don't know, Rose. I guess I didn't think I would make a good mother, and men come and go. I guess I didn't want to have to raise a child alone." She tried not to show it, but there was a certain sadness.

"But…that's just it, T. You wouldn't have been alone."

"I'm so glad you're here." She stretched her arms out. We hugged.

"Me too, T. Me too."

T got me a job as a nurse's aid where she worked. I really liked the job a lot. I worked mostly with the elderly. Listening to them, my problems didn't seem so bad.

Months had passed. Sister sent me a picture of her progress. She was coming along quite nicely. She told me Daddy came up to visit, thinking I was still there. He was disappointed I had moved. With everything that was happening, I forgot to tell him. I called him and explained. When I told him everything and about what was happening, he didn't have very much to say.

So many feelings came up. I wrote a poem.

Floating in life's sea
her body surrounds me, protecting me from all harm. So warm,
so safe knowing only that
I am hers.
I hear her voice, songs, laughter. I am hers.
I sense her doubts, burdens, fears. I am hers.
I feel her anger, sadness, cries. Through it all, I am hers.
I want to meet her, see her, touch her, tell her, I am hers.

I heard a sudden knock on my bedroom door.

"Rose? What are you doing?" she asked, holding a newspaper.

I quickly closed my notebook and said, "Nothing…why?"

"You want to go to a movie tonight?"

"T, I'm tired. Would you mind if we didn't go? I really would just like to lie here and do nothing, okay?"

"Sure, I just thought you were bored," she said as she put the newspaper under her arm.

"No, not at all."

"Okay…I think I'll go down the hall and play some cards. I should be back in a few hours. If you get hungry, there's some junk food in the bottom cabinet. See you later."

After T left, I took out my notebook again and wrote Sister a long letter. I told her about my new job and asked her what she needed for the baby. There was a mail slot down the hall. I thought I had some stamps. I forgot I'd used the last one when I wrote to Jamal. T said she had more if I needed them. I went into T's room to see if she had any. I loved T's room. It was simple but cute. Everything in there was either black or white. She had a wall full of pictures. They were black and white as well. I walked over to her dresser to see if she had any just lying on top of it. She didn't. I was drawn over to the wall of pictures. I noticed several pictures of T and a young man. He wasn't ugly, but he wasn't cute either. She seemed to have liked him a lot. I wondered why she never mentioned him. I giggled when I noticed a picture of Mama and Daddy. The black-and-white contrast made it look like it was taken before I was born. As I moved down the wall, there were pictures of Sister and me. Actually, there were only a few of Sister and quite a few of me. I was surprised to notice how well dressed I was in all of them. Some of them I remembered taking. I remembered Mama telling me to put on Sister's dress because she wanted to send T a picture of me. I'm sure T thought all of those dresses were mine. T had the most beautiful hope chest sitting at the foot of her bed. It was a shiny black with white hinges. "That's where she probably keeps her stamps. The smell of cedarwood tickled my nose as I opened the chest. Everything inside was so neat with several smaller chests inside. The first one I opened contained combs and hairpins. I knew there were no stamps in there. I noticed in the far corner of the chest there was a smaller one with a heart on it. There were more pictures inside. They were of the same man that was in the pictures on the wall, only these were in color and taken much later. I saw writing on the back.

I hope this picture makes you smile, like it made me smile when I thought of you, David.

I didn't think nothing of his name being David. I thought it was cute her and Mama both liked a man named David. I was getting ready to put the chest down when I saw a folded-up piece of paper hiding under the pictures. It was old. I could tell by the discoloration. I know I shouldn't have, but I couldn't help myself. I opened it up and read it.

Dear Fannie Mae,

I know you don't like me calling you that, but I only do it because I think you're so sweet. How are you? I've been really busy. I should be coming home soon. I get a leave next month. I loved the pictures you sent. You're really getting big. What did the doctor say about your last checkup? I know you don't like talking about it, but the only reason I liked your sister at first was to get your attention. You thought I was crazy about her, and I wasn't. You didn't think anyone could like you, especially when you were with your sister. I thought you were more beautiful than she was. You were pretty. I know you didn't think you were. But I do, and I still do. We both know your sister seduced me that night.

I know it was wrong, but it got the best of me. I hadn't been with anyone in a long time. I didn't think you cared for me at all. So I just gave in. I never would have if I had known how you felt. I know we've gone over and over this. I still know that you haven't completely forgiven me, even though we now have a child on the way. I love you, Fan. I hope we put this behind us so we can continue on with our future and raise the child we're going to have.

I love you, David

"So T had been pregnant before!"

I folded the letter and put it back. I felt something hard. Just as I went to pull it out, I could hear T coming through the door. I quickly closed the lid and stood by the dresser.

"Oh! Rose!" she said, putting her hands up to her chest. "You scared me. What are you doing in here?"

Clearing my throat, I said, "I was looking for another stamp."

"Oh sure. They're right over here." She went to a basket that was sitting under her nightstand. "This is where I keep all my paper, pens, and of course, stamps," she said, handing me a book of stamps. "You're staring at me."

"I'm sorry. I didn't realize I was. I only need a couple. How was your card game? You didn't stay very long."

"I know. I was tired. I played one game and made my excuses."

T walked over to her hope chest and pushed on it. It made a noise as if it hadn't been closed all the way. She didn't look at me differently. Maybe she thought she left it open.

I went back to my room and lay down on the bed. My head was aching something terrible. I wondered why she lied about having any children. Miscarriage? Abortion? Maybe it hurt too bad.

Several months passed. Sister gave birth to a beautiful baby girl. I received pictures about a week later. It read: Roselyn Ann Sinclair, 6lbs,7oz. To (Aunt) Rose. With love, Sister.

"Oh, hi, Rose. Dinner will be ready in a minute. I hope you're hungry."

"Yes, it smells good. T?"

"Yeah, sweetie."

"Look, I have a picture of Sister's baby. She named her after me."

"Rose?"

"Close. She named her Roselyn with an *e*."

"Oh, that's so sweet," T responded.

"I love my sister so much."

"I'm glad to hear it, sweetie."

"Did Grammy love you and Mama the same?" She stopped stirring the sauce, took a pop out of the refrigerator, and sat down beside me.

"What do you mean?"

"I just wondered if Grammy treated you and Mama the same."

Looking at me strangely, she asked, "Why would you ask me that? Don't parents treat all their children the same?"

"No," I responded in a tone that made her want to know more. "Mama didn't like me very much."

"What! Rose, that's absurd. Of course she did. Maxi wrote me letters all the time, telling me all the things you all were doing, all the fun—"

"What letters?" I asked. "Do you still have any of them?"

"Yes, I have them all."

"Can I see them?"

"Sure." T got up and went into her room to get the pictures. She had a hat box full.

"Oh my goodness, you have all these? I thought you and Mama didn't talk much."

"We didn't talk much, but I didn't say anything about letters."

"Can I read some?"

She hesitated for a moment and answered, "Yes."

Dear Fan,

Sorry, I haven't written to you in a while. I've been really busy. The kids and I are going to Disney World. It should be a lot of fun. Everyone is really looking forward to it. I'll send you some pictures when we get back. I bought Rose a lot of new clothes just for the trip. You should see her. She's growing like a weed. She's also invited to a birthday party next week. She's real excited about that. I need to go and make some travel arrangements, so I'll write you again soon.

Maxi

"I don't believe her," I said, shaking my head in disbelief.

"What?"

"Did Mama ever send you those pictures of Disney World?"

"No. She said they didn't turn out right. As a matter of fact, she said that a lot."

"I'm sure she did," I said. "Mama never took me to Disney World."

"You all didn't go?"

"Yes, they went. But Mama didn't take me."

"Why not?" T was angry.

"Some stupid reason."

"But she took Sister!"

"Mama did that all the time. She never bought me a lot of clothes. She bought me some clothes, but they weren't like the clothes she'd buy for Sister."

"Rose, I can't believe what you're telling me."

"It's true! Ask Sister. She wouldn't let me go to parties. She didn't let me do anything. She'd let Sister go. She was ashamed of me, my hair, my skin." T became furious.

"That bitch!" T got up from the table and walked to the sink and banged both hands on it.

"I'm telling you, T. She treated Sister like a little princess, and Daddy and Mama would always argue about it. I think that's why he left. He couldn't take it anymore. When Daddy left, she really treated me like shit. Do you know she let us think he was dead?"

"What!"

"Yep. It wasn't until recently that we knew he was alive. Sister happened to see him one day. Mama couldn't deny it."

"That bitch promised!" T screamed.

"Promised? What did Mama promise?"

T just looked at me, like in a staring contest.

"You know all I've been through, T. I don't need you to start keeping secrets from me too."

T came back to the table, sat down, looked at me and said, "I have to go visit Maxi."

"What? Why? I'm going too."

"I don't know, Rose. Maybe you should stay here."

"No. Besides, I want to see my niece." T couldn't deny me that.

"All right. We'll leave the day after tomorrow. I have some business I need to take care of first."

"T, since we're talking, I wanted to ask you about a picture."

"I know about that picture, Rose. I promise I'll tell you anything you want to know when we get back. Dinner's ready."

T was very angry at Mama. She wouldn't call Mama to let her know we were coming. I could care less. I was only concerned with seeing Sister and that gorgeous baby of hers.

Early the next morning, I heard T leave, assuming she was taking care of some business. But when I got up, there was a note on the kitchen table.

Rose,

I'm sorry, I needed to handle this one alone. Please try not to be angry with me. Besides, it's not very good for you to take off work so soon after starting. I promise I'll tell you everything when I get back.

T

I slammed my fist on the table. "I can't believe she left me." As I was walking back to my bedroom, I heard the phone ringing.

"Hello?"

"I'm sorry. I hope this is not a bad time?" I quickly changed the tone of my voice.

"Oh! Jamal, of course not. Hi."

"Hi. If you're busy, I can call back later."

"No, I'm not busy. As a matter of fact, I'm bored. My aunt just left for California for a couple of days."

"Good…I need to see you. Can I come up?"

"Sure."

"Okay, I'll need to call and get flight information."

"I know there's a flight out every afternoon at four."

"That's perfect. I'll see you later tonight, okay?"

"Sure, baby. I'll be here." I started dancing around the living room, singing, "Heaven, I'm in heaven." Thank you, God. If T hadn't left me, I would have missed out on seeing Jamal. "Heaven, I'm in heaven," I continued to sing.

When Jamal arrived, I had dinner prepared. As soon as I heard him knock on the door, I quickly lit several candles, including the two I had sitting on the table separated by a gorgeous centerpiece. "Just a minute," I said. I quickly glanced around the room to make sure everything was in order. T's apartment looked like a romantic dream. The flickering candles danced softly with the music. I opened the door.

"Hi, honey!"

"Hey, baby." He stared at me. "You look so pretty."

"Thanks," I said, smiling. *Mission accomplished*, I thought, but he had a strange look in his eyes.

"What's the matter, baby?" I asked. "Oh, I'm sorry. Come in," I said.

"Your aunt has a beautiful apartment." I looked at him.

"Jamal? What's wrong?" As he started to speak, we walked over to the couch.

"Baby." He took my hands. My heart started beating rapidly. "I can't stay."

"You can't? But I made dinner."

"I know. It smells delicious, but I really just came to talk to you about something." I didn't say a word. "Rose…I can't see you anymore." I gasped and quickly stood up. He stood up too. He took my hands again, and we sat down. "Rose…it's too hard. The closer I try to get to you, the more distance you put between us. I can't continue to put my life on hold. I told you I would never cheat on you. I've been there, done that. So I think the best thing for me to do is to move on. That way, neither one of us gets hurt."

"What? You don't think I'm hurting right now?" I said, crying.

"Rose, this is not easy for me either."

"Then why?"

"Baby, I can't. I just can't. I live in California. You live here in Chicago. I don't want that kind of relationship. There is another flight out in two hours. I'm going to be on it."

We just looked at each other. My tears just flowed. He grabbed me and held me tight. "I'm sorry, baby. I'm sorry." When he let go, I noticed he had been crying as well. He got up and went to the door, took one last look at me, and left.

I felt as if my heart was going to explode. I sat back down on the couch and rocked and rocked and rocked, tears streaming down my face. I'd never experienced such pain. I didn't know what to do. I continued to rock, my arms folded as if I was trying to hold myself together. I supposed I was.

CHAPTER 42

I got the story later, in full detail.

T said Mama wasn't home when she arrived. Mama never locked the door, so T was able to go inside. She had only been there a little while when Sister came through the door.

"T? Hi. When did you get here? Where's Rose?" she said, walking over to T and giving her a big hug.

"She's at home. She couldn't come. She started a new job a couple of weeks ago, so it would not have been good for her to ask for a leave of absence so soon, you know?"

"Well, of course," Sister responded.

"Where's the baby? I saw the pictures. She's gorgeous." Sister grinned.

"She's with her daddy."

"Oh, how sweet. Does he help you out a lot with her?"

"Yes, he does. He spends a lot of time with her…and me too."

"Do I hear wedding bells for you two?" Sister grinned again.

"I don't know. Maybe."

"That's great, Sister. So how's your illness?"

"What illness?" she said with a smirk

"Oh!" T said. "It's like that. The medication keeping it under control?"

"Yes, I'm so happy. I told Henry about it, and he's fine with it. So yes, T, I'm doing fine."

"Sister? Can I ask you something?"

"Sure, T. What is it?"

"Well…I'm not quite sure how to ask this."

"T, just ask."

"Okay. Did your mother treat you and your sister the same?"

"Why do you ask?"

"Your sister and I had a long talk, and she said your mother made a definite difference between you and your Sister." Sister became slightly angry.

"Rose talks too much."

"Don't say that. Don't say that, Sister. Your sister was really hurt by that."

"I know she was," Sister responded.

"So it's true then?"

"Yes, it's true. Mama did make a difference between us." T continuously shook her head from left to right. "I didn't realize how much Rose was hurt by it until we were older, and we talked a lot about it. Mama's still doing it, telling her that her father was a rapist. I mean, come on. What kind of person would want her daughter to believe something like that? Mama's crazier than I ever was. T, is that why you're here?"

"Yes, something like that. Where is your mother?"

"I don't know. She's never here. Is that the phone? It's probably Henry."

Before Sister picked up the phone, T quickly asked, "Does your Mama have any photo albums?"

"Yes, they're in the drawer under the hutch." While Sister was on the phone, T looked through Mama's photo albums.

"Was that Henry?"

"Yes, his mother invited me to come over for dinner. I promised her last week I would, so do you mind?"

"Of course not, Sister. I mean, you didn't know I was coming. No…you go on. I'll just look through these albums and hopefully your Mama will bring her ass in here soon. She has very few pictures of Rose…hm!"

"Well, happy waiting, because you never know when Mama is coming back once she leaves. Well, all right. I'm leaving. Make yourself at home. Maybe Mama will come in soon. Bye."

"Hey!" T opened the door and yelled. "Hurry up and bring that pretty baby home so I can kiss them cheeks!"

"Okay!" Sister yelled back.

CHAPTER 43

"Hello?"

"Rose! It's Nina. I got your message. What's the matter?" I started to sob all over again.

"Come on, baby. Stop crying. Stop crying and tell me what's the matter. Is there something wrong with Sister? Your mother? Come on, Rose. Stop crying." I wiped my eyes and blew my nose and tried to collect myself enough to speak.

"It's Jamal."

"Oh my god, Rose! He's been in an accident?"

"No, no. He broke up with me this evening." Nina was quiet for a few seconds.

"What?" she responded. "What happened? He's found someone else, that son of a—"

"No. I wish I could blame it on that, Nina, but I can't. He told me that he can't deal with the distance anymore. He said the closer he became, the more distant I became, emotionally and physically." I started to cry again.

"Oh, Rose."

"And you know what, Nina? He's right. He's right. I put everyone else in my life ahead of him. Everyone and everything. I don't blame him. I wish I had moved in with him now. I had no really good reason not to, just excuses." I blew my nose again. "I love him, Nina."

"I know you do. Is it too late?"

"Too late for what?" I asked.

"To move in with him. I mean, if he really loves you and you change your mind, don't you think he'd still say yes?" Nina gave me a ray of hope.

"You think it could work?"

"Hell, yes. Jamal seems to be a good man. He treated you like a lady. He tried to be there for you. He's never disrespected you. I say go for it, girl. Go for the gold!"

"What should I say?"

"Say just what you said to me. That he's right, and you realize everything he said to be true. Tell him how much you care for him, although I'm sure he already knows."

"I think I will," I replied.

"Are you going to call him?" Nina asked.

"No, I think I'll write him a letter. That way, I won't be nervous, and I can say all the things I want to say. And then if he likes the idea, he'll call. Besides, I'm really good with words on paper."

"Letters don't move as fast as phone calls."

"I know. I'm scared. Too scared to call right now."

"What will your aunt have to say about it?"

"I don't know, and I don't give a f—"

"Watch it!" Nina chuckled. "That's what I want to hear. Are you feeling better now?"

"Yes, I am. And, Nina?"

"Yeah."

"Thank you."

"You're welcome, dear. That's what friends are for. By the way, was your aunt there when this all happened?"

"No. She's in California."

CHAPTER 44

This stuff was hard for T to tell me. She was not the crying type, but she cried through a lot of this.

She had been drinking a cup of coffee and reading a magazine when she heard Mama come through the front door.

"Fannie? Hi! What are you doing here? Where's Rose?" she said, giving her a hug.

"At home. She'd started a new job so she couldn't come," T said. And besides, I wanted to talk to you about Rose."

"What about her?" Mama said, continuing up the stairs. T followed close behind.

"She said some things I found disturbing."

"You know what? Every time Rose goes out of town to visit family, she starts trouble."

"What do you mean?" T asked.

"She went to visit Mama in Mississippi. She hadn't been there a week and Mama called me, all upset asking me what lies I had been telling her."

"Well, what lies had you been telling her?"

"You know what, Fannie? You're just as bad as she is."

"Who? Mama?"

"No. Rose. All I've done was try to raise her, give her a nice home, love her."

"So lying to her about her father being a rapist is raising her?" Mama didn't say anything. "I'll bet you wouldn't have told Sister that."

"What are you trying to say, Fannie?"

"Rose told me how you treated her when she was growing up. How you treated her like shit, and how you bought Sister dresses and barrettes." Mama turned to T abruptly.

"Now you wait just a minute! I gave Rose just as much as I gave Sister. I love them both the same."

"Yeah, what about that trip to Disney World? Did Rose go?"

"No. Rose...no...Rose had done something. I can't remember what it was now, but she did something to keep her from going. She acted up a lot."

"Yeah right! You're such a liar!"

"You got a lot of nerve. You talk about me lying. You let her believe the biggest lie of all. Who do you think she's going to hate when she finds out?" T was stunned. She looked at Mama with tears in her eyes.

"I don't believe you went there, Maxi. You know I did what I had to do," she said, wiping her eyes. "I love Rose."

"You loved her so much. That's why you were breaking my door down to visit her."

"That's not fair, Maxi. We agreed."

"Yes, Fan, we did agree." They just looked at each other. "So don't come in my house telling me I was a bad mother. I also did what I had to do." Mama lit a cigarette with a silly smirk on her face, like she knew she had won.

"Maxi, I just don't understand why you told Rose her father raped you."

"Because Rose was asking so many questions. She wanted to know why she looked different from Sister. I didn't know what to tell her. That was the first thing that popped into my mind," Mama said.

"To tell her her father is a rapist?" While Mama and T were arguing, Sister came through the door unheard. She heard them. She laid the baby on the sofa and continued halfway up the stairs, stopping on the stairs to listen.

CHAPTER 45

I went into T's room to get some stationary, but mostly to search her footlocker. As I pulled out the box of stationary, I noticed something silver. A diary. It was locked. I put it back, satisfied for the moment, and went into my room to compose the most important letter of my life.

I sat about ten minutes, not sure how to start. I let my mind wander through everything that had been a stumbling block in my relationship with Jamal—my mother's drug habit, Sister's illness, my need to find out about my father. "The key!" I realized the key went to that diary in T's locker. I got up and went into the closet where I kept it, but couldn't find it. I started to pull everything out of the closet, from dirty clothes on the floor to boxes I had on the shelf. I became frantic. I started to sweat. "Oh my god!" I pulled out a pair of jeans I hadn't worn since I arrived and looked in the pockets. It was there. I quickly walked into T's room and pulled out the diary. "Please, God, let this be the key." I put the key into the lock and turned it. It popped open. I sat there, wishing my sister was here.

* * * * *

Sister could hear everything Mama and T were saying.
"What should I have told her?" Mama asked T.

"I don't know, Maxi. But I'm sure you could have come up with something better than that Maxi! Something that wouldn't have hurt her so much. Did you want her to be hurt?"

"Why would I want that, Fannie?"

"You didn't think telling her something like that would hurt her?"

*"I keep telling you. I **didn't** think."*

"I'll bet you wouldn't tell Sister anything like that."

* * * * *

I opened the diary and skimmed through the beginning. I found a page that contained David's name.

> *Dear Diary,*
>
> *May 16, 1974*
>
> *I missed my period again. I think I'm pregnant. I don't know what I'm going to do. Mama is going to kill me. I can't think about anything else. Lord, help me to sleep tonight. Tomorrow I think I'll go to the free clinic downtown. I hope I don't see anyone I know. I heard that I can find out right away if I'm pregnant. I'm so scared.*
>
> *Dear Diary,*
>
> *May 17, 1974*
>
> *I'm pregnant. The doctor says I'm a little over two months. What am I going to do? Mama is going to kill me…and David. How am I going to tell him? I wonder if David will help me pay for an abortion.*

Dear Diary,

June 12, 1974

I'm going into my third month. I've decided to tell David tonight. He told me he never really liked my sister. He said Maxi was stuck on herself. I felt good when he told me the only reason he hung around her was to get my attention. I wonder what he would say about the baby. I wonder what Mama's going to do. I'm so scared. I told Maxi. She said she'd be with me when I tell Mama.

Dear Diary,

June 22, 1974

I was scared to face Mama and tell her, so I wrote her a long letter. I'm so scared. I left it on her night-stand after she told me I could spend the night at a friend's house. She'll probably beat me all the way home. I won't sleep a wink tonight. David said he'd stay at my friend's house with me. I hope he keeps his promise.

Dear Diary,

June23, 1974

I thought Mama was going to shoot me for sure. I almost had my baby right then. I hurt my Mama. I feel so bad. She cried and cried.

Dear Diary,

November 6, 1974

I didn't think this baby was ever going to be born. She is so beautiful. David is so happy. He's been working real hard to give us everything we need so Mama won't have to spend a dime. She weighs five lbs., ten oz. I named her Rose.

I was beginning to feel sick. I couldn't breathe. "Oh my god! Oh my god! No!"

* * * *

Sister moved closer to Mama's bedroom door as the conversation became more interesting.

"Well, you know what, Fannie? You should have raised your own daughter."

"I wish I had, Maxi. I wish I had. I regretted every day knowing I let you have her. I should've listened to Mama." Sister took a tissue out of her pocket and wiped her eyes.

"Think again, sister dear. You didn't let me have her. The courts gave her to me. Mama was sick and, well, you..."

"If Mama had been able to take care of her, she would have loved her like one of her own."

"You go to hell! You go to hell, Fannie! I was doing you a big favor. Rose could have been adopted out of the family!"

"You'd rather tell my daughter her father is a rapist, a hurtful lie, instead of telling Sister her father was a rapist. You just hate the truth about anything!"

Mama yelled some choice words.

"Everyone tried to tell you," T continued, "but you wanted to have a white man so bad, you refused to believe it." Mama started to walk away from T, but T kept at her, yelling, "I heard he raped you!"

"That's it, Fannie. Get out!" Mama screamed.

"He did, didn't he? Steven raped you!" Mama kept walking around the room, shaking her head. "He kept on seeing you, trying to get you not to tell, and you didn't! He bribed you into marrying him. I was sick then, but I remember!"

Mama put her hands up to her head. "Shut up! Shut up!"

"He bought you that car you said you won!"

Mama lunged at Fannie. "Shut up, Fannie! Shut up! You don't know anything!" she said, hitting T with her fist.

Sister put her hand up to her mouth to keep from making any noise. She could not believe what she had just heard. She started to weep.

"What's that?" Mama asked.

"What's what?" T asked, stopping them in their tracks.

"I heard a horn blow," Mama said as she went toward the window.

"That's Henry out there." T looked quickly toward the door.

Sister ran down the steps and picked up her baby. T went rushing out of the room while Mama continued to look out the window. T saw Sister just as she went out of the door. T ran down the steps after her, calling her, but Sister kept running, her eyes blurred from the tears. Mama saw a car coming and hollered out of the window, calling Sister's name as loud as she could. Henry struggled to get out of his seat belt, calling Sister's name. Sister kept running. Just as T got to the door, her and Mama both screamed as the car struck Sister, sending her and the baby flying through the air. Everything went silent. Then screams came from everywhere. Sister's body lay bloodied, broken, little Roselyn close by in a pool of blood. People came running out of their homes only to turn away when they saw. T ran into the street and screamed and screamed until a strange man grabbed her, trying to console her. Henry was beating his head against a nearby pole. The ambulance and police arrived a few minutes later. They quickly jumped out of their vehicles, running over to each one, shaking their heads. Mama came running outside just as one of the paramedics covered Sister's head. Mama started screaming, pulling her hair, not knowing where to run to first.

A voice rang out.

"This baby's alive." The paramedics worked desperately on little Roselyn as the police asked everyone to stand back. Mama, T, and Henry were holding on to each other for dear life. The street was silent except *for the low sobbing coming from T, Mama, and the driver of the car, a young female.*

"Hurry! Hurry! Let's get her out of here!" cried one of the paramedics working on Roselyn. Her little body was wrapped tight to keep her from moving. "Let's go!" the paramedic yelled as they put her little body into the ambulance.

"Here, Ms. Sinclair. You take the keys. I'll ride in the ambulance," Henry said. Mama and T followed closely behind the ambulance, not saying a word to each other, only feeling their own pain of what they knew to be their fault.

CHAPTER 46

I felt a sharp pain in my chest as I called my sister's name. I wanted to talk to her. I went to the phone and dialed Mama's number. I let the phone ring a half dozen times before I hung up. I sat back down on the bed and put my head in my hands. Hearing the phone ring, I almost didn't answer. But I thought, *What if it's Jamal?* I quickly ran to the phone.

"Hello."

"Rose?" It was T. My body tightened.

"Yeah?"

"Rose, listen carefully. I have some money in my footlocker in a red canister. I need you to take the first flight out."

"Why, T? What's the matter? You sound funny." T took a deep breath before starting again.

"So do you. I just need you to take the next flight out."

"Tell me, T! I'm not budging until you tell me." I don't know why, but I started to cry. Something was wrong, desperately wrong. I could feel it.

"Get out here." The phone went dead.

When I arrived, there was a note waiting for me on the table, telling me to go to a hospital. My stomach sank. I started shaking and couldn't stop. When I got there, Mama was standing outside, smoking a cigarette. She noticed me and quickly turned and went inside the hospital. Before I could make it to the door, Mama and T were coming outside. I ran up to them, breathing hard.

"What happened?"

Mama tried to take my arm.

"Come over here and sit down."

I snatched it away from her.

"I don't want to sit down." Tears started to stream down my face. "It's Sister!"

Mama couldn't get words out. T took over.

"Rose, your sister got hit by a car." Her voice started to shake. "She died."

She said it once, but to me it sounded like she said it over and over. I shook my head.

"That's not possible."

"She was killed instantly," Mama said, choking up again. I started to scream. Mama and T were sitting there. They came rushing over to my bedside, trying to settle me. I screamed and screamed. A doctor came in and administered a sedative. I calmed down and drifted off. I woke up several hours later, only to find T in the room.

"Where's Mama?"

"She's down with the baby."

"She's got the baby here? Where's Henry? Couldn't he have taken care of her?"

"Henry's out helping with the funeral arrangement. But, Rose, the baby was in Sister's arms when she got hit." I sat up. T could tell I was getting ready to freak, so she quickly responded with "She's okay. I mean, she didn't die. She was hurt pretty bad. The doctors said by her being a baby, she didn't tighten up when she hit the ground, and also her blankets had helped her a great deal. Her arm was broken. A little piece of the bone came through."

"Oh my god. T! What about her head?" I asked, crying.

"The doctors say she landed on her arm, which helped. She also had a hooded sweater on, so there was very little damage to her head. Her brain was slightly bruised. She's strong."

"I want to see her, T. Help me up," I said, struggling to rise. I felt like I had been hit with a brick.

"I don't know, Rose."

"I am fine! I want to see my niece. I've never seen her. Help me up."

"Okay, Rose, but she looks a whole lot worse than she actually is. The doctor says her eyes will be dark for a little while, but it's nothing to worry about."

"Okay, okay! Take me down now."

Mama was just getting ready to feed her when she saw me come into the nursery.

"Do you want to feed her, Rose?" I looked up at Mama but couldn't speak. I had tears in my eyes. She looked so frail, kind of like Sister did that day when she was sick from bulimia. I sat down in the rocking chair that was there. Mama handed her to me. I looked down into her face and couldn't keep the tears from falling. She looked like a little raccoon. But the most beautiful raccoon I ever saw. I saw my sister peeking through those eyes. I said hi and gave her a kiss. Mama and T left us alone.

When I went to Mama's house, I put myself in seclusion. However, it did feel good to be back in my own room. I was tempted several times to go into Sister's room. But as soon as I walked up to the door, a lump filled my throat, and her scent filled my nose. I was lost. Mama called me to get the phone.

"Hello?"

"Rose." It was Nina. "I'm so sorry to hear about your sister." I started to bawl.

"Thanks, Nina. Can you come up?"

"Sure. That's why I'm calling. I'm on my way out. I hope you won't be mad at me, but I called Jamal and told him about Sister."

"That doesn't bother me. I don't care. What did he say?"

"He'll be there tomorrow. He said he needed to tie up some loose ends first."

"Thanks, Nina. I need him so much."

"Don't cry, Rose. How did it happen?"

"I don't know. I haven't talked to Mama about any of it yet. What time will you get here?"

"I'll be there in a couple of hours. I'm just waiting for the inn to call and confirm my reservations," Nina explained.

"Nina, would you mind if I stayed in the hotel with you?"

"Of course not. But you don't want to stay with your mama and aunt?"

"No. I'll explain later."

"Okay. I'll come and get you before I register, okay?"

"All right. And, Nina?"

"What?"

"Hurry."

CHAPTER 47

Nina arrived a couple hours later. She came in, said hello to Mama and my aunt and a host of other people at the house, then we left. Nina gave me another hug when we got outside the door.

"Oh, I forgot to tell you. Kiki and Samara will be here. They have a room next to ours." I hugged her again. "Let's get out of here." Nina and I didn't talk much on the way to the inn. She understood and let me have my time. We ordered pizza.

"Rose, I wish there was something I could do to make you feel better," Nina said.

I just stared out of the window.

"Mama is not my mother," I said, continuing to stare out the window, not really seeing anything out there.

"What?" Nina asked, walking over to me. I think I was scaring her.

"I was looking for some stationary inside of my aunt's foot-locker to write Jamal's letter. I found a silver diary. Remember the key I told you about a long time ago?"

"Yes."

"It fit the diary and…"

"Take your time, Rose."

"I read that my aunt is my mother. She gave me to her sister to raise."

Nina dropped down in the chair that was there and put one hand to her mouth.

"I wanna die, Nina," I said between gulps. "I just wanna die. I can't take it anymore."

Nina came closer, holding me and rocking me.

"It's going to be okay. I promise. It may not seem like it now. But it will. It's going to be okay."

"No, Nina, it won't. My sister is gone. Nina, she's gone. I wanna die too."

"Rose…shhh……shhh…it's okay, baby. It's okay," Nina kept repeating.

"I wanna die…I wanna die." I cried and cried.

The next morning, Nina and I went over to Mama's house. She said she was on her way to the funeral parlor to take Sister's dress and comb her hair.

"Mama, let me."

"Are you sure?"

"Yes…please…Nina, would you take me?"

"I can take you, Rose."

"No, Mama!" I snapped. It was funny to hear myself call her Mama.

"Nina, would you?"

"Of course. Are you ready?"

"The bag is over by the door," Mama said, pointing.

"Nina, I need to run upstairs and get something. I'll be right back down and we can go."

I remembered the last time I entered a funeral parlor. It was to comb my Grammy's hair. I stopped when I reached the steps.

"Rose, are you sure you want to do this?" Nina asked.

I looked at her and said, "Yes, Nina. I have to."

The funeral director greeted us at the steps and told me how sorry he was. He then led me down a long hallway. Nina waited for me in the foyer.

The funeral director pointed to a room at the end of the hall. "If you need anything, my office is right down these steps."

"Thanks," I said, not taking my eyes off the door where Sister lay. I stood there for a couple of seconds and took a deep breath before entering. I walked slowly over to the most beautiful white casket trimmed in pink and gold. I thought I was going to be afraid, but when I saw my sister lying there, there were no fears. The director did a beautiful job. She was gorgeous. I walked closer to her and took out the comb and brush and plugged in the curling irons. I gently lifted her head. The sun shining through the window made her skin warm as if she was only sleeping. I felt the tears becoming heavy on my lids and gently wiped them away.

"Your hair always did grow fast. I was always jealous of your hair, how long it was, how rich." I didn't notice Nina had come and stood by the door. "I miss you so much, Sister. I don't know if I can make it without you. Who am I going to talk to? I need you so much right now. They're trying to say you're not my sister. But you are my sister. You will always be my sister. I never told you, but...you are the shining star in my life." I brushed Sister's hair up in a bun and started curling her hair toward her face. "You always looked pretty with curls around your face. Remember all the fights we got into when we were young? We always made up. You'd climb into bed with me and hug me all night, or I'd climb into bed with you. We'd talk all night long. We could always depend on each other. I'm sorry for leaving you. You might've still been here today if I hadn't left. You begged me not to, and I left anyway. Can you forgive me?

"I saw Roselyn. She's beautiful. She looks just like you. Yes, I'll take care of her for you. I won't let them have her. I'll raise her like my own. I'll love her. I'll give her the best of you with stories, pictures, and memories. She'll know you as I do, and she'll love you as I do. We won't forget you." When the last curl was done, I placed a white pin in her hair, two doves I gave her for her birthday once. Two doves joined together in spirit, one never being without the other. "I love you, my sister." I stared at her beautiful face, leaned over, and kissed her gently as I said goodbye.

Nina was standing at the door, wiping her eyes.

"I'm ready, Nina." I turned and gave my sister one last look as I left the funeral home.

When we returned to Mama's house, there were cars lined up everywhere. Some cars were parked a couple of blocks down. Mama must have seen me coming because all of a sudden, Kiki and Samara came out of the front door. We all hugged, Nina joining us. We didn't want to let go.

"Thanks for coming."

"You didn't have a doubt, did you?" Kiki asked. I couldn't answer. I shook my head no and hugged them all again.

When I walked inside, Henry was there. I went over to him. He gave me a very tight hug.

"You know, Rose, Sister talked about you a lot." My eyes filled up. "Yes, she did. She loved you a lot."

"Thanks for telling me that. She loved you a lot too."

"I know." We hugged again.

Mama was in a lot of pain. I wish I could have grieved with her. I couldn't. Our pain was the same but separate. My friends and I huddled in our own corner. I broke away when I saw Tweety come through the door.

"Hi, Tweety." He could barely speak.

"Hi, Rose. How are you doing?" he asked.

"I'm doing, Tweety. I'm doing." Just as I was getting ready to join my friends again, I saw Daddy coming up the walk. All the warm feelings I should have had for my family was lying with my sister. I said hello to him and walked away. I felt bad, but I couldn't help but wonder how much he knew, how much he knew about everything. He looked at me strangely and went to find Mama. Mama was upstairs with T. They were looking over the eulogy when Steven knocked on her door. When Mama saw him, she screamed and attacked him.

"It's your fault! It's your fault!" I was on my way upstairs when I heard her screaming. "It's all your fault!" Mama was hitting him with both fists. She then grabbed him, holding him tight, rocking and crying. T pulled her away from him.

"It's okay, Steven. She's just upset," T explained.

I couldn't make sense of that and went downstairs, gathered my friends, and left.

CHAPTER 48

My friends tried to keep me busy with conversation, but it didn't work. I had too much on my mind. We flipped through the cable channels, trying to find something decent to watch.

"Stop! Kiki, turn back one."

"What?"

"Come, Rose, you don't want to watch that," Samara said.

"Why not? I love *Sparkle*. This was Sister's and my favorite movie. She used to pretend like she was Sister and I was Irene Cara. Let's finish watching this." But just as Irene started to sing at her sister's funeral, I got up and left the room.

"I told y'all we shouldn't have watched that movie," Nina said angrily.

"What? How were we going to stop her?" Kiki said.

"I know, I'm sorry," Nina said. "Well, the funeral is at eleven a.m. I'm going to bed."

"Hey, Nina? Wasn't Jamal supposed to be here?"

"Yes, he said he was coming. I don't know what happened. Well, good night. I'll see you in the morning."

"Tell Rose we said good night."

At ten the next morning, there was a knock on the door. I was still dressing, so Nina answered the door. She peeped through the keyhole and was glad to see Jamal standing on the other side of it. She quickly opened the door.

"Hi. I didn't think you were going to make it," Nina said.

"Nothing could have stopped me. How's Rose?" he asked.

"Not good. She didn't sleep a wink."

"That's expected. What happened?"

"I don't know for sure. Rose said she was hit by a car right in front of the house."

Jamal could only shake his head.

"Will you tell her I'm here?"

"Sure thing. Have a seat. I'll get her for you."

"Nina, was that the girls? Are they ready?"

"Someone for you," Nina said.

I came out of the bathroom and saw Jamal standing there." I stared at him. He stared at me. My eyes filled up again and I ran to him. His arms felt so good around me. He kissed me.

"I'm sorry about your sister, baby." I didn't want to let go. "Are you okay?"

He took a tissue out of his pocket and handed it to me.

"I'm so glad you're here. I didn't think you were going to come."

"Now I'm hurt. Do you think I would desert you when you need me the most?" I hugged him again.

"Are you all ready?" Nina asked. "Let's go." We all rode in the car with Jamal. I didn't want to ride in the funeral car. I told Mama and T I would meet them there. The church was full. Jamal sat up front with me, keeping my hand in his. I couldn't believe how calm Tweety was as he delivered the most beautiful eulogy. When he concluded, Mattie, a black heavy-set girl, went up to the mike and started to sing "Walk Around Heaven." It was time to view the body. Mattie's voice rang out strong.

One of these mornings won't be very long / You'll look for me and I'll be gone / I'm going to place where there'll be nothing, nothing to do / I'll just walk around, walk around heaven all day.

I stood up, but I couldn't move. Tears were streaming down my face. I could feel Jamal trying to lead me closer to the casket. I couldn't. Mama and T were both screaming. I felt like I couldn't breathe. I broke away from Jamal and swiftly walked out of the church, Jamal close behind. I needed him.

Jamal stayed an extra day after everyone left. We talked a lot. Everything I wanted to tell him in the letter I told him face-to-face.

Even though we had broken up, I asked him if it was too late to share our lives together. I told him I was ready and how I had planned to write him and ask him about it before my sister died. He said the offer was still good and asked how soon I would be ready. Long enough to tie up some loose ends and to pack. He said I didn't need to pack. Everything I need, he'd get for me. I told him to give me a few more days.

Although I was going to be moving in with him, I hated to see him leave, but there were some things I needed to do. Jamal said he left something for me. He told me to look in my purse just as he was getting ready to drive away. I went into my bedroom and opened my purse. There was a package wrapped beautifully, and a letter.

Dear Rose,

On my way here, I stopped and picked this up for you. I realized after I left how empty my life was. Although we didn't see each other every day, there was a comfort in knowing that I was yours and you were mine. I've decided I don't want to live my life without you. I love you. If you're not ready, I'll understand and won't bother you again. One thing is for sure. I do not want to live my life without you. Will you marry me? I know this is not the most romantic way to ask you, but with everything that's going on, I thought you might need a little time to think about it without the pressure of me standing there, waiting on an answer I want to hear but you might not be ready to give. Take your time. Hopefully, not too much time. Please, will you marry me?

Jamal

P.S: Whatever the answer, what's in the package is yours to keep.

I started shaking. *Yes*, I thought as I put the most beautiful ring on my finger.

The next morning, I went to the hospital to see Roselyn. She was doing much better. The doctor said she would be ready to come home in a couple of days.

Mama and T were acting awfully funny. Whenever I'd come around, they would stop talking immediately. It happened more and more. I hadn't gotten the true understanding of what happened the day Sister died, but one day I walked in on Mama and T arguing. Mama was crying.

I heard Mama say, "My baby would still be alive if it wasn't for—"

"You stop!" T screamed. "Don't you dare try to blame this on me. You never should've—"

"What! More lies?" I blurted out all of a sudden. "I want to know what happened the day Sister got hit."

"What do you mean?" T asked. There was a loud banging on the front door. T quickly ran down the steps to answer, thinking she was saved by the bell. It was Henry. He pushed his way in.

"It's all your fault," he said, pointing his finger at Mama as we came down the stairs. "It's all your fault! Yours and hers," he said. "I saw her face when she came running out. You did something!" He shouted as he stumbled toward Mama. Mama was shaking her head. "What did you do to her?" he asked, trying to grab Mama's throat. I quickly grabbed Henry and led him to the couch.

"Come, Henry. Sit down." My heart broke whenever I'd see him.

"They did something, Rose! I know it. Sister would have never come running out of the house like that, not with the baby. I tried to get to her." He started crying. "I couldn't get out fast enough." I turned around and looked at Mama and T.

"She ran right into it."

"I know, Henry, I know. Why don't you go home and get some sleep?" I said, trying hard to keep my composure.

"I can't sleep. I see it over and over. My baby! Flying through the air," he cried.

"Little Roselyn's going to need you now. You have to be strong for her," I said.

"I can't, Rose. I can't. You take her!" he blurted out. I saw Mama and T shift their bodies when Henry said that.

"What?"

"Sister loved you. She told me if anything was to ever happen to her, she wanted you to take care of little Roselyn."

"Why would she say something like that?"

"It was her illness. She didn't know if she could take care of her at first. We had a long discussion about it. She made me promise. Rose, please! All I ask is that she knows who her Mama is and to be able to see her from time to time. She loved you so much." He cried.

"But what if you decide you want her back?"

"I'll get a lawyer. My mother has a good lawyer. I'll have him draw something up."

"You don't have to do that. I'd give her back," I said.

"I'm not worried about you," he said, looking over at Mama and T. Mama moved closer.

"Henry, do you think that's a good idea? I could—"

"You could what!" he screamed, trying to stand. "Kill her like you killed her mother!" Mama stared at Henry. He then looked at me.

"Rose...please!"

"Yes, of course. I'll take her, Henry."

"I'll talk to a lawyer right away...well, tomorrow," he said trying to stand again, only this time I helped him up.

"You go home and try to get some rest. Should I call you a cab?"

"No, I have one waiting." I kissed him on his forehead and led him to the door and watched him get safely into his cab. When I closed the door, Mama and T were starting to go up the steps.

"Stop! Sit down!" Mama and T both looked like children as they sat down on the couch. "I want to know what happened to my sister," I said sharply. "And you can start by telling me who my mother is. T?"

Mama and T talked for hours as I listened to the most horrendous story I could ever imagine.

"Daddy raped you? And Sister heard this?" I said.

"We didn't know she was there! Rose!"

I stood up.

"Oh my god! Sister!" I cried. After a couple of minutes, I walked back over to them. I had no more anger. My sister was gone. That wasn't going to change.

"Where is David now?" I asked T.

"New York. He's a professor at the university there," T said, wiping her eyes.

"He never tried to get in contact with me?"

"He tried over and over again. Somehow I was able to convince him that this was for the best."

"No wonder you never loved me," I said, looking at Mama. T looked at Mama.

"I did love you!" Mama said.

"I wasn't white enough," I added, laughing a hurtful laugh as I went up the stairs, leaving them sitting there.

T tried many times to talk to me after that. She told me Roselyn and I could both come and live with her. I said nothing. I said nothing to either of them. T went to visit little Roselyn in the hospital, and then she left.

CHAPTER 49

The lawyer called for Henry and I to come to his office to finalize the papers. When I left the lawyer's office, I had the cab driver drive to the cemetery and wait.

I walked up to Sister's headstone and placed two single black roses at the foot of her grave, crossing their stems.

"Sena Ann Sinclair, I always thought you had a beautiful name. But for some reason, I liked calling you Sister. I remember Mama used to say, 'It's easy, Rose. Just say Sena.'" I laughed. "But I wanted to call you Sister, because that's what you were. My sister. No matter what, in my heart, my mind, my soul, you are always my sister. You were there for me even when Mama was at her meanest. I'm so sorry I wasn't here for you. You have given me the most precious gift. When I look into her eyes, I see you. I will love her and care for her as if I'd given birth to her myself. I will teach her about God, and teaching her about God will be teaching her honesty and love, love of herself and others. I will tell her about you. She will love you as I do. And if God blesses me with another little girl, I will raise them as sisters, each knowing who they are and being secure in knowing that. So rest now, my dear sweet sister. And when you sit with the Father, you can smile, knowing that he is taking care of us as I know he is taking care of you."

I blew my sister a kiss and walked away, knowing I would never come there again.

Shortly after that, we left my mother's house, Roselyn and I.

I walked with a higher spirit.

The End

ABOUT THE AUTHOR

Linda Kay Jones was born and raised on the south side of Chicago. She is the fifth daughter born in a family of seven sisters and one brother. Linda moved to Cedar Rapids in 1991 with her husband, Richard Goodall, and three children. After several years, Linda divorced, and after a ten-year courtship, she married her current husband, James Jones. Linda furthered her education by attending Kirkwood Community College, where she won the Jeff Smith Award for best outstanding essay in English. Linda lost her sister Beverly, who was one year younger, to a mental illness. It was that loss that inspired the creation of *Sena's Black Rose: A Different Kind of Love Story*. It's a story of unimaginable situations and what it took to endure them.